MORE THAN WORDS
UNDERSTANDING THE ANCIENT BOOK IN A MODERN WORLD
MINDI JO FURBY

© 2013 Mindi Jo Furby. All rights reserved.

No part of this book may be reproduced, stored in a retrieval system, or transmitted by any means without the written permission of the author.

Published March 2013

ISBN: 978-0-615-76729-1

Library of Congress Control Number: 2012918784

Printed in the United States of America

Editor: Christina Miller

Graphic Designer: Jenna Leigh Moore

Scripture, unless otherwise noted, taken from the NEW AMERICAN STANDARD BIBLE®, Copyright © 1960, 1962, 1963, 1968, 1971, 1972, 1973, 1975, 1977, 1995 by The Lockman Foundation. Used by permission.

Dedication

■■■■■■

"Sanctify them in the truth; Your Word is truth."

■■■■■■

These simple words of Christ spoken two thousand years ago burn in my heart every time I think of you, dear reader.

You motivated the countless hours spent sunken into a couch typing this manuscript. My posture thanks you.

Every time my energy waned, God seared *you* into my mind and rejuvenated my aching fingers as the keyboard welcomed them back.

Inversely, the dedication of this book came before it even began. For reasons yet unknown, God prepared and delivered this book into your hands for *this very moment* in your life.

He simultaneously extends *His* hand for you to hold through this journey, because it will shatter your categories of Him and His Word. But demolition will birth new life as He rebuilds your perspective and shapes you into a good steward—one who accurately handles His Word of Truth.

■■■■■■

That's my prayer; you're my dedication. Read these pages with great expectations—He's got far more in store for you than either of us realize!

Praise for MORE THAN WORDS & Mindi Jo Furby

"Mindi Jo Furby has written this book in a conversational tone that will be easy reading for anyone wanting to know the Word of God and how to apply it to their lives. Those who hear her will want to take the next step to understand how God's Word can give stability to their life."

Elmer L. Towns
Co Founder, Liberty University, Lynchburg, VA

"Vibrant, informative, proactive instruction...her grasp of Scripture, love for the Lord Jesus Christ and insight into the Holy Scriptures revealed to me an understanding and interpretation of Scriptures that I had not been exposed to before."

Fran Barrick
Lay Ministry Leader

"Mindi Jo Furby has an infectious energetic personality that compliments her quick wit and deep and abiding thirst for God's Word. What sets her apart is her unique ability to take complex and deep concepts from Scripture and translate them into everyday words...and having fun all the while."

J. Mark H.
Financial Advisor, Elder of Christ Community Church, NC

"I have studied Hermeneutics under Mindi Furby, and it is a pure delight to find a young woman so enthusiastic, well informed on her subject, and with a Holy Spirit given gift of teaching. She has a dynamic personality and an encouraging spirit...The LORD is going to use this girl to further His Kingdom!"

Deborah Savage
Children's Ministry Teacher

"Mindi Jo Furby is an excellent teacher! I was able to gain a better understanding of how to study the Bible correctly, which furthermore enabled me to grow deeper in my relationship with God."

Kaci Hollingsworth
UNC Graduate

"Mindi's teaching and her insight into interpreting God's Word and how it relates to us draws you closer to the Holy Spirit. She opened my eyes to an entirely new and informative way to not just read Scripture, but understand, interpret correctly, and how to apply it. This book will catapult your walk with Christ to another level and transform your life."

Teresa White
Financial Administrative Manager

"Mindi brings new light to ancient Scripture. Her instruction teaches you how to study the Bible for yourself and glean a new and more complete understanding of God's Word. Mindi stirs up a hunger for knowledge and truth and provides you with the tools you need to do the research and find the answers for yourself."

Linda Mann
Grace Church, Southern Pines, NC

Table of Contents

Chapter 1: What Is the Bible? 1

Chapter 2: The Canon 29

Chapter 3: Paving the Way 59

Chapter 4: Hermeneutics—What Is It? 69

Chapter 5: The Rules 83

    Rule #1 83

    Rule #2 94

    Rule #3 101

    Rule #4: 103

Chapter 6: Old Testament Genres 107

    Historical Narrative 108

    Law 123

    Poetry 134

    Wisdom Literature 137

    Prophecy 142

Chapter 7: New Testament Genres 153

    The Gospels 153

    Acts 160

    New Testament Letters 165

    Revelation 171

Chapter 8: Step One 177

Chapter 9: Step Two 209

Chapter 10: Step Three 219

Chapter 11: Step Four 235
Chapter 12: Step Five 243
Chapter 13: Let's Wrap it Up! 249
About the Author 253
Bibliography 255

PREFACE

I grew up in a culture defined by one word: image. Every thought, action, word and decision was made through an "image filter," and if it didn't enhance how the world perceived you, it didn't make the cut. Everyone lived with an agenda, and part of it was coercing others to believe their points of view.

The depressing part was that the Church wasn't a sanctuary from this perspective; it often served as an incubator for it.

I was taught "the right way," and lived with an unspoken (and uninformed) understanding that everyone of alternative perspectives should be ignored or "converted". People must not only come to know Jesus, they must convert to our version of Christianity via our particular practice of faith. They had to look like us and abide by our image, which was the best one, naturally.

The antidote for this behavior, (as I came to realize after a dramatic and personal journey with God), is quite simple: a correct understanding of Truth. Though all truth is God's truth, not all of it reveals Him in the same way. His Word, the Bible, is the truth given for us to understand, abide by, and know Him through. A proper understanding of and surrender to it leads to a transformed life and God's glory revealed.

Our image needs a serious makeover, and it's only going to happen if we get serious about the Word.

Scripture, unfortunately, remains mystery to many, and is left on bookshelves far more often than it's pursued with any kind of intensity and passion. We far too often leave it to our pastors to make sense of it for us rather than seeking its truths on our own.

Ninety-two percent of Americans own a Bible. Of this 92 percent, each household owns an average of three Bibles.[1] Are those Bibles being used, or do they collect dust? If used, to what extent? As an accessory to church every weekend or as a lifeline pored over daily?

My heart's cry is that we would encounter God in an (un)expected place—like His Word—and discover an unrelenting passion for it in our lives.

Nothing in this book is new or novel in concept. In fact, you notice lots of footnotes indicating where this topic's real geniuses can be found. This is simply a collection of several years of study—a conglomeration of material from books, lectures, articles, and personal research conveniently gift-wrapped for you in a way that will challenge your "image filter" to center on Him.

What makes this book unique is that it is written for you. It's not for the professor-type who knows Scripture inside and out. It's not for pastors, seminarians, or PhDs, although all of these are more than welcome to read it!

This is written for you—who know Jesus or are thinking about getting to know Him. You don't have to be a professor of theology to know Jesus or dig deep into His Word. If you'd like to know more about Scripture and how to apply it to your life, buckle in. If you could do without the fancy words and academic-speak, then this informal, down-to-earth book may be for you.

---

[1] Gasque, Ward. "Bibles: Available, Accessible, Ignored." Christian Week, February 1, 2008, 22. http://www.christianweek.org/features.php?id=15

What Is the Bible?

Scripture. The Bible. The Holy Word of God. The Canon. The Good Book. God's Word. It goes by many names and titles and comes in many styles and versions. Most people are familiar with it, and many own at least one—some large families claiming four or five. Many of these books rest somewhere deep within the confines of a bookshelf, collecting dust. Others are displayed in grandeur as family heirlooms, passed down for generations but unopened in years.

Most Americans are quick to claim to know the Bible (after all, they're church-going folk) but have a difficult time defining it. It's easy to define Scripture with a synonym, but few can ascribe a definition to it that surpasses catch phrases and synonyms. So let's get personal. Can *you* define it? Can you answer the question of this chapter: What is the Bible?

Is it simply an ancient text? Or a good book with moral values and guidelines that supposedly help us along the way? Is it a collection of ancient manuscripts that tells us how to get to God or please Him? Or just a gathering of myths, written as a practical joke on humanity?

People in both the past and present define Scripture in a plethora of ways, each coming from different perspectives, biases, and beliefs. By way of informal research, I went to YouTube.com and typed in

"What is the Bible?" Quite an entertaining slew of responses came up! For example, in one particular clip, several children are asked this question. The first answer was, "It's a *super* thick book, like *this* thick" (as his friend holds up his little hands to mimic the depth), "that says 'The Bible' on it."

Truer words were never spoken! Another child answered, "It talks about God and has a whole lot of words and pictures in it" (got to love children's Bibles) "and is the place to go to find out more about God." All true (minus the picture part, but you get the idea).

The Bible has been defined in many ways throughout history, and though the YouTube examples above come from children, most adult responses are no more elaborate or insightful. For example, it's not uncommon to hear responses like the following:

- "It's a self-help book."
- "It tells you about God."
- "It puts a whole bunch of restrictions on your life . . . the 'thou shalt nots' and such."
- "It has some good advice. It's a good reference tool for living well."
- "It's a mythical representation of God, written by mankind."
- "It was created as a tool to control people—make them do what others want them to do."
- "It has made-up stories that are supposed to explain things."

A pretty sad tribute, considering almost every household in America owns one.

These definitions are particularly frightening when we consider that most "Christians" who own a Bible also claim to believe it and base their eternal destiny on its truth! This is precisely why we are going to begin our journey by defining Scripture. We can't be productive in discussing how to read, interpret, and apply Scripture if we don't have solid foundational knowledge of what it is!

But before we get too immersed in interesting facts and definitions for Scripture, I must say without apology that I steadfastly hold that Scripture is the written word of *the* God it describes—the Holy, Almighty God Who created this universe and still holds it in His hands. How can I or any person hold to that kind of statement with such confidence and authority? How can anyone know for sure what the Bible is and whether it's worth putting his or her faith into?

That's what we're about to find out! Let's discover it together by answering the timeless and not-often-asked question, "What is the Bible?" We're going to let the Bible speak for itself, of course, but we'll also throw in some fascinating historical facts that substantiate its claims.

INERRANT

Scripture is first inerrant, which simply means without error. Not exactly groundbreaking, right? But since I prefer slightly more elaborate definitions, here's another one for you:

> Inerrancy is "being wholly and verbally God-given. . . . Scripture is without error or fault in all its teaching, no less in what it states about God, than its witness to God's saving grace in individual lives."[1]

This is quite the claim! Scripture asserts itself to be absolutely, positively, 100 percent without error in any way, shape, or form. In other words, it claims to be truth!

Contrary to many people's claims and presuppositions, Scripture

---

[1] James Montgomery Boice, *Does Inerrancy Matter?*, Oakland: International Council on Biblical Inerrancy, 1979, p. 13.

is inerrant, but not in the way you might think. Genuine inerrancy does not apply to the myriad of translations and versions we have in our homes today. It's surprising but true. Scripture's inerrancy refers only to the original written manuscripts (also known as autographs) when they were first penned by their human authors. That'll probably cause a whiplash for some. It certainly did for me! But hang with me.

We must realize that Scripture has been copied and translated hundreds of thousands of times throughout the years since its original penning. The process of copying and translating has paved the way for some variations to creep into the text, leaving the pretty, leather-bound copies we have today slightly less accurate than the original documents.

One needs only to go to a local bookstore or open an Internet browser to discover quite the assortment of translations and versions of the Bible. If there are so many versions and translations, which one is right?

Precisely the point. These dozens of translations (just in English, not to mention the hundreds of other languages Scripture has been translated into) confirm that somewhere along the centuries of copying and translating, discrepancies arose and created the grammatical and textual variations we have today.

You wouldn't believe how many ongoing debates address the correct way to translate a specific verb tense of a certain Hebrew word. Scholars have been debating for centuries how to interpret Scripture correctly and keep it as close to the original autographs as possible. But because no two languages are the same, this is an impossible task. But don't worry. These variations are few and far between, and we'll talk about it lots more in coming chapters.

For now, to help us understand how discrepancies sneaked their way into the copies of Scripture, let's take a moment to think about the world as it was two thousand years ago, around the time the New Testament was written. No phones. No computers with Internet access and more information at our fingertips than we could ever want. No text messaging, e-mail, cell phones, digital cameras, online calendars, and yes, it's true: no Skype, Twitter, or Facebook!

Communication was limited to speech (the verbal, face-to-face kind) and the written word. And communication with those who didn't live nearby was left to—you guessed it—snail mail. Gasp!

Needless to say, technology was a far cry from what we have today. However, those living two thousand years ago were content in their blissful state of ignorance as to what mankind would accomplish technologically, so they made full use of what was available to them.

Let's zoom in on the snail-mail factor for a minute. Today, letters or other important documents can travel across a continent in one to three days, depending on whether the sender is willing to pay a little extra to overnight it. In biblical times, however, letters had to be carried and delivered (hand and foot) by a messenger. Yes, the human kind of messenger who probably took along a donkey or camel for good measure. And yes, I'm serious. Pages had to be hand-written (it's true; no Microsoft Word), and copies were created by written hand as well. Quite tragic that copy machines were not available. Even more astounding, the printing press had yet to be thought of!

Many of you already know this, but it is important to understand that the world was much different two thousand years ago. Why must we understand this? Because only then do we realize how easy it was for copies of the autographs to fall prey to textual and grammatical variations. Copiers of Scripture had to write out each book—letter by letter, sentence by sentence, page by page. They had to cross every "t" and dot every "i." Considering the three-quarters of a million words in the Bible, that's quite an undertaking![2]

Despite all these complicating factors, most textual discrepancies in the Bible are minor and limited to spelling and/or literary style, not compromising or distorting theological truths. In fact, the New

---

[2] http://www.christiananswers.net/bible/about.html. This site also has a plethora of other interesting facts about Scripture that are worth a glance!

More Than Words

Testament "can be regarded as 99.5 percent pure," and the remaining .5 percent are often figured out through a practice known as textual criticism.[3]

Impressive. And this fact possesses several profound ramifications for our inerrancy study.

First, it means that all those hundreds of thousands of people who hand-copied Scripture over hundreds of years made a shockingly tiny number of copying mistakes. Try to imagine working on that project, spending your whole life copying page after page of the most holy book in existence. Talk about pressure and a job I admittedly would not sign up for!

Also, the few mistakes these copying heroes (that's how I see them) committed were limited to issues like sentence structure and spelling, not discrepancies in the truths and principles taught in Scripture. Scribes didn't change what Scripture was saying; they simply made an error here and there in spelling and grammar.

That's amazing if you think about it. Many people today change the Bible to suit their purposes. They ignore or skip over some verses and hone in on others when it benefits them. Can you imagine what would have happened if one of the copiers of Scripture held that perspective? What if some Hebrew scribe of ancient times decided he didn't like a certain verse, so he left it out? Or what if he shortened a story or two because his hand was getting tired? Then we'd have one branch of copies that had the deleted lines and others that didn't. Talk about confusing and definitely not inerrant!

But that's not the case. God preserved the copying and translating of His Word in miraculous ways. Its only errors are minor textual discrepancies, not hypocrisies in its truths.

Let's draw this home for a moment with a modern-day example. Are you familiar with the game Telephone? One person says a phrase

---

[3] Boa, Kenneth. "The Reliability of the Bible." Bible.org. www.bible.org/seriespage/reliability-bible. Textual criticism refers to the practice of determining what the original autographs of Scripture said. Three different types of textual criticism will be introduced and explained in chapter five.

or sentence to the person next to him. That person repeats it to the next person in line and so on. At the end of the game, the last person repeats what she heard. But is it ever the same as the original sentence? Nope! Not unless only two people are playing, and even then it's hardly the same. Not only are words different, but usually the phrase or sentence ends up being completely dissimilar to the original.

Now, this obviously is not a perfect example, but you get the idea. It is a big deal that people copying the entire Bible made so few copying mistakes! A technologically inferior society managed a pretty impressive feat. The biggest motivating factor in this whole process (aside from the power and sovereignty of God) was undoubtedly the scribes' regard for Scripture as the holy, sacred, written Word of God, given to a people who would be utterly lost without it. They didn't think of the Bible as did the hypothetical lazy scribe we mentioned earlier. They didn't think of Scripture as something to pick and choose, depending on their current mood. Rather, they took it as the most holy of books ever penned on earth, and their meticulous practice of copying reflected that.

Get this: scribes in the Old Testament took this responsibility so seriously that if they made an error of any kind, they would destroy the entire manuscript they were working on.[4] No joke! They didn't have erasers or the convenient backspace button back then. But they did have a high regard for what they were copying, which should tell us something. Scribes realized how sacred and important Scripture is and did everything within their power to preserve its inerrancy to the best of their ability.

How often do we think of Scripture in those terms? How thick is the layer of dust on our Bible's cover? How stiff has nonuse made its binding? This book—which many dedicated their entire lives to copying in scrupulous and strict form—we hardly give notice. When we do, we rarely ascribe the reverence it deserves.

It's time we wake up and realize its heritage and power—how

---

[4] Boa, "The Reliability of the Bible."

carefully God preserved His Word for all these centuries so we can read and have access to the truth He penned long ago.

This is important stuff! We can hardly hope to understand inerrancy if we don't put it in a modern-day context. Along with the immaculate quality of the copies of Scripture, we must also take into consideration the quantity of the copies. Quality is grand, but not if there isn't anything to observe!

Let's take a look into the Old Testament scrolls. Because of their age (3500-2400-ish years old), existing manuscripts of the Old Testament are few in number. But those we do have are substantiated and supported by other discoveries made on archeological digs and such. For example, you surely have heard of, or are familiar with, the Dead Sea Scrolls (pictured below)

Photo courtesy of www.facsimile-editions.com

found in 1947 by a couple of young Bedouin shepherds.[5] These shepherds initially found a cave containing seven scrolls, which turned into a lottery of scrolls discovered during an extensive search over the next decade.

---

[5] Sweet little side note: the Dead Sea Scrolls have been placed online for anyone and everyone to see! Yay! Visit http://dss.collections.imj.org.il/ to check them out!

What is the Bible?

Why such an important find? Because these scrolls are fragments of Scripture, and some not just fragments! One scroll they found was the entire book of Isaiah, which is identical to the one we have in our Bibles today.

The dates of these scrolls (third century BC to 68 AD) astound us even more.[6] That's old, and the fact they still exist leaves us quite impressed! Scrolls dated as copies of the third century BC confirm, most *verbatim*, the copies of the Old Testament we have today—the entire book of Isaiah and fragments of every other book in the Old Testament except Esther.[7] This does wonders in confirming the inerrancy of Scripture, don't you think?

But the Dead Sea Scrolls are hardly the only confirmation we have of the Old Testament's accuracy and inerrancy. The Septuagint (a third century BC Greek translation of the Old Testament) also confirms the books from the Old Testament, along with the Samaritan Pentateuch (the first five books of the Old Testament, which the Samaritans confiscated from the Jews when they were freed from captivity in the fourth century BC)[8], the Targums (a collection of ancient paraphrases of the Old Testament), and the Talmud (an enormous collection of ancient Jewish laws and traditions).[9]

That's a lot of data, but all confirm the authenticity of the Old Testament manuscripts. The Old Testament books are substantiated not only by its own copies, but by the writings of other ancient Jewish literature preserved (although not nearly as well) through the centuries.

If you thought the Old Testament talk was impressive, wait until you hear about the New Testament. Copies of the New Testament are much easier to track down and evaluate because they are much younger than their Old Testament counterparts. Yet far more ancient

---

[6] Library of Congress. "Dead Sea—Introduction." ibiblio - The Public's Library and Digital Archive. http://www.ibiblio.org/expo/deadsea
[7] LaSor, William Sanford. *The Dead Sea Scrolls and the Christian Faith.* Chicago: Moody Press, 1956. Read more: http://www.answers.com/topic/dead-seascrolls#ixzz1OPC7gp2X
[8] http://www.biblehistory.com/Samaritans/SAMARITANSThe_Samaritan_Pentateuch.htm
[9] http://www.sacred-texts.com/jud/talmud.htm

More Than Words

manuscripts than just the Old Testament exist to compare the New Testament to. In fact, the number and quality of New Testament copies are unparalleled in all other ancient literature.[10] A pretty big claim, but oh, so true!

Some interesting facts for you: there are over five thousand Greek New Testament manuscripts, eight thousand Latin, and about one thousand in other languages (Coptic, Syriac, etc.).[11] That's a lot of copies! And remember our earlier discovery? In all these copies, the New Testament is still 99.5 percent without error. Amazing!

Like the Old Testament, New Testament books are confirmed and cited thousands of times over by early church fathers. This further substantiates the accuracy and inerrancy present within such enormous quantity. So, how does the New Testament rate with other ancient literature in terms of quantity? Glad you asked! The number of existing copies of other ancient works (from those such as Plato, Caesar, Tacitus, or Aristotle) ranges from one to twenty.[12] Not one to twenty thousand, but one to twenty, period. You can easily see how those can't compare to the New Testament, which has well over *ten thousand* very well-preserved copies!

The bottom line? Scripture's inerrancy remains well documented historically and archeologically by quality *and* quantity. No other ancient text or literature comes close in comparison. Logically, if we quickly believe the authenticity of other ancient writings, such as those of Plato or Aristotle, we'd better be willing to trust Scripture! Scripture's inerrancy—being without error—proves astounding and overwhelmingly true. Even though the copies we have today contain slight errors, they rank near perfection—varying in only spelling and slight grammatical discrepancies from the original autographs. Scripture deserves our trust, folks, and within its pages we find the truth by which we can and must base our lives. Conveniently, we will address this in the next part of our biblical definition.

---

[10] Boa, Kenneth. "The Reliability of the Bible."
[11] Ibid.
[12] Boa, Kenneth. "The Reliability of the Bible."

INFALLIBLE

Since we mastered the concept of inerrancy, let's look at another claim about Scripture: its infallibility. Merriam-Webster defines infallible as (1) "incapable of error," (2) "not liable to mislead, deceive or disappoint," and (3) "incapable of error in defining doctrines touching faith or morals."[13] This doesn't seem much different than inerrancy. In fact, many scholars and believers alike interchange the terms synonymously. But I am persuaded a difference exists between the two, even if slight.

Inerrancy promotes the Bible as error-free—grammatically, structurally—perfectly and wholly complete as God's true Word. When the authors penned the first autographs, they recorded truth from the Living and True God to us, His created people and children. His Word holds true in every aspect—physical, emotional, historical, etc. Infallibility agrees with inerrancy yet walks it a step further. Inerrancy claims the Bible *cannot* make a mistake, deceive, or mislead those who place their trust in its truth. The words of Scripture stand not only as accurate; but absolute truth in all they record, assert, and claim.

This, of course, throws many people off because astonishing ramifications inevitably follow such a claim. If true, if Scripture really exists without error in what it says, commands, implies, and promises, I must obey it and adhere to it. Otherwise all the warnings and promises of judgment it describes will apply to me without exception. I will be without excuse because I have the error-free truth in my hands but have refused to listen to and/or obey it.

See the predicament? Asserting Scripture's truth and inerrancy is not an action for the weary-hearted. As soon as we admit its infallibility, we bind ourselves to its truth and place ourselves under subjection to it.

This is why many people either refuse to believe that Scripture is infallible or do their best to avoid the topic altogether. I'll say this

---

[13] http://www.merriam-webster.com/dictionary/infallible

several times throughout this book, but the phrase "Ignorance is bliss" is true. Many people would rather remain blissful in ignorance than humbled in knowledge. What you don't know can't hurt you, right?

Unfortunately, that's deceptively wrong. Truth is truth, regardless of what you do with it. It's our choice as human beings to discover truth and either surrender to it or ignore it and hope for the best. I heartily recommend the first option. I am a life-long student of it.

Pursuing truth inexorably brings us to the infallibility claim about Scripture because Scripture claims to be the truth. And not just *a* truth; *the* truth. Scripture asserts itself as the only total and complete truth available to us in this universe. We receive a choice, Scripture or something else, never Scripture *and* something else.

Scripture's inerrancy serves as an unavoidable claim to test in our conquest for truth. Think of it this way: if someone told you he had a fool-proof and guaranteed way to pay off all your debt and then endow you with unlimited treasures of greatest worth, he'd pique interest, right? If he said the way to do this is found only in the box he's holding, would you still be interested? And if he proceeded to tell you he desired to give it to you freely, without hesitation or qualification, would you still want to take a peek?

The claims of inerrancy and infallibility of Scripture compose only parts of Scripture's story until this point. They get us curious enough to take a peek, which is all He asks of us. However, if you search outside the box and discover the truth of its claims, you realize your accountability to it. We're all accountable to truth, whether or not we want to know about it. Consider yourself challenged. Decide whether you want to know the truth and let it set you free, or if you want the man with the mysterious box to pass you by. It's your choice. Unfortunately, you're held accountable to what's in the box regardless of your decision.

So do you want to know what you're accountable to? I highly recommend an answer of "yes!" If you agree, let's get started and see what's in the box!

What is the Bible?

Not much in life qualifies as infallible—incapable of making a mistake or misleading us. In fact, the only examples the dictionary gives us of the word infallible are double-negatives. It refers only to items that are *not* infallible.

No person escapes fallibility (even couples madly caught up in puppy love find this out eventually!). But what about objects or possessions? What about a calculator? Do they make mistakes? Not if programmed correctly. We rely heavily on a properly functioning calculator; otherwise we find ourselves in big trouble with our taxes, budget, and a lot more!

We place our confidence in these little mechanical devices because they distribute objective and accurate mathematical information. They hold no bias against us (though some may think otherwise, especially during tax season!). They exist to state the facts, and we base decisions on those facts accordingly. Since calculators don't err mathematically, (barring malfunction or human error), they seem to qualify for definition of infallibility. But only until we realize being error-free is only part of the equation. We mustn't neglect the part that claims an infallible thing/person/object cannot mislead, deceive, or disappoint.

Calculators, though seemingly sure, render disappointment on many occasions. Consider this: John uses his calculator to gather all his financial statements and creates a plan to become a millionaire in five years. He's got a plan and the calculator backs it up, so by golly, he runs with it!

What the calculator fails to factor into its calculations is the impending economic recession. This error causes John to lose his job and plunges him into an upheaval reaching far beyond finances. The calculator suggested a possibility of becoming a millionaire but remained significantly limited in its perspective—leaving ample room for disappointment.

So when we assert Scripture's infallibility, we not only claim its incapability of error, but also its inability to mislead, deceive, or disappoint. However, we must assert its infallibility on *its* terms. Truth is truth no matter what, and oftentimes we don't much appreciate what we discover. But if we submit to Scripture's authority and follow its truth with humble obedience, disappointment will evade us in the end.

In Scripture we find many stories of people differing in opinion from God's. But if they submit to God's truth and direction, they inevitably find contentment and peace in the end. Many scholars, pastors and theologians have penned a multitude of volumes about the subject of Scripture's infallibility. Nonetheless, we will explore a bit more by focusing on two distinct parts of infallibility: being "without error" (though with a little twist from our previous section), and infallibility's relationship with being "God's Word." Both are crucial, so let's dig in!

WITHOUT ERROR

You'll recall from the previous section of inerrancy all the facts and data providing evidence of the inerrancy of Scripture in the original autographs. Now we'll see why Scripture must be inerrant in order to be infallible if, indeed, it is the Word of God.

We've established Scripture contains no error (at least, 99.5 percent inerrant in the copies available today). Would it matter if it had a mistake or two? Why would one theological error be significant among all those chapters and books?

If one part of Scripture errs, then the Bible by definition fails as God's written Word. The inerrancy of Scripture rides on the wave of God's inerrancy and perfection. If the God of the Bible lives as He claims to—alone in perfection and holiness—He is incapable of error. His Word, as an extension of Himself, is also incapable of error.

Our journey together stops at this point unless we grasp the inextricable relationship between God and His Word. Scripture ascribes perfection to God. He alone exists as omniscient (all-knowing),[14] omnipotent (all-powerful),[15] omnipresent (everywhere at all times),[16] holy,[17] truth,[18] the Creator of all things,[19] sovereign,[20] and much more. He chose to reveal these things about Himself through His Word. If His Word is faulty in any way, the revelation presented in it cannot be defended beyond doubt. There can be no partiality with God or His Word. He decided to make His Word a direct reflection of Himself; thus, it must be infallible. Anything less would negate the truths presented in it.

At this point we move beyond discussing the mere words of Scripture and focus instead on the *meanings* of those words. In the inerrancy section, we realized Scripture's words are without error to an unparalleled degree among ancient texts. But now we move beyond the language itself into the *meaning* God wants to communicate through it.

Pause for a moment and put on your thinking caps as we delve into the philosophical. Since God desires communication with us through written word, we need to understand the relationship between words (language) and their meaning. Many neglect to realize such a relationship, which is why we must address it!

God authored all language, correct? Think back to the Tower of Babel in Genesis 11. Until that point in history, everyone spoke the same language and had no difficulty communicating with each other. Their harmonious communication fared too well for them, for through it they began disobeying God. Perhaps you know the story. God's anger burned, and He decided to strike the people with

---

[14] 1 John 3:20; 2 Kings 19:27; Psalm 50:11; Isaiah 66:18; Jeremiah 29:11; Ezekiel 11:5; Revelation 2:2, 9, 13, 19; 3:1, 8, 15. These are some of many verses declaring God's omniscience.
[15] 1 Chronicles 29:11-12; 2 Chronicles 20:6; Job 42:2; Isaiah 40:26; Ephesians 1:21, 3:20; Philippians 3:21; Hebrews 1:3; Revelation 4:11. These are a sampling of the many passages of Scripture that assert God's omnipotence.
[16] Psalm 50:11; 139:1-10; Isaiah 20:15-16; Jeremiah 23:24. Evidence of God's omnipresence saturates Scripture; these are just a few examples to serve as a starting point.
[17] Leviticus 11:44-45; 19:2, 21:8; Psalm 22:3, 93:5; Isaiah 48:17; Ezekiel 36:22; 1 Peter 1:16.
[18] Psalm 25:5, 10; 31:5, 40:11, 108:4, 119:142; John 3:21, 14:6, 16:13, 17:17; 1 Timothy 2:4
[19] Genesis 1:1; Isaiah 40:26-28,42:5, 43:1, 7; 45:8, 12, 15, 18; Romans 1:25, 1 Peter 4:19
[20] 1 Timothy 6:15, Deuteronomy 32:4, Isaiah 25:1, Romans 12:2, Philippians 3:12

confusion by causing them to speak different languages. The inability to communicate paralyzed their idolatrous task of building a tower to the heavens. A universal language instantly morphed into several, making communication frustrating and impossible.

Now back to our infallibility discussion. No language exerts more holiness or is less prone to infallibility than another. Language is language. God created every language spoken on this earth. None hold more intrinsic value than another, nor are any less valuable than another. For whatever reason, God chose three languages to write Scripture: Hebrew, Aramaic, and Greek. There's nothing innately special about these three. As we'll learn later, they were simply the most logical choices based on the times and people Scripture addresses. The point here is that language itself exists as a mere tool through which God communicates His truth to the world.

Language expresses itself via words, yet *meanings* are what's important, not the words themselves. This is where hermeneutics (i.e. the proper study of Scripture) comes into play. Together, we're learning how to read, interpret, and apply Scripture. Our responsibility as believers in Christ includes learning to take the words at face value, but not to the extent of neglecting what God is trying to communicate through them.

Our perspective must remain proper: only God's intent and truth matters. Our job is to interpret it on His terms. Gordon Lewis articulates this point wonderfully when he says, "An important distinction between the Bible as given and the Bible as interpreted should be noted. The doctrine of infallibility applies to the Bible as a given, not to the interpretation of any individual."[21] Infallibility applies to what God wrote in Scripture, not to whatever we may think is there or our opinion of what it says.

Infallibility reaches beyond mere words into the meaning of those words as God intended them. The pages of Scripture contain no

---

[21] Gordon R. Lewis, "What Does Biblical Infallibility Mean?" *Bulletin of the Evangelical Theological Society* 6.1 (Winter 1963): 18-27.

hidden meanings. We must not get caught up in technical details of words, but rather concentrate on the communication moving through them. For example, if one version translates a phrase "his height was like the height of cedars"[22] as opposed to "he was tall as the cedars,"[23] the translators are hardly committing egregious sin.

The point of the text remains, does it not? This is what we mean by pointing out the difference between honing in on words over and above their meanings. No matter what we're reading or listening to, the meaning or message communicated through the words is more important than the exact words themselves. Though without error, the language and words of Scripture serve merely as tools God uses to communicate His truth. We still must seek His truth and meaning on His terms, but it's wise to understand what we're looking for so we don't get caught up in an unnecessary quarrel of semantics.

Let's now turn our investigation beyond inerrancy and determine why Scripture is incapable of misleading, deceiving, or disappointing those who hold it as their ultimate authority. There's quite a difference between being error-free and being incapable of misleading or deceiving.

GOD'S WORD

We'll get deeper into the subject of the Bible as God's Word a bit later, but it's too important to ignore now. Scripture claims to be God's Word (2 Timothy 3:16-17, among others), which means it is the word God specifically chose to speak to humanity.

The words of God must logically reflect the character and nature of God. What He says reveals who He is. This is true with everyone in some degree or another. We hold people responsible and accountable for what they say and who they present themselves to be. If someone

---

[22] Amos 2:9 in NASB
[23] Amos 2:9 in NIV

presents himself in a false manner and the truth surfaces, he finds himself in a tough spot.

Let me give you an example. A man named Mike wants to court a pretty young lady. She captivated his attention from the moment he laid eyes on her, and he exercises extreme measures to elicit her attention as well. When he finally rallies enough nerve, he introduces himself in a thoughtfully articulated presentation—designed to warrant her immediate approval.

Mike runs into a dire problem, though. His brilliantly crafted introduction fabricates facts. He exaggerates some of his stories, thinking they will impress her. You can imagine the outcome. If she remains interested, it won't take long to discover all those awesome stories that drew her to him weren't true at all. Then what will happen? She'll be gone faster than he can blink and realize what happened!

Here's the point: people's words reveal, directly or indirectly, who they are. Mike claimed to be someone he wasn't, but the girl discovered the truth in the end. Truth always surfaces, and God's truth in Scripture bears no exception. (Well, He *is* truth, but you get my point).

The concept of infallibility of Scripture depends completely on this point. The Bible contains God's Word—words about Himself along with many other assertions—which reveals His character traits and attributes. If His character is flawed in any way, then His Word is flawed. If His Word is flawed or untrue, then *He* cannot be completely true. See the connection? One is dependent on the other and vice versa. If the Bible's claims are true, if God is incapable of making a mistake, then His Word, by default, is true and infallible—incapable of deceiving, misleading, or disappointing you if your perspective corresponds with His.

Admitting that God and His Word are true, without fault, and incapable of deceiving us is a big step. How can He expect us to believe His Word to the extent that we base our lives on it? At this point it gets personal. Consider this a challenge to do some investigation of your own. Yes, it seems like a copout answer. But think about it. Personal theologies cause heated debates. They range everywhere between those who believe Scripture is completely true and those who believe the exact opposite—that Scripture is fallible and not worth pursuing. Two opposing sides, two different arguments and evidentiary claims. The only way to investigate this argument, if you haven't yet settled it, is by reading Scripture and finding out whether its claims about itself and God prove true. He'll answer. I promise.

Regardless of what side you're on or leaning toward, you always come to a point of decision. Then you must take a step of faith. Here's some food for thought: it sometimes takes more faith to believe Scripture than to doubt it.

So investigate. Investigate Scripture's claims about God and about itself, then investigate the God of those claims. Has He ever failed? Has anything written of Him in His Word ever proven false in the end? Read Scripture, read books, discuss with others, pray. At some point you will have to take a step of faith—either for God and His infallible Word, or in yourself and your guaranteed fallibility (sorry to tell you, but it's true: you are quite fallible!).

It's your choice. Be encouraged and challenged to make the right one. No one can do it for you. But remember, truth is objective. It exists whether you're on board with it or not. So make sure your beliefs correspond with it!

INSPIRED

Unlike our first two terms—inerrant and infallible—we must examine the term "inspired" with a biblical definition, not merely with an English one. Though a number of definitions correspond with the concept of inspiration (English and non-English), we must ascribe Scripture's definition of inspiration with the highest priority. A quick visit of the basic concept of inspiration will help us ascertain such a definition.

Instead of writing Scripture Himself—speaking the Bible into existence as He did creation—God used people to write Scripture in a tangible form. He inspired human authors to write His Word, which reveals Himself to the world. Just as He used language as a tool, He used human authors as His instruments to capture His words with ink on a page. These human authors were, of course, bound by time and space (unlike God). Therefore, Scripture was written at a particular time, in a particular place, to a particular people. God doesn't directly address people living in every point along the timeline of history in one broad sweep. Instead, He limited the compilation of Scripture to a particular time and people by inspiring human authors to write His Word for their particular situations. In light of this, a splendid definition/explanation of biblical inspiration follows:

> God did not dictate most of the Bible in the first person. He did not say, "Because I'm God I will speak directly to everybody in all times and cultures." Instead, God (the ultimate source) spoke through the human writers of Scripture (the immediate source) to address the real-life needs of people at a particular time in a particular culture. This is how God chose to speak.[24]

God could have communicated however He wanted, but ultimately He chose the way of written word. He confirms His decision in 2 Timothy 3:16-17:

> All Scripture is inspired by God (or God-breathed) and profitable for teaching, for reproof, for correction, for training in righteousness; so that the man of God may be adequate, equipped for every good work.

---

[24] Duvall, J. Scott, and J. Daniel Hays. *Grasping God's Word: a Hands-on Approach to Reading, Interpreting, and Applying the Bible.* Grand Rapids, Mich.: Zondervan, 2001. 99.

Inspiration simply means that God impressed His words upon the minds, hearts, and hands of the biblical writers so they could write His inerrant, infallible, and inspired Word for generations to come. We don't know exactly how He inspired each individual author. Did He direct their thoughts, supernaturally take over the feather and ink, or give them an incredibly strong sense of what to write? We don't know. But that's not the important part.

Not knowing *how* doesn't negate knowing that He *did*. God desired to bestow a message to the world, and He chose to communicate it through ordinary, nothing-astronomical-about-them men who practiced other occupations and lived vastly different stories. One commonality weaved among them, however, and that was the Lord. He inspired each of them to write down His truth, which they did obediently and thoroughly. The end product? His inerrant, infallible, inspired, and (next point) living Word.

LIVING

> For the Word of God is living and active and sharper than any two-edged sword, and piercing as far as the division of the soul and spirit, of both joints and marrow, and able to judge the thoughts and intentions of the heart. (Hebrews 4:12)

Don't you love that verse? It accomplishes what it promises—piercing through the distractions and chaos threatening to sidetrack you even as you sit here and read. It captures your attention with its rich descriptive words, graphic similes, and drastic comparisons. This verse alone proves the point that Scripture is living, but we're going to take a deeper look at this concept anyway, because it's worth it!

Let's recall some of the questions we asked about Scripture at the beginning of this study. Is it simply an ancient text? Or a good book with moral values and guidelines that supposedly help us along the way? Is it a collection of ancient manuscripts telling us how to get to God or please Him?

Now let's add a new one. Does it have any relevance or practical meaning for today? If Scripture is just a good book, it falls short of some unforeseen expectation and leaves us disappointed. We have lots of good books. Many even claim to show us how to get to God and please Him. What makes Scripture different?

The Quran, the Buddhist's Theravada or Mahayana, the Book of Mormon, and hundreds of others claim 1) to be crucial in your personal faith, and 2) to know how to relate to God (or gods—assuming they believe in Him/them). Scripture claims these things too yet stands unique because of its other claims: inerrancy, infallibility, and inspiration. Quite a rare (and by rare, of course, we mean *only*) combination in existence today.

But something else sets it apart as well. It's living. No, that does not mean it breathes, moves, or is going to sprout legs and begin walking around. But it does mean it's relevant and impacts our lives daily and practically, if we adhere to its truth.

Though God chose to write His Word with ink and paper (or parchment or scrolls), His communication with us isn't restricted to words on a page. Those of us who enter a personal relationship with Him through Jesus Christ are still in communication with, guided, sharpened, strengthened, comforted (and about a million other descriptive words) through His living written Word. God didn't instruct the human authors to pen His words just to leave them for humanity to do with them what they would. No! He preserved them and uses (note the present tense, not *used*) His Holy Spirit to breathe life and truth from them into a believer's life every time she reads it. This is powerful! This is what having a living Scripture means! God uses His Word as much today as He did when He originally inspired the authors to pen it.

The life of His Word is yet another direct reflection of its Author.

The Bible lives because the God who wrote it lives and uses it daily to teach, reprove, correct, and train us in righteousness. He remains active in the lives and hearts and minds of His people through His Word. He empowers His Word to interact with us by means of His Spirit. The same Spirit, by the way, who "dwells in you, He who raised Christ Jesus from the dead will also give life to your mortal bodies through His Spirit who dwells in you."[25]

The Holy Spirit and Scripture intertwine, especially in reference to this living aspect of the Word. Consider Ephesians 6:17, where Paul talked about putting on the armor of God: "The sword of the Spirit . . . is the word of God." The two cannot be separated. At the beginning of the church in Acts, "the place where they had gathered together was shaken, and they were all filled with the Holy Spirit and began to speak the word of God with boldness."[26]

The Holy Spirit preceded the preaching of the Word. We see them linked again with a promise of Jesus: "When He, the Spirit of truth, comes, He will guide you into all the truth; for He will not speak on His own initiative, but whatever He hears, He will speak; and He will disclose to you. . . ."[27]

Paul sheds light on their relationship with salvation as well, saying, "In Him, you also, after listening to the message of truth, the gospel of your salvation—having also believed, you were sealed in Him with the Holy Spirit of promise."[28]

A multitude of passages sheds light on the relationship between the Holy Spirit and the Bible, but I hope the aforementioned examples gave you a glimpse into this beautiful relationship. The Holy Spirit is God, along with the Father and Jesus Christ. He's alive. He is not some impersonal or mystical cosmic force that cannot be understood or fathomed. He allows us to understand Himself and His role within the Godhead (at least to the extent that's possible for our little, finite

---

[25] Romans 8:11
[26] Acts 4:31
[27] John 16:13
[28] Ephesians 1:13

brains) through His Word. He operates and functions with the Word to reveal the truth that sets us free, if we choose to live by it.

When we approach Scripture humbled and hungry to seek and know Him more, He speaks through His Word to touch and transform our lives, leaving us speechless and in awe of Him. This assumes, of course, we're willing to obey what it says. James writes,

> Therefore, putting aside all filthiness and all that remains of wickedness, in humility receive the word implanted, which is able to save your souls. But prove yourselves doers of the word, and not merely hearers who delude themselves.[29]

We can have utmost knowledge of Scripture and the best intention to know the truth no matter the cost. But if we find the truth and don't obey it, we don't accomplish much. God's Word is living, but the rate at which it lives in and through us depends on us. Those who approach it eagerly and with great expectation of being conformed into the image of Christ will experience its life far more than those who open it once a week during the preacher's sermon. We've got to give it and the Holy Spirit opportunity to live and move in our lives.

Scripture is not just some book with a bunch of rules or outdated proverbs bearing no practical ramifications for today. It is God's inerrant, infallible, inspired, and living Word, as real and impactful today as the sword of Hebrews 4:12: two-edged, "and piercing as far as the division of the soul and spirit, of both joints and marrow, and able to judge the thoughts and intentions of the heart."

It gets personal because it is personal. He is personal, and He uses Scripture as a tool to communicate with us intimately and profoundly on a daily basis.

---

[29] James 1:21-22

WORD OF GOD

This point may seem redundant in light of the thirty-plus times we have referred to Scripture as the Word of God thus far. But skipping this point would result in grave injustice. Please take a brief journey with me, engaging your bright and creative imaginations.

We're going back to a time before the world existed. Only God and His splendor and glory exists. In all His holiness and perfect contentment, God decides to speak a perfect and beautiful world into existence, knowing full well that complications would arise because of sin. He creates this awesome and magnificent place for the next part of His creation: mankind. He then gives them a mandate to work, rule, and subdue His home, Earth. God didn't have to give Adam and Eve the mandate to love, worship, or have a relationship with Him; they naturally lived in perfect harmony with Him and each other.

Imagine what it must have been like to take luxurious strolls through the most astounding and serene environment the world has ever known. Can you picture the vibrant blue skies mixed with the lush green of the vegetation and the intoxicating colors of the birds and animals? The word "dull" didn't exist at this point, friends! Every aspect of creation exudes perfection and fascination. Every blade of grass stands at perfect attention, and the fluffy-tailed bunnies frolic through the cool dew of morning. Adam and Eve wake up to the radiant, golden sunshine warming their pink, rosy faces, speechless once again. Daily they walk, chat, laugh, and have an intimate relationship with God. They have no hindrances. They behold glory face-to-face and are filled with ecstatic joy like a Midwestern child seeing the beach for the first time. Every single detail is perfect and awe-inspiring, including the relationship Adam and Eve share with God.

Communication in the Garden of Eden was completely unhindered and unmarred, freely flowing between the created and their Maker.

No fear, shame, disappointment, pride, or brokenness. Just goodness left only to our imaginations.

But we all know that perfection does not last. With a swift decision, the story turns tragic. The beautiful harmony and awe-inspiring relationship between man and God plunge to a crashing halt when Adam and Eve sin. It's a story preached from pulpits all over the world. Because sin pronounced people unfit for God's presence, a barrier erected between them that day. Adam and Eve lost the privilege to walk with God in intimacy and freedom when they chose themselves and creation over Him—the Creator. It was the most tragic day the earth ever endured and created an incomprehensible dilemma for the relationship between God and people.

Typically, teaching on this topic focuses on the severed relationship. Yet one less-frequently taught aspect remains—that communication also broke that day.

Think about it. Wrap your brain around it and let it seep into the depths of your being. No longer could Adam and Eve walk freely with God. No more late-afternoon walks in the garden or unbridled intimacy, which defined their relationship. Awkwardness crept in, along with shame and disappointment. Adam and Eve's eyes were opened to a world and life outside of God—one of their choosing, and one they undoubtedly regretted.

Before we get too carried away, we must realize that communication didn't cease, but the *way* He communicated with them changed drastically. No longer were the Creator and created on the same page, hearts beating harmoniously with each other. From then on, all communication, love, adoration, and worship were forcibly filtered through the chasm of sin separating them.

This is where our topic of Scripture arrives on the scene. It is God's Word to us! We now possess His Word, which Adam and Eve didn't appreciate nearly enough, in written and permanent form. Granted, communication between God and us is still hindered, but now we see what a vital role Scripture plays. Scripture mends that which was brutally torn in the communication between God and mankind. Not perfectly as before, but enough to reestablish communication with God again through Jesus.

Scripture is not only God's way of giving humanity something tangible and sure to base our lives upon, but also the means through which He communicates with us today. The Bible is God's Word to us. Slow down and ponder this for a minute. It is God's—not Buddha's, not some ancient guru's or drunken loony's, but God's—the almighty, all-powerful, sovereign, holy, and awe-inspiring Lord of all. It is His Word, impressed upon human authors to compile in written form, preserved immaculately for hundreds of years. He offers it as a free and precious gift to us—yes, us! He offers it to our families, neighbors, friends, co-workers, employers, church family, and on and on and on. It is His method and message of communication to a world hopelessly lost without Him.

What is the message He graciously tries to communicate to us? The simple, beautiful, profound truth of the gospel—though humanity fell past reconciliation, redemption is possible and guaranteed to those who choose to accept Jesus Christ and make Him Lord of their lives. That's the bottom line of Scripture. It's why we're all still here—why God hasn't called the whole thing off. The message of our redemption through Jesus Christ is the thread that weaves all of Scripture together. It's God's message through His Word to us on a personal, powerful, and profound basis. Can we say "Wow," or are we all too speechless at the moment?

Let this truth drench every fiber of your being. We are unworthy of such a gift, much less a written record explaining it to us! Be thankful. Be humbled. Be amazed. That's what the big fuss is all about. We have in our homes, on our dusty and probably neglected bookshelves, the very Word of God recorded and preserved for humanity so we could communicate with God and understand His plan for us.

It's a big deal, folks. Remember that every time you hold a Bible in your hand or sit down to read it. Savor what it is and taste each morsel of truth you glean from its beautiful and holy pages. It doesn't disappoint!

We've now successfully given Scripture a working definition, which we'll base the rest of our adventures on. Scripture is the inerrant, infallible, inspired, and living Word of God given to us so we may know Him in a personal and radical way. It is 100 percent accurate. It is not capable of disappointing or letting us down. It can penetrate the depths of our core and reveal truth to us in ways we never imagined. It's the tool He uses to communicate His message of hope to us—His people.

We worship an amazing God. Gaining access to such a gift as His Word goes beyond human comprehension. Take a few moments today and a few times throughout the week to pause and reflect on the gift of His Word. It would have been awesome enough with only one of its characteristics, yet it has all of them and more. Treasure it, friends. We've been given the gift of a lifetime—the gift leading us to eternity with Him through His glorious gospel.

The Canon

We've covered what the Bible is—the inerrant, infallible, inspired, and living Word of God. Now let's turn to discover where it came from. First we'll look at how it's put together (many little books all in one). Then we'll discover who wrote it (human authors), what languages it was written in, how long it took to write, and finally, how exciting it is. It's much more than an instruction manual!

How is this cool, old book put together? It's sixty-six books total, divided into two categories, the Old Testament (thirty-nine books) and the New Testament (twenty-seven books). God endows us with far more than just *a* book, He lavishes us with *lots* of books for us to observe, study, interpret, and apply to our lives. Can you imagine if we received only one book? Or one page? Our faith would look much different. Our theology would be stinted, our understanding of the gospel limited, and our grasp of His character traits and attributes weak at best.

But He didn't give us just one page. He presents us with page after page, book after book, testament after testament of His beautiful truth in written form! We could spend our entire lives poring over one book without digesting all it has to offer about God. Yet we get the opportunity to pursue sixty-six of them!

We must approach Scripture with a posture of eternal thanks to God for giving us so much of His Word. We don't deserve one word. God could have left Adam and Eve alone and let Satan exercise total dominion on Earth until it self-destructed. But He didn't. Rather, He involved Himself with His creation by communicating with them, primarily through His Word. Now we have access not only to the history of the world and our faith, but also to His heart, character, personality, and goodness. We couldn't hope to know even a fraction of what we do today without the Bible, and He crafted its extravagant volume so we can pursue more than our fill for this lifetime!

Here's a question to ponder. Who decided that those particular thirty-nine books of the Old Testament qualified for inclusion in the Bible? Why not thirty-five or forty-two? What about other books written at the time?

If this question remains unanswered, we'll have a hard time defending our faith because we won't know where its bedrock came from. The Bible is the foundation for Christianity—for our relationship with Christ. Knowing about this foundation is crucial to understanding our faith. That's one of the many reasons we're talking about the canon and its history.

The books of Scripture were written as time progressed throughout both Old and New Testaments. God carried out His plan of redemption and recorded every necessary step of the way.

Genesis explains where we came from—Creation, the Fall, the Flood, and how humanity multiplied and God chose a people to be His instruments to the world. From there it describes the ups and downs of His chosen people (Israel). God establishes Israel as His chosen nation, and as it turns out, they are a high maintenance bunch! They fall into a crazy sin-repent-forgiven-sin-again cycle, which they repeat over and over and over again throughout their history. Scripture records these cycles, along with a plethora of other historical narratives and facts. It is then collected, memorized, studied, and indoctrinated into the minds and hearts of believers. This basically describes the Old Testament.

Fast forward a few hundred years to the first century AD. The Old Testament stands complete, and Christ arrives on the scene. The New Testament begins by recording His time on Earth and many items He did, said, and accomplished. The rest of Scripture reflects the next phase of redemption that Christ brought to the world. Because of Him, people can enter God's presence and begin a relationship with Him. Access to God is no longer restricted to His people, Israel. The New Testament describes this shift in detail, and like the Old Testament, still contains historical documentation of church history. It explains the new theological understandings the early church encountered, based on the new perspective Christ extended to them.

Both the Old and New Testaments revolve around Christ. The Old Testament points to Him; the New Testament introduces and elaborates on Him.

Over time, the books of the Bible were written and collected. Then the time came for them to be solidified as a canon—to receive their stamp of approval as being from God. Enter the Canon Committee (or so I like to call it).

A committee usually involves a bunch of people with a title, wondering what to do with it. Some of you may serve on one. Some are good, productive, and beneficial. Others can be a waste of time, energy, and focus. It may come as a surprise to learn that a committee decided which books would be included in the Bible (though the formal term for that committee is council). If there was ever a committee that was worth its weight in beans, it was the committee that determined what books would be included in Scripture!

Imagine for a moment what it would be like to sit on such a committee. You bear responsibility for confirming what books are worthy of inclusion into the most holy book the world has ever known.

Can we say *pressure*? You can rightly imagine the people serving on that particular committee took their positions very seriously. How, then, did they make such decisions?

Let's take a look at the term canon first. What does it mean? The term itself has a long history of meanings (yep, words do change meaning over time! Consider: gay, awesome, coke, hot ... you get the point). The basic historical meaning of canon in Greek and Hebrew is a "measuring rod." This changed slightly over time and ended up as "the standard that books had to meet to be recognized as Scripture."[1] Basically, to be considered for Scripture, each book had to be canonized—deemed worthy of being included.

Ultimately, God alone determined the canonicity of every book in Scripture. He inspired and approved sixty-six books as worthy to be a part of His Word. He chose every word written in His canon and preserved it immaculately from the moment of its writing. The books He inspired were widely accepted and debated little at the time of and after their writing.

Yet, a time did come when others tried to introduce uninspired books, claiming they originated from God. In order to maintain the unity and preservation of Scripture—true Scripture—councils were formed to affirm (or confirm, more than decide) what books were indeed inspired, and which ones would not be included in the canon. These councils were made up of church leaders God chose to acknowledge His work amidst the rising heretical books being written in that day. These councils pursued this calling with utmost reverence.

Back to the big question: how did the councils perform such a weighty duty? In an effort to make a complicated subject easier, we'll limit our study to the specific guidelines they used to canonize the books of Scripture. The biggest confirmation of a biblical book's worth in Scripture is Jesus Christ. Why? Because

---

[1] Keathley III, J. Hampton. "The Bible: The Holy Canon of Scripture | Bible.org - Worlds Largest Bible Study Site." Free NET Bible and Thousands of Bible Studies | Bible.org - Worlds Largest Bible Study Site. http://bible.org/seriespage/bible-holy-canon-scripture.

It was He who confirmed the inspiration of the Hebrew canon of the Old Testament; and it was He who promised the Holy Spirit would direct the apostles into all truth.[2]

While on earth, Jesus quoted (directly or indirectly through reference) from almost every book of the Old Testament.[3] If it was recognized as God's Word by God's Son, then we can do the same! The councils agreed. They realized that if Christ quoted or referred to a particular book of the Old Testament, it was authoritative and approved by God to be canonized.

The councils also used other standards to determine a book's canonicity. Here are a few of those standards:

Canonicity[4]

- If it (the book) is **authoritative**—contained words clearly claimed to be directly from God; i.e., phrases like "Thus says the Lord."
- If it is **prophetic**—if it was written by a prophet, king, judge, scribe, apostle—an authoritative spiritual leader anointed by God and recognized as such by the people.
- If it is **authentic**—not contradicting other revelation of truth; historically accurate.
- If it is **dynamic**—containing evidence of God's hand working and confirming His truth.
- If it is **received**—if it was accepted by the people as God's Word and continued to have that reputation long after it was written.
- If it is **doctrinally accurate.**

---

[2] Geisler, Norman L., and William E. Nix. *A General Introduction to the Bible* . Chicago: Moody Press, 1968. 207.
[3] The only books not quoted by Jesus were Esther, Ecclesiastes, and Song of Solomon.
[4] Litke, Sid. "Canonicity | Bible.org - Worlds Largest Bible Study Site." Free NET Bible and Thousands of Bible Studies | Bible.org - Worlds Largest Bible Study Site. http://bible.org/seriespage/canonicity.

These are no-joke requirements, taken seriously by the councils that used them to solidify the canon. "Making the cut" was no laughing matter. These men pursued their work diligently and approached their task with reverence. Many false books existed, and weeding through the false to authenticate the true was not an assignment taken lightly, especially when considering that they were dealing with God's Word! Now let's take a look at who these men were and when they began this task.

The books of the Old Testament were highly recognized and accepted before the time of Christ, which helps explain why people were not surprised to hear Him quoting from them. The Jews were content with their Old Testament Scriptures, and Jesus quoting them only authenticated what they already believed—the Old Testament is God's Word.

Since the people already accepted and believed that the Old Testament books were of God, the council didn't have to do much to confirm it later, when the New Testament was being written. There are rumors (some weightier than others) that a council existed (the Council of Jamnia) to solidify the Old Testament canon in AD 90. Some scholars adamantly assert this council existence, while others completely refute it. The bottom line is that it doesn't matter all that much *when* the Old Testament was confirmed, but that it *has been confirmed*. Case closed. No more books can be added; none can be taken away. Straightforward and simple, the way we like it.

Next is the New Testament. We have a bit more information with this Testament, largely because, well, it's newer! Here's its story. The New Testament books (both gospels and letters) were written and distributed among the churches over a period of about forty-five years and continued to be collected and distributed as time went on. As they were written, they were recognized as being from God (a good example is 2 Peter 3:14-18), which made the job of the councils easier in confirming them. As we mentioned earlier, as time progressed, other books from uninspired authors began popping up and claiming they were from God—clearly not a good thing.

These uninspired books were the primary reason councils formed to confirm Scripture. If everyone had gone on their merry way and accepted God's Word for what it was (not trying to make up more of it), everything would have been fine.

But they didn't. Instead, some people started writing their own books and calling them Scripture. Christians then realized they needed to take action, to combat the false and heretical books that were being written.

This is precisely what they did! Two councils got together and confirmed the twenty-seven New Testament books once and for all. These were, of course, in addition to the Old Testament books already confirmed. These councils were called the Council of Hippo in AD 393 (yes, Hippo . . . couldn't make this stuff up!), and the Council of Carthage in AD 397.

You may be thinking, "Why did it take so long to confirm them (nearly AD 400) if they were originally written in the first century AD?" Well, the other pseudo-Scripture books we've been talking about weren't exposed until the middle of the second century. The New Testament was complete by around AD 90 with John's Revelation; these pseudo-books began appearing about fifty years later. Again, no one questioned the authenticity of the gospels and letters already in circulation. But as soon as the false books started appearing, you can be assured that Hippo and Carthage got on top of it, baby!

To wrap all this up for you in a neat little package: the canon of Scripture simply references the collection of books deemed worthy of being included in God's Word. This canon is two-part: the Old (thirty-nine books) and New (twenty-seven books) Testaments. From the moment these books were written, they were and have been accepted as God's Word. Even still, as the church began to grow and develop, councils came together to stamp the canon as completely official—sixty-six books total—no more, no less. No other books, writings, documents, etc. can be included in Scripture or held on the same level. The canon of Scripture is complete. Learn it, know it, accept it, and live by it, because it's truth!

AUTHORS OF SCRIPTURE

Now that we are experts on the canon and how the Bible was put together, we can go a little further and ask, "Who were the human authors who wrote the books of Scripture?"

Many of you can answer this question for at least a handful of books. Glance at the first couple verses of New Testament letters and you'll see who wrote them. Others are easy because the book bears the name of the author (i.e. Isaiah, etc.). But what about books like 1 and 2 Chronicles? Or Leviticus?

In a general sense, the books of the Bible were written by over forty men who witnessed the events they wrote about. We reach a caveat, though. Not all of these men directly witness events, because some weren't around at the time they happened (creation in Genesis), and some didn't write about events at all (Proverbs). But generally speaking, the human composers of Scripture personally witnessed the events they wrote about. Let's take a look at 1 John 1:1-3 as evidence for this point (emphasis mine):

> What was from the beginning, *what we have heard*, what *we have seen with our eyes*, what *we have looked at and touched with our hands*, concerning the Word of Life—and the life was manifested, and *we have seen and testify* and proclaim to you the eternal life, which was with the Father and was *manifested to us—what we have seen and heard we proclaim* to you also, so that you too may have fellowship with us; and indeed *our fellowship is with the Father, and with His Son,*

Jesus Christ. These things we write, so that our joy may be made complete.

In this passage John verified that his words did not originate in his imagination. Far from it! Rather, he writes about things he saw and experienced firsthand. He didn't merely hear about Christ and all the awesome things He did. No, John walked, lived, moved, followed, and was mentored by Christ. He knew Him personally and on an intimate level, surely beyond what he could capture in words. John was with Christ—both when He walked the earth and after the resurrection. That's the kind of detail and assurance we have of Scripture's truth.

The human authors lived and experienced the words they wrote and desperately wanted their readers (yes, that means us too!) to understand and experience them for themselves. What an honor and privilege! We've already found ourselves thankful that God would give us His Word written down and preserved for hundreds of years. Our thankfulness grows even more when realizing we're reading about real events and encounters between men and women (just like us) and God Himself.

These men witnessed and were transformed by the events they experienced at the hand of the God they wrote about. No doubt they were eager to share them with us. But who were these men? What were their names and backgrounds? Let's get down into some nitty-gritty but awesome details.

Have you ever heard the term Pentateuch? If you have, you'll probably recall that the Pentateuch is the first five books of the Bible, also known as the Books of Moses. I'll bet you can guess who wrote those. Ding, ding, ding! Moses!

We discover quite a bit about Moses from these books. See for yourself in the book of Exodus. He was born a Hebrew but raised in the Egyptian king Pharaoh's household. A few years later he murdered an Egyptian, fled to the desert for forty years, got married, and became a shepherd. God called him to go back to Egypt to lead the Israelites out, trading Egypt for the wilderness until their hearts were prepared for entering the Promised Land. That is a brief version of Moses' biography, but you get the gist of it.

Not every author of biblical books holds that much of a biography. In fact, we're not sure who authored several books. The book of Hebrews is probably the most widely recognized in this category. Theories of its authorship span the spectrum. Some scholars believe it was Paul; others have suggested Barnabas or even John. Though it would be fascinating to know, some books were left anonymous when written, so it's silly to spend much time trying to figure it out.

However, we can discover a lot about the authors we do know about. What's even more fascinating is realizing that God used each of their personalities and personal experiences/backgrounds to shape the uniqueness of the books they wrote. God worked through the human authors of Scripture and used "their background, personality, cultural context, writing style, faith commitments, research, and so on" to give each book its own literary flair.[5]

Don't misunderstand. God exerted complete control of the entire writing process. He was sovereign over every paragraph, word, letter, and punctuation mark. Nothing went into the original autographs without His approval.

However, in His sovereignty and creative awesomeness, He worked through the individual personalities of each author to give that particular book an extra creative boost. The point: we do not have a mundane and monotone Bible! Over forty men with different personalities, backgrounds, walks of faith, experiences, etc. penned the sixty-six books of the Bible over a 1,600 year period of time, and each book bears the distinct mark of those men as well as the multifaceted nature of its true Author, the Lord.

God could have given us a bland and boring instruction manual of the dos and don'ts in the life of a believer. But He didn't! Instead, He inspired over forty different men to portray many different accounts

---

[5] Duvall and Hays, *Grasping God's Word*. 159.

of His hand at work—written in many different linguistic styles. Ah, what a nice segue to our next topic—the literary styles of the Bible.

LITERARY STYLES

We've seen how Scripture is hardly a collaboration of monotone rules and guidelines. It is inspired and living, written by real people with real stories who had real experiences with God. Yet there's more evidence for the vivacity of Scripture, which is admittedly found in an unexpected place—literary styles. (Don't accuse me of being an academic nerd just yet; though you certainly have some ground to do so!).

Let's give this subject a bit of context before we begin. We all have a man in our lives (or are one). Whether a husband, father, son, employer, co-worker, or friend, we all know of their wonderful (or frustrating) tendency to ignore instruction manuals. When a man purchases a package including the phrase "some assembly required," women lower their expectations of seeing a finished product (at least as it looks on the box). Why? Because men feel the need to express their macho-ism and prove their manliness by not needing the instructions. Can I get an "amen"? Oy vey.

Women, on the other hand, being the multi-tasking, reasonable creatures we are, consider carefully what's before us:

>   one box with contents unassembled
> \+ one complimentary instruction manual
> <u>+ one individual willing to use the latter to help with the former</u>
> = a successful mission: an assembled product.

No mystery. Black and white. Easy-breezy. A no-brainer. Neither men nor women particularly enjoy reading instruction manuals, since they are not the most fascinating of literature. But they are a necessary evil and, in fact, a crucial part of completing a task with any hope for timely and non-agonizing success.

Where's this all headed? The Bible, as we've learned, is God's tangible way of communicating to us. Through it He reveals Himself to a broken and utterly lost people, via the revelation of His truth and His Son, Jesus Christ. But let's take a deeper look at the *method* He chose to communicate His truth to us. He could have given us an instruction manual akin to the one in our *man vs. assembly* parallel. It would have been straightforward and effective, depending on the willingness of the recipient to read it and obey. But He knew human nature and realized that such a manual would be seriously neglected and devalued of its purpose.

So what does the Author of Life decide? He spoiled us (yet again) by giving us several different types of writing styles and literary techniques. This means that within the Scriptures we have many different styles of writing, including historical narratives, poetry, letters, parables, prophecy, the gospels, proverbs and more. Several types can often be found within a single book.[6] We don't hold a methodological heap of pages with line after line of rigid and detailed instructions as our Bibles. Rather, we engage lively, creative, interactive writing styles that intrigue and inspire us not only to read, but to relate to and obey.

When we read stories of people struggling to conquer their fears and doubts, we relate to them and are inspired to pay close attention to the way they overcome their struggles. Why? Because we can learn from them and follow suit.

Consider Abraham—called by God away from his family, friends, and hometown to an unknown place. He held no assurance that it would work out—except for God's word. How often do we find ourselves in situations that seem downright impossible, and we have no idea how we're going to make it? Abraham (and about a hundred others in Scripture) must have asked the same question. Time and again God gives His answer. By answering the people represented in the narratives, God answers us, because we, like the people in the stories, are real.

---

[6] Chapter four addresses the individual genres of Scripture.

God not only gives us account after incredible account of people who dealt with issues just like we do, He gives the assurance that those stories are real and still applicable today. They're not just some fantasy with fictional characters designed to break us from reality. No, these stories *are* reality. They are real-life events that happened to real people who were changed by those events. These people—the authors and others—endured real experiences, highs and lows, and were touched by God to such an extent that they wanted to share it with everyone they met.

I can't help but wonder whether the authors of Scripture, especially the Old Testament, realized the significance of what they were penning. Here they are, writing what they assumed was important because it was from God. Yet they probably remained clueless to the extent to which their work would be known, read, and abided by millennia later. Can you imagine writing something forever known all around the world for the rest of human history? Or that your writings were inspired by God Himself and would be preserved by Him for the rest of time so others could come to know Him as you did?

Though unable to speak for the authors of Scripture, I can imagine their goal was for others to see Him as they did and commit themselves to Him, no matter the cost. These men experienced the power, life, and sovereignty of God first-hand. Anyone who has experienced Him to that extent can't help but share Him with everyone—whether they listened or not! The authors shared Him by obediently writing His Word, which is as alive and vibrant as the God they experienced. His Word reflects and extends God's beauty and character to this world. The authors penned His truth in a way that all of humanity could know Him and make Him known.

See how this is all coming full-circle? God authored Scripture. He used real men to write about events they experienced. Their writing is expressed in different and creative ways, using a variety of literary styles and techniques so we could relate to and be captivated by them, realizing the truth they are trying to convey.

This is seriously mind-blowing stuff! The Bible is not just a book. It is His inerrant, infallible, inspired, and living Word, written by real people in various ways to mesmerize us into realizing His astounding truth. He went through all this trouble—this whole crazy yet beautiful process of canonizing Scripture—for *us*. He desires us to know, know Him more, and make Him known. Are we making the most of it?

LANGUAGES

Literary styles are fascinating because they reflect the writers' personalities and backgrounds. We normally don't think of or question the different literary techniques used in the Bible, but knowing them boosts our knowledge and wonder of Scripture. The same can be said for our next topic—the languages of Scripture. As with literary styles, understanding the original languages of Scripture reveals much about its history, which amplifies our grasp of its truth.

Have you ever wondered what language Scripture was originally written in? Maybe not, but it's time to learn! Let's refer back to a word we learned at the beginning of our study—autograph. Autographs refer to the original manuscripts of Scripture, not the myriad of copies that we have today. What language(s) were the autographs written in, and why does it matter?

To answer the first part of that question, let's break Scripture down into testaments. The majority of the Old Testament was written in ancient Hebrew, which was Israel's primary language back in the day. The parts not written in Hebrew were written in Aramaic (Ezra 4:8-6:18, 7:12-26; Daniel 2:4-7, 28; and Jeremiah 10:11).[7] Surprisingly enough, Hebrew and Aramaic (along with Arabic and Akkadian) are sister languages from the umbrella of languages known as Semitic.

One interesting fact about Hebrew is the length of time it has been preserved. It is one of the world's oldest languages. Although there's

---

[7] http://biblescripture.net/Canon.html

evidence of local dialectical differences arising as time progressed and the nation of Israel spread out, it survived as the language of the Israelite people and is still spoken today.[8] This is remarkable, considering how many ancient languages are now extinct, in addition to the fact that existing languages change and adapt as culture ebbs and flows. Hebrew is a beautiful and complex language. I continually stand in awe of those who have followed their passion and become scholars of it.

On the other hand, many of us are familiar (at least on a recognition basis) with the language of the New Testament: Greek. But the phrase "it's all Greek to me" exists for a reason! The Greek language "is the presumed parent of all the other languages of Europe except Basque, Finnish, Hungarian, and of Sanskrit" from India.[9] This means all other European languages stem from Greek in some way, shape, or form. Isn't that fascinating?

But there's more. Let's dive into some Greek history, shall we? Greek became the head-honcho language due to the efforts of Alexander the Great. Remember him from your history classes in middle school? He's the guy who conquered almost the entire ancient world 300 years before Christ. Big-time dude. And his goal? To have one world empire. An easy way to get what you want is to conquer everyone who opposes you, and that's exactly what Mr. Great did. He made Greek the common language, and even though Alexander's reign didn't last long, the Greek language survived him and became the universal language of New Testament times.

Please take a moment to reflect on the timing of this universal language push. Do you think it was coincidental that the established world of that day spoke a common language? Granted, a great many other languages were spoken in addition to Greek, but Greek was the language that bridged the masses together—the language that united

---

[8] Hebrew is still spoken today, but NOT in the same form or pose as the ancient Hebrew of Scripture.
[9] Utley, Bob. "The Bible | Bible.org – World's Largest Bible Study Site." *Free NET Bible and Thousands of Bible Studies | Bible.org - Worlds Largest Bible Study Site*. N.p., n.d. Web. 13 July 2011.

the known world. The timing becomes significant when we realize this is precisely the time that Jesus Christ entered our world with His gospel! Christ came at a perfect time—when world communication was at its peak. When something major happened, everyone knew about it. Word would spread quickly because language complications were few. Because of this universal language (yes, a minor reversal of the Tower of Babel), news of Christ and the gospel exploded into the deepest and most remote crevices of society faster than would've ever been possible before.

How easily do you think the gospel, Scripture, and the church would have spread if there had not been a universal language? It wouldn't have been as easy, would it? As we've seen God's hand reign sovereignly in every aspect of Scripture so far, now we can see Him working through outside worldly events to make way for the distribution and intense spread of His church. This is divine orchestration at its best!

Even though all this information about Hebrew and Greek is fascinating, how does it impact our lives today? One word: translations. As time went on and other languages grew in popularity and use due to the rise and fall of kingdoms and such, Hebrew and Greek began fading in the relevancy department. Fewer and fewer people spoke them as new world powers, countries, and nations were established and other languages arose. The world's population spread out, and the concept of a universal language inevitably faded. But Scripture was still written in Hebrew and Greek. It had to be translated in order to remain available to the masses as they continue spreading out over the world. Thus, it's a worthy cause to explore how we ended up with it translated into hundreds of other languages.

Without the copying and translating process, we would be forced to become multilingual in order to read, interpret, and understand Scripture. Considering that getting through the English portion on our SAT was a chore, how many of us would discipline ourselves enough to become fluent in two ancient languages? Probably not many! So let's learn about the translation process—the end result of which we are pretty big fans, whether we've ever realized it or not.

TRANSLATIONS

As society continues to "progress" and technology advances beyond most folks' comprehension, what profession flourishes? Well, there are several, but for this point let's choose law. Lawyers. Or should we say, laaaawyers. People tend to draw out that word with smirks of cynicism, bitterness, disgust, and several other adjectives that we'll leave to your imagination. One particularly frustrating aspect of the lawyerly profession is that of nit-picking. You know what we're getting at.

We're required to sign sixteen pages of legalese when we get cavities filled at the dentist. These pages are crammed with reasons why we cannot file any kind of lawsuit over anything that may happen while we're in the chair—bombs going off, tornadoes ripping through the building, the Flood making its comeback, and, of course, unmentionable and intentionally-left-generic "complications." We're on our own, and we enter that chair at our own risk.

Lawyers believe they need to articulate every possible scenario so patients can't sue if something goes wrong. What they fail to realize is that it leaves us more scared of the chair than of anything else! If they're warning us of all these things, does that mean that all these things have happened at some point? If so, is it safe to go to the dentist at all?

Lawyers scrutinize every paragraph, word, and syllable that comes across their desks, because if they don't, they will be the ones defending it.

Although legalese is mundane and way too detailed for us normal folk to care about, it's not difficult to imagine why such documents must exist. People file lawsuits for stupid and frivolous reasons, and lawyers are held responsible for their actions. Some documents actually bear some significance, but many legalese-filled papers are serious wastes of trees. The topics simply don't compensate the time or effort spent on them. However, some topics excel as worthwhile in the realm of time and energy.

Let's shift gears to the copiers and translators of Scripture. It's easy to imagine these men as lawyerly types because, like lawyers, they were intensely detailed and thorough—enough not to overlook a single punctuation mark from their work. Copying Scripture ranked as their number one priority, which demanded perfection. They fully accepted the seriousness of the copied material—that any error would mar the Word of God as He intended it to be read and received by humanity.

We have already mentioned that some errors inevitably arose in the process of copying—a word left out here, a punctuation mark missing there. But for the most part, the copies of Scripture we have today are nearly identical to the autographs. To whom can we credit this accomplishment, after the Lord? The copiers (a.k.a. scribes), and translators who arose later. If we wanted any document to be treated with the utmost respect, it would be Scripture, would it not? Therein lies the key difference between modern-day legalese and ancient-day scribes—the object of their work.

How does this all relate to translations? Translating any work or document from one language to another poses a difficult task, because no two languages are identical. If you've ever studied a second language, you realize languages are the products of much more than words. Grammar, syntax, sentence structure, and lots of other complicated factors make languages what they are.

Case study: English. English is an incredibly complicated language for many reasons, one of which resides in the slang creeping into it over the years. And you contribute to the complication every day! Think about it. When you type a text to a friend or an e-mail to a family member, do you write in formal English? Are all your sentences perfectly formatted and congruent? I doubt it! Or consider accents from different parts of the country. If a New Yorker and a Southern gentleman meet,

The Canon

there's a good chance they will have difficulty communicating. Why? Because the dialects in which they speak and understand English are vastly different. They'll be lucky not to leave the conversation thinking each is from another country, much less that they are speaking the same language! This, and many other reasons, makes the translation process an enormous and time-consuming process.

Not only must translators achieve intimate familiarity with extinct languages (Hebrew and Greek are still spoken today, but remain in a different dialect and form than the types written in the autographs), they're expected to reach even more intimacy with English words and their function—which changes almost daily. Talk about frustrating!

That's why so many translations pop up as years go by. It's not that a translation from the 1970s isn't accurate or good; it's just not current with the English spoken today. Consider for a moment the word "awesome." What probably flashed through your mind resembles it being used flippantly about something hardly serious—a motorcycle, a chef's new recipe, a surfer's ride. You can imagine without any serious effort how the word awesome would be used in those contexts. But do you remember what it used to mean? Awe-some, or awe-struck, breathtaking, leaving one speechless, worthy of awe. A far cry from how it is used today, don't you agree?

Herein lies the translators' frustration. It's almost impossible to translate Scripture in a way that will last because languages don't last. At least, not in their current form. Neither the translator nor his translation is at fault. It's simply the way it is.

TWO CAMPS OF TRANSLATIONS

Now onto the translations or versions we use today. Before we get too deeply engrossed in this fascinating topic, we must recognize a critical distinction between the two camps of Bible versions in existence today: translations and paraphrases. They must not be confused or seen as synonyms. One prioritizes maintaining Scriptural authenticity and accuracy to the original autographs, while the other focuses on making the Bible easier to understand in a modern-day language.

Are we saying that if we can understand something in modern-day language, then it is not authentic? Not at all. But remember our previous discussion. The most complicated and frustrating part of translating the Bible or any other document is keeping in line with what the original document says (and means) while simultaneously making it linguistically relevant to the reading audience. A balance between these two must be maintained. If the translator sacrifices the integrity of the biblical manuscripts in order to make them sound good in English, he fails miserably at his job.

On the other hand, if a translator focuses only on translating the manuscripts as closely as possible to the Hebrew or Greek, the translation will result in choppy, broken, and hard-to-comprehend English. No one will want to read it, which defeats the purpose.

What's the solution to this feud of focuses? How do translators balance Scriptural integrity with relevant language for today? Time to discuss translations and paraphrases.

CAMP ONE: TRANSLATIONS

Translations arise from people who translate the original Hebrew or Greek manuscripts into English (or whatever language being pursued). Translators are groups of Ancient Hebrew, Aramaic, and Greek scholars hired to translate the ancient manuscripts of Scripture into modern-day English. For example, the New American Standard Version of Scripture was translated by "conservative Bible scholars who have doctorates in biblical languages, theology, or other advanced degrees."[10] When a difficult decision about a translation issue arose, an ultimate decision was made:

---

[10] http://www.lockman.org/nasb/

> By a consensus of a team composed of educators and pastors who were directed by their faith that the original words of Scripture were inspired by God. Therefore, their work was treated reverently and carefully, and . . . we passed to critical consultants for a thorough review of the translation.[11]

This particular process took more than twenty translators and almost three years of full-time work. In other words, they meticulously tended to their task, as do the vast majority of committees and groups given the assignment to translate Scripture from the original languages into modern-day English.

In their efforts, translators try their hardest to remain linguistically relevant for today. But if they err, it will be on the side of caution—not sacrificing biblical authenticity for the sake of easy reading. They accomplish this in two ways.

The first is a sub-camp (so to speak) called word-for-word. They pursue the goal of translating Scripture as closely as possible, or word-for-word, to English from the original manuscripts/languages. Please understand, a literal word-for-word translation between any language is impossible because sentence, grammar, and stylistic structures are different and can be incredibly complex. But word-for-words put forth a valiant effort.

Even a language as simple as Spanish is impossible to translate word-for-word because Spanish arranges its sentences and uses its tenses differently than English. Adverbs and adjectives man different posts in a sentence, along with nouns and verbs, direct objects, prepositional phrases, and every other grammatical nuance imaginable. Translating is complicated, regardless of the subject or languages at hand. Languages are beautiful, intriguing tools for communication. Word-for-word translations do well in remaining true to the original

---

[11] Ibid.

languages by limiting a third-party interpretation of the original text as much as possible.

These translators refuse to draw conclusions for readers and forsake popularity and ease of reading as primary concerns. They desire the text to speak for itself by providing the readers with a translation as close to the original manuscripts as possible. They don't want to assert themselves into the interpretation phase of studying Scripture. Instead, they limit their work to strict translation so English readers read as close to the original Hebrew and Greek as possible. Word-for-word translations include New American Standard Bible, New King James Version, and English Standard Version.

The other sub-camp of translations is known as thought-for-thought. These translators also concern themselves with maintaining Scriptural integrity, but they exercise a bit more in the interpretation department than their cohorts, the word-for-words.

Thought-for-thought translators focus on the thought or meaning of a given passage or verse and translate it as thoroughly as possible according to its *thought*—not necessarily the exact *words* used in the original languages. This in no way implies they add or subtract ideas from Scripture. They simply focus on communicating the *thought* the original author was trying to get across (factoring in language and cultural barriers), rather than being strict about precise word choices.

The rising issue with these translations is the measure of interpretation translators bring to the text. Unlike word-for-words, who try to be as objective and personally removed from the process as possible, thought-for-thoughts interpret the main concept/thought/meaning for the readers. They work hard to ensure correctness and authenticity, but the reader shouldn't assume total accuracy. When translating thought-for-thought, an element of objectivity is removed because they interpret (albeit slightly) the meaning of the text for their reading audience instead of leaving it for them to discover.

You'll recall from previous conversations that language is a tool to communicate the point an author wants to make. No language is better or more useful than another, nor is any more important than another. The most important component is being communicated *through* the language at hand. Here's where it gets tricky. Word-for-word translations let you, the reader, determine what God is communicating through His Word under the guidance of the Spirit in diligent and reverent study. Word-for-words give us an opportunity to see what God is saying through His Word as He originally wrote it.

Thought-for-thoughts, on the other hand, still care about what God is saying. However, they walk a step further by telling readers what the message is. They translate the message behind the precise words as they understand the message. They remove an element of research by giving us their interpretation of the original languages, not a strict translation of them. The foundation of thought-for-thoughts is the concept of language being a tool to communicate a message. But instead of letting the readers determine that message, they help by providing the message in their translations. Neither is right or wrong, good or bad. Your choice in translation is determined by preference. The goal of this discussion is to help you better understand your choices.

Thought-for-thought translations are easier to read than word-for-words because, again, their intent is to communicate the message over and beyond the precise words of the originals. And as you might expect, they can be quite different than their word-for-word siblings. Some examples of thought-for-thoughts include New International Version, Holman Christian Standard Bible, New Living Translation, and the Contemporary English Version.

Let's look at a real-life example of the differences between word-for-words and thought-for-thoughts. In Philippians 2, Paul tells the Philippian believers to follow Christ's example of obedience—obeying the Father even if it calls for sacrifice. Verse 7 of the NASB (New American Standard, word-for-word) translation says Christ "emptied Himself, taking the form of a bond-servant, and being made in the likeness of men."

The word "empty" used in the NASB is *keno* in the original Greek, which literally means "to empty, make empty." This, of course, makes the word-for-word translation's choice "emptied" an easy one. The NIV (New International Version, thought-for-thought), on the other hand, translates verse 7: Christ "made himself nothing, taking the very nature of a servant, being made in human likeness." Quite a bit different than the NASB translation. Let's look at them side-by-side.

NASB	NIV
"emptied Himself..."	"made Himself nothing"
"taking the form of a bondservant"	"taking the very nature of a servant"
"and being made in the likeness of men"	"being made in human likeness"

See the difference? NASB practices a word-for-word approach, while the NIV concentrates more on getting the basic thought or meaning across. Both translate from the original languages to English but do so in very different ways. Can you see how the NIV's "made himself nothing" could mean a lot of different things to a lot of different people? So could "emptied Himself" by NASB, but we start closer to the original intent with NASB than we do the NIV.

Is this nit-picking, you wonder? It certainly can be. And lots of people use it as an excuse to nit-pick to their hearts' content. But the intent of this study is not to split hairs. Rather, it's to empower you as a believer and a reader of God's Word by raising your awareness of what you're reading. The goal is to help you understand that although the English translations we have today do their best to communicate God's Word through its original languages, they sometimes err and are prone to subjectivity.

Are English translations trustworthy at all then? Absolutely. They offer a remarkable presentation of the original languages' content—especially since most of us will never become Hebrew and Greek scholars. But if you come across a verse/word/phrase that stands out to you, don't be afraid to research it and go deeper. Look at other translations and then look up the original Hebrew or Greek word by conducting a word study.[12] Never succumb to timidity when pursuing your studies in the Word.

CAMP TWO: PARAPHRASES

Now we have good grasp of the translation camp, so let's move to the other camp of Bible versions available today: paraphrases. To paraphrase something means to write or say it in your own words. Or, if you'd like a more official definition, it is "a restatement of a text, passage, or work giving the meaning in another form."[13]

Paraphrases translate the Bible not from the original languages, but from other English translations. Remember how we talked about thought-for-thoughts being one more step removed from objectivity in translation because they slightly interpret Scripture? Paraphrases take it even further by paraphrasing the already-translated text.

That's the equivalent of the sixth person in succession during a game of Telephone. Person One: God inspiring His Word to Persons Two, the human authors. Persons Three are the copiers of Scripture, who copied diligently and purposefully for centuries until Persons Four and Five came around and started translating those copies into other languages. Some translated as closely as possible, using the word-for-word approach (Persons 4), while others conducted their translations by targeting the meanings or thoughts of the text (Persons 5). Persons 6 arrived on the scene and decided not to concern themselves with the original languages at all. They stick with the English translations already available.

---

[12] Word studies are explained briefly in chapter five, along with further resources available to you to learn more about them.
[13] http://www.merriam-webster.com/dictionary/paraphrase.

More Than Words

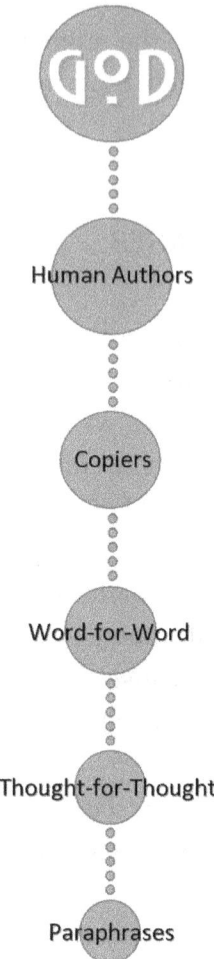

See the progression? With each "person" who comes on the scene, we walk one step further away from the original autographs of Scripture. Now, most of these cannot reasonably be avoided since not all of us are jumping in line to become Hebrew and Greek scholars. And that's fine, as long as we remember that the Bibles sitting on our shelves (hopefully not collecting dust as we move along in our studies!) are not the original autographs. They're extremely close and still very much worth basing our lives and relationships with God upon. Yet we can no longer be ignorant of the translation telephone progression. We can, however, learn how to utilize it fully and as well as possible.[14]

Let's return to the Persons 6 category, also known as paraphrases. These include the Living Bible, the Message, and the Amplified Bible. Rather than giving you a harsh or negative impression of them, I'd like to explore their positive aspects. Arguably the most prominent/best aspect of paraphrases is their ease in reading and comprehending the material. In fact, that's how one of them, the Living Bible, came to be.

A man named Kenneth Taylor noticed how difficult the Bible was for his young children to understand. He decided to paraphrase the American Standard Version (NASB's daddy) so his children could digest the text better. Is that a bad thing? Of course not! Can it be a bad thing if that's the only version people ever use as they grow up and continue in their faith? Yes, indeed. Paraphrases are subjective because they concentrate on modern-day, easy language more than a strict translation of the text.

We probably need to voice a caveat at this point. Some English versions of the Bible claim to be translations (having been translated from the original languages, not English), yet still should be considered paraphrases. Why? Because they emphasize easy reading in modern language more than careful translation of the original languages.

Here's an example. Are you familiar with the Message Bible? The Message was written by a man named Eugene Peterson who, although he worked with the original Greek and Hebrew texts, ended up writing a paraphrased Bible. Peterson "'paraphrased' the original [languages] by selecting [modern-day] language that communicates the style and flavor of the original Bible times."[15] This, of course, is all according to him.

Therein lies the biggest problem with paraphrases, whether driven from the original languages or not. The translator, in this case, Eugene

---

[14] This, of course, is the purpose of this book and will be addressed and explained in further beginning in chapter four.
[15] http://www.christianbook.com/Christian/Books/cms_content?page=253967&sp=65298&event=1003MSG%7C14764%7C65298.

More Than Words

Peterson, decides what he thinks the passages meant in biblical times and what they mean for us now. Is he wrong? Not necessarily. A number of verses in the Message accurately communicate what the original text is trying to convey. But with the Message and other paraphrases, accuracy is not a given. It should not be assumed.

At risk of hitting you over the head with this again, remember: the further we get from the original biblical text, the further we get from what God was communicating through it—which is the entire point of reading His Word. Paraphrases, whether or not masked as translations on technicality, should be used with caution.

If a paraphrase writes a particular verse in a way you like, and you find yourself drawing a theological conclusion from it and it alone, check with other translations to legitimize it. Don't assume it is accurate and worth basing your entire theological foundation on. To drive the point home, let's return to our wonderful Philippians 2:7 verse. This time, we'll bring in the Message with our comparisons of a word-for-word like NASB and thought for-thought like NIV.

NASB	NIV	THE MESSAGE
"emptied Himself…"	"made Himself nothing"	"he set aside the privileges of deity"
"taking the form of a bondservant"	"taking the very nature of a servant"	"took on the status of a servant"
"and being made in the likeness of men"	"being made in human likeness"	"became human!"

Can you see our telephone progression from the NASB to the Message? The Message may be straightforward and easy to understand, but it is quite far removed from the original verbiage of Scripture. Again, this can be helpful for those who have a difficult time reading or comprehending other translations. But remember: let the Message and other paraphrases serve as a starting point or extra reference, not your primary choice for study. Be challenged to go deeper and against the telephone current! Get back to the source on the source's terms. Then we can start the true adventure of reading, interpreting, and applying Scripture—which is our goal and the best part.

We've loaded our brains with information about the languages, the translation process, and the different translation camps (translations and paraphrases) of Scripture. Hope your head doesn't hurt! Let's briefly review what we've learned so far, because we're about to make a substantial transition, and it helps if we're all on the same page!

REFLECT

We began our journey asking what the Bible is. Just an ancient text? A cool, old book with lots of stories? A composition of writings from a bunch of drunken kooks? Or something more? We learned that the Bible supersedes all those things in value and authority. It is the inerrant, infallible, inspired, and living Word of God. Definitely a good start!

Next we looked at one of our new vocabulary words: the canon. What, pray tell, is the canon of Scripture? We learned the canon is the collection of books that met the required criteria to be included in Scripture. Biblical books were never doubted as the Word of God, but because heresy started to arise, the Councils of Carthage and Hippo solidified once and for all the books of the Bible—the canon of Scripture.

After looking at how the Bible was put together, we gave some attention to the men whom God inspired to write His holy Word. These men, we discovered, number around forty and were mostly eyewitnesses (helping their credibility significantly) of the accounts they wrote about. Even if they wrote of events they didn't witness, they had God as their inspiring Author, so they could hardly go wrong. And they didn't!

More Than Words

In fact, they were given the freedom not only to write what God put on their minds, but they also wrote in ways that reflected who they were—their backgrounds, personalities, and experiences. We certainly do not have a mundane or monotone Scripture! Instead, we have a vast collection of different styles and literary techniques, which God used to communicate His truth.

Discovering different literary styles God gave us in His Word led to our discussion about the languages of Scripture. Scripture was written primarily in only two languages—ancient Hebrew and Greek, and those languages (especially Greek) just happened to be popular at the perfect time in history—enabling the super-fast spread of His Word to the world.

Studying languages naturally led to questions about how those languages compare with the languages we have today, namely, English! We made good headway in the translation department, understanding how complicated and serious the process is, especially when God's Word is at stake! Then we got into the specific English translations of today and the two camps of translations and paraphrases. After a thorough exploration of those, we're ready to proceed into the invigorating world of hermeneutics! Don't be afraid; we will thoroughly define it as our new vocabulary word.

3

Paving the Way

Hermeneutics. This intriguing, mysterious, yet empowering word is tragically little-known among the majority of Christians today. You've probably gathered from the title of this book that Scripture is more than words. Well, hermeneutics emphasizes this point by helping us understand the Bible—an ancient book—in a modern world.

Before we begin our journey in hermeneutics, we need to make sure we're in harmony. We've established a working definition of Scripture and have learned how it's put together, who wrote it, the different versions available today, etc. However, we must be on the same page in more ways than just knowing *about* the Bible if we are to begin hermeneutics. We must believe in and submit to its authority over our lives. That means we need a personal relationship with its Author—God, our Heavenly Father.

To pave the way for our hermeneutic journey, we must resolve two issues. These issues prevent people from conducting proper and effective hermeneutics. The first issue is stated above: having a genuine relationship with Jesus Christ, not just saying we do. The second builds on the first: actively pursuing Him in every aspect of our lives, with evidence to boot. Hermeneutics reaps no benefit if these two issues remain unresolved.

Ascribing truth to something does not render it true. Similarly, we should not always assume an individual possesses an accurate understanding of what she claims. People sometimes don't know what they're talking about yet choose to open their mouths anyway. This happens a lot in the world of religion nowadays—particularly Christianity. The last I heard, America is still considered a "Christian" nation, which should give us the first glimpse into how differently people define the term "Christian."

People quickly claim the name of Christ as a sort of default when asked their religion. Saying, "I'm a Christian" is an easy and safe response for most living in America today. It goes with the flow and will hardly step on anyone's toes (though that's becoming increasingly untrue because of society's rapid movement toward an anti-Christ mentality). When people claim the name of Christ, few provide a biblical answer regarding what makes them Christians. Most people respond with answers like, "Well, I read the Bible and go to church on Sundays," or "my parents and grandparents were Christians," or "I give money to the poor."

Biblically, these answers do not cut it. Jesus says all too clearly that:

> Not everyone who says to Me, 'Lord, Lord,' will enter the kingdom of heaven, but he who does the will of My Father who is in heaven will enter. Many will say to Me on that day, 'Lord, Lord, did we not prophesy in Your name, and in Your name cast out demons, and in Your name perform many miracles?' And then I will declare to them, 'Depart from me, you who practice lawlessness.'[1]

Many people think they're right with God. They believe they're good people and will easily earn their place in heaven when they meet

---

[1] Matthew 7:21-23.

Him face to face one day. Their good deeds outweigh their bad (at least, according to their estimation), so they have nothing to worry about. They're not "big" sinners anyway—they don't get drunk, don't cheat on their spouses, and certainly don't intentionally harm anyone. They are good enough, so they give themselves a pat on the back, certain that heaven sweetly awaits their grand entrance.

This train of thought blatantly contradicts Scripture. A gross percentage of folks who think they're okay eternally will be in for a rude awakening one day. Look at the passage we just read. People in this passage accomplished marvelous and miraculous things in the name of Christ. They prophesied, cast out demons, and did miracles. That's more elaborate than what most of us do for Him today! Yet what is Christ's response to them? He will say, "Depart from Me, you who practice lawlessness." Only those who do the will of God the Father in heaven will enter.

What is the will of God the Father?

> [He] desires all men to be saved and to come to the knowledge of the truth. For there is one God, and one mediator also between God and men, the man Christ Jesus, who gave Himself as a ransom for all, the testimony given at the proper time.[2]

Knowing Him differs entirely from knowing *of* Him and claiming His name. Many people don't know Jesus from their next-door neighbor, yet they remain convinced their eternal destiny rests securely with Him in heaven.

This is not meant to be a scary, fire-and-brimstone diatribe. It is meant to prompt you into a moment of spiritual reflection and evaluation. Enter into a time of prayer right now. Read the following verses and see whether you have accepted and affirmed them personally.

---

[2] 1 Timothy 2:4-6

> Jesus said . . . I am the way, the truth, and the life; no one comes to the Father but through Me.[3]

∎∎∎

> Whoever believes will in Him [Jesus Christ] have eternal life. For God so loved the world, that He gave His only begotten Son, that whoever believes in Him shall not perish, but have eternal life. For God did not send the Son into the world to judge the world, but that the world might be saved through Him.[4]

...

> Everyone who calls on the name of the Lord will be saved.[5]

∎∎∎

> If you confess with your mouth Jesus as Lord, and believe in your heart that God raised Him from the dead, you will be saved; for with the heart a person believes, resulting in righteousness, and with the mouth he confesses, resulting in salvation. For the Scripture says, 'whoever believes in Him will not be disappointed.'[6]

Scripture is clear about what it takes to be saved—to accept Jesus Christ as your personal Lord and Savior. You must at some point in your life recognize and believe that 1) you are a sinner, and as such, have fallen short of achieving salvation on your own merit. You cannot do it on your own. 2) Jesus Christ is the Son of God. 3) Jesus was sent to this world and to the cross as the sacrifice for our sins. 4) He was raised from the grave and lives today at the right hand of God in heaven. 5) He is our Advocate before the Father, securing our status with Him as children and preparing a place for us to be with Him in heaven for eternity.

---

[3] John 14:6
[4] John 3:15-17
[5] Acts 2:21
[6] Romans 10:9-11

Believing those truths fuels the first step, but then you must surrender to Him and make Him Lord of your heart and life. Believing is not enough on its own. James tells us "the demons also believe, and shudder."[7] An intellectual comprehension of facts does not put you in a relationship with God any more than learning all about someone puts you in a relationship with him. We can read a biography of someone famous and believe everything we read, but that hardly puts us in a relationship with the person.

Faith is our response to what God has said in His Word. It's more than lip service and an acknowledgement of facts. We cannot achieve salvation on our own. Only through His sacrifice on the cross are we forgiven of our sins. Only then can we have a relationship with God the Father. Faith is not only believing those facts, but acting on them and surrendering to Him. We must ask forgiveness for trying to live on our own apart from Him, and we must repent—turn 180 degrees in the opposite direction by embracing His truth and will for our lives. We must die to self and be born again in Him.

Accepting God's incredible offer of grace—salvation through Jesus Christ—is the first and crucial step to hermeneutics. Without belonging to Him, we can't hope to understand and/or gain much from His Word.

The second group in danger of missing out on the point of hermeneutics are those who know Christ, who have a relationship with Him but aren't growing, aren't being challenged in their faith, and don't care to be. God tells us:

> No longer to be children, tossed here and there by waves and carried about by every wind of doctrine, by the trickery of men, by craftiness in deceitful scheming; but speaking the truth in love, we are to grow up in all aspects into Him who is the head, even Christ, from whom the whole body, being fitted and held together by what every

---
[7] James 2:19

joint supplies, according to the proper working of each individual part, causes the growth of the body for the building up of itself in love.[8]

I'll save the are-we-truly-Christians-if-we-aren't-growing-and-maturing-in-our-faith talk for another time; but this nonetheless exists as a real concern within the church, especially in America—the growing and maturing of our faith.

I continually find myself astounded at the lack of Bible knowledge among Christians who occupy the pews week in and week out. I've talked with many people who know little of the Bible, including elementary facts like the names of the four gospels. Are we growing if we don't know anything about the Word? No. We cannot grow in our faith and love and knowledge of Jesus Christ without becoming intimate with Scripture. It's simply not possible.

The Word of God is our lifeline, the only object, person, or being in this world directly connecting us to God. What about prayer? What about the Holy Spirit? Those are absolutely crucial too. But how would you know about prayer or the Holy Spirit without the Bible? How would we know anything about God, other than evidence of His existence through nature, without it? We wouldn't. Then why aren't we more dependent on the Bible? Why do we praise, acclaim, and rely on our pastors, Sunday School teachers, and devotional books as our sole sources of bringing us into the Word and keeping us there?

These questions address nothing that I have not found myself guilty of at some time or another. The point is that we must change our perspective of this Holy Book in order to grow in our faith, love, and knowledge of Jesus. Time and again, the apostles address this very issue—they command and exhort believers to "be filled with the knowledge of His will in all spiritual wisdom and understanding,"[9] "increasing in the knowledge of God,"[10] "being renewed to a true

---
[8] Ephesians 4:14-16
[9] Colossians 1:9
[10] Colossians 1:10

knowledge according to the image of the One who created Him,"[11] and reveal that God "*desires all men to be saved and to come to the knowledge of the truth.*"[12] None of this can happen without the Word. We possess no knowledge of God if He doesn't reveal Himself to us, which He chose to do in written form.

That's why we began this book by defining Scripture and giving a brief history lesson of it. It's the most crucial aspect of our faith, because without it we wouldn't know about any other aspects of our faith! We would know hardly anything of God other than what had been "passed down" to us through other means, which may or may not be reliable.

What does this all have to do with hermeneutics? Your journey in hermeneutics begins with your journey with the Lord. If you haven't made a decision for Christ, then everything you learn in this book will remain merely an intellectual accumulation of facts. There's nothing wrong with learning facts, but a mere growth of intellect stints the goal at hand significantly.

The goal of hermeneutics is to be transformed by God into His image and become more like Christ. This cannot happen if we do not accept His Son and know Him on an intimate and eternal basis. For those who make Christ the Ruler of their hearts and lives, my prayer is that along with an increase of head knowledge about hermeneutics, you will be transformed through practicing it properly. Nothing short of transformation reaches the goal, and I beg Him to remove the veil of confusion and sin by tuning us to His truth and letting it seep into the deepest and most remote crevices of our hearts.

We can't do this on our own; the Spirit has to help us not only come to Christ, but to continue to be transformed into His image:

> Not that we are adequate in ourselves to consider anything as coming from ourselves, but our adequacy is

---

[11] Colossians 3:10
[12] 1 Timothy 2:4, emphasis mine.

> from God, who also made us adequate as servants of a new covenant, not of the letter but of the Spirit; for the letter kills, but the Spirit gives life . . . therefore having such a hope, we use great boldness in our speech, and are not like Moses, who used to put a veil over his face so that the sons of Israel would not look intently at the end of what was fading away. But their minds were hardened; for until this very day at the reading of the old covenant the same veil remains unlifted, because it is removed in Christ. But to this day whenever Moses is read, a veil lies over their heart; but whenever a person turns to the Lord, the veil is taken away. Now the Lord is the Spirit, and where the Spirit of the Lord is, there is liberty. But we all, with unveiled face, beholding as in a mirror the glory of the Lord, are being transformed into the same image from glory to glory, just as from the Lord, the Spirit.[13]

Transformation into the image of Christ—becoming *like* Him, (the word *Christian* means "little Christ") is the goal of hermeneutics. And as we saw in this passage, this cannot be done without the Spirit, who enters our lives when we accept Christ as our Savior.[14] That's why it is crucial to address these two issues before we continue in our studies. Knowing Christ and making Him Lord of our lives is the first nonnegotiable step. Purposefully striving to glorify Him and be transformed into His image is just as nonnegotiable, following a decision of His lordship in our lives.

Conduct a mini-evaluation of yourself for a moment. Do you know Christ? I don't mean an intellectual assent to His existence and what He may or may not have done for you on the cross. If you don't, pursue Him. Keep reading, of course, but do so with the intent to understand Him at His Word, and then make a decision based on

---

[13] 2 Corinthians 3:5-6, 12-18.
[14] Ephesians 1:13.

whatever you conclude. If you do know Him, then read carefully, with full anticipation that what you learn will be the platform from which you will be transformed by His truth into the image of your Savior and God. That is what it's about, ladies and gentlemen! Let His truth rock your world and make you what you claim to be: a Christ-follower!

4

Hermeneutics—What Is It?

Time to dive into hermeneutics. The proper definition of hermeneutics is "the study of the methodological principles of interpretation; a method or principle of interpretation."[1] Simply put, hermeneutics is the art and science of interpreting Scripture. Through this process we read, interpret, and apply Scripture to our lives correctly and responsibly. We interpret the ancient book in a modern world in a way that honors its Author.

We've seen in no uncertain terms that Scripture is unlike any other book written in all of history. It's the inerrant, infallible, inspired, living Word of God Himself. This, among other attributes, puts it in a different category than all other books. Thus, it should be treated that way. We shouldn't read it like every other book we come across; otherwise, we would do it a grave injustice. Scripture is the holy Word of God!

That's kind of intimidating when we think about it, right? How do we, mere fallible mortals, begin to read such a precious gift? And once we read it, how do we interpret it without messing it up with our limited, scarred knowledge? And how can we apply it correctly to our lives? That's what we're about to find out!

---

[1] http://www.merriam-webster.com/dictionary/hermeneutics.

REACTIONS TO HERMENEUTICS

Black and White

You're probably experiencing a range of reactions right now. If you're a world-is-black-and-white person, you're probably thinking, "How difficult can that process be? Scripture is straightforward." Consider the verse, "Children obey your parents in the Lord, for this is right," (Ephesians 6:1). This is hardly rocket science. However, not everything in Scripture is conveniently packaged in straightforwardness.

For instance, what do we do with James's command to "consider it all joy, my brethren, when you encounter various trials?" When we go through the pits of life, are we supposed to dance around the ice-cream truck like children on a scorching-hot day? Is that what James is saying? Not exactly. Things aren't always as they seem with Scripture (or with anything else in life, for that matter.).

The Complacent

Another camp of reactions includes those who think, "Eh, whatever. I'm perfectly content with my good ol' Christian life. Why bother with something crazy like hermeneutics?"

With utmost respect, we should never be perfectly content with our Christian life. We can be content in Him, with Him, with our lives revolving around Him, but never content to the point of complacency and lack of drive. God beckons us as Christians ("little Christs," Christ-followers), to yearn with utmost intensity, perhaps borderline obsession, for more of Him. We should ache for Him like the child who aches for the ice cream in the truck driver's hands.

What is the good news for those who aren't there yet? That

yearning arrives as we know Him more. The more we know, the closer we get. The closer we get, the more we love. The more we love, the more passionate we become!

How do we get more of Him? Through His Word. Thus, it's important to know His Word. And how do we get to know it? By understanding how to read, interpret, and apply it correctly. Don't ever get complacent! Always strive for more.

The Timid

One more reaction group that's probably worth mentioning is the timid. Those who say, "Look, I've lived my whole life not knowing this stuff. I'm not an academic, and I learn quite well through my pastor's preaching and other studies. To be honest, all this makes me nervous."

Good. I'm glad it makes you uncomfortable because that probably means change is in the air. You'll be challenged, and with challenge comes growth. This may not be what you want to hear, but it's the truth. We should never rely on someone else for our spiritual growth. Others can nurture, challenge, and sharpen us. But our relationships with Christ and the health thereof should never completely depend on a third party (Bible not withstanding). Scripture is worth pursuing and discovering for yourself. From this point on, let any intimidation be the driving force behind motivation.

A host of other reactions could be included here, but despite the thoughts circling around in your brain right now, take a moment and consider something: the journey we are about to embark on will change your life. Not in a monumental and crazed way, altering every aspect of your life, but you will now realize you can study God's truths on your own. I pray that you will no longer be able to look at a Bible without getting a tingling sensation in your toes, goose bumps along your spine, or a big smile on your face because you know that when you open it, you will meet with and grow closer to its Author.

You will have your own little secret love affair with the Creator of this universe! If you've ever wanted to know what a perfect date looks like, pull up a chair, grab a beverage of your preference, get comfy, and open the book that reveals the most dashing, mysterious, beautiful, and intimate Being who ever existed. Meet with your God. Meet with the One who has given everything to be with you, who has sacrificed His own Son so that you could be called His own. That's Who we're pursuing with this study.

We're in hot pursuit of His Word—reading, interpreting, and applying it in a way that brings a smile to His face. We're hearing from Him and letting His Words wash over and cleanse our minds, hearts, souls, and spirits. If you're anything like me, this journey will turn your world upside down, and it will only be the beginning. You've heard the expression "ignorance is bliss." Well, they can't say that about Scripture, because it—the truth—is bliss! It is totally satisfying, convicting, and awe-inspiring bliss that will leave you speechless yet hungry for more. No more ignorance in the Bible department, dear friends! Get ready for the adventure of a lifetime!

Let's elaborate more on our definition of hermeneutics—the art and science of interpreting Scripture.

AN ART

How, may we ask, is hermeneutics an art? Don't worry, left-brain friends who get nervous even thinking about painting by number, we're not talking about drawing, composing, or designing. Rather, we're saying the interpretive process contains an artistic component; it is not an entirely objective process.

An artistic component will always accommodate hermeneutics because, like its subject, it is multifaceted. Consider a diamond. Imagine a five-carat brilliant, perfectly cut diamond perched up high in its splendor, positioned in a seductively poised setting. After picking your jaw back up (ladies), imagine holding it up to a light.

What happens when you look at it? All sorts of sparkly reflections of light dance about the room. Move the diamond around a bit, and you'll notice those reflections changing and moving with the diamond, like your own very expensive yet fabulously gorgeous disco ball. Stand at another angle, and the dazzling lights dance in another brilliant display.

The point? Diamonds are multifaceted. One diamond produces a host of reactions, depending on how we hold or look at it. It's the same with Scripture.

Scripture is one book, yet it creates a multitude of reactions and yields just as many observations, depending on the individual reading it. Does that mean its truth is dependent on the reader? Not hardly. But it does mean that within the process of hermeneutics, the Holy Spirit will reveal various (and many similar) observations to different readers in order to shed light on a particular truth.

Remember our discussion about the different authors of Scripture? How God used each man's cultural upbringing, religious background, experiences, and relationship with Him to impact the way the man wrote his particular book? The same can be said of the reading audience (us) today. We all come to Scripture with different backgrounds, experiences, beliefs, etc., which will inevitably impact the way we practice hermeneutics, the way we see the truth. Does it change the truth? Not in the slightest. But the way we see it greatly depends on who we are and how He made us.

Our differences make this point even more incredible! If we were all the same, we would have a boring, humdrum existence. We're not all clones of each other, and we're happy about that! Sure, we would all change a thing or two about ourselves if given the chance—less plumpness around the lower quadrants of our bodies, washboard abs that remain chiseled no matter what we eat, long, luxurious locks requiring little to zero maintenance—but that's a different sidebar for another time.

What we tend to overlook due to our fantasy distractions, however, is how amazing we all are and how beautifully diverse (yet united) we live as His children! Think about it. Type A needs Type B, otherwise the word "fun" would not be in existence. Just the same, Type B needs Type A, or nothing would ever get done. We need a balance of work and play, art and science, fact and feeling. We need everyone's strengths to balance society and the body of Christ, which makes hermeneutics an enjoyable group adventure as well as an individual one.

By studying His Word together, we display our strengths and weaknesses for others to enjoy and learn from. Some of us will notice a passage detail highlighting one aspect of the truth being portrayed, while another notices a sequence of events that adds even more depth. Get a whole bunch of people together making observations and studying His Word, and you get serious benefits of hearing how the Spirit reveals His truth in lots of ways!

Each detail and insight acts as a piece of the puzzle, filling it in and giving it dimension and depth that we could only have hoped to imagine on our own. God's Spirit reveals His truth to us individually. Although His truth never changes, the perspective through which we see it varies quite a bit and makes for a fabulous time of study!

This is what we mean when we say the process of hermeneutics is an art. It's artsy because our methods of finding the truth of Scripture vary and depend on each of us as individuals. We will not always see the same things, but we will always arrive at the same truth if we go about it correctly. And our interpretive journey will benefit when we do it together!

A SCIENCE

A warning, however, must follow this point. While our differences can make us stronger, taking those differences to the extreme leads to hermeneutical demise. Enter the science portion of our hermeneutics definition. We cannot neglect the scientific process of hermeneutics for the sake of our uniqueness and artistic diversity. God extends us freedom in observing details creatively, but those observations must be conducted under the umbrella of objectivity.

We must leave behind any personal agendas, vendettas, beliefs, and opinions because we seek truth—His truth, not our own. Truth rarely follows our fallible opinions. We must not try to make Scripture say something *we* want it to say rather than what it *does* say. Doing so results in major consequences. Truth is our priority—His truth on His terms. We'll get into that more, but for now, let's turn our attention back to our definition. Hermeneutics is both the art and science of— what? That's right—interpreting Scripture.

INTERPRETING

What does it mean to interpret something? The first thought that comes to mind usually involves languages—interpreting a document or speech from one language to another. Or perhaps you have children and find yourself interpreting grown-up answers to young children who prefer black and white ones. Both are matters of interpretation.

Interpreting the Bible is far weightier and more serious. We're not talking about merely interpreting Scripture from one language to another, but rather from the written Word to our minds and comprehensions. Interpreting Scripture this way requires us to think. We must use our brains and bridge the gap between God's mind and ours.

Fun fact time! Did you know there are roughly 775,000 words in the Bible?[2] We must not only read them but also interpret/understand them so we can apply them to our lives. We've got the reading part down, but the next two parts are just as crucial.

Hermeneutics now arrives on the scene in blazing glory. Knowing how to read does not automatically translate to total understanding of what we're reading. If we arrive at an incorrect understanding, we'll surmise an incorrect application, which is not good! Especially when our relationship with God is affected.

---

[2] http://www.christiananswers.net/bible/about.html

Consider an example. A little boy is learning how to read. He shows off his new skills for Mommy and Daddy whenever he can. In the car on the way home from school one day, the boy sipped his Hi-C and recounted every detail of his busy school day to Mom. Suddenly, he became visibly perturbed and put down his drink.

"Is everything is all right?" Mom asked.

The boy lowered his gaze. "I never knew it was against the rules to drink in the car."

"Where did you hear that?"

"I just saw a sign that said, 'Don't drink and drive!'"

The little boy's reading skills are accurate, but his understanding is incomplete.

People make the same mistake with Scripture every day. This is why hermeneutics is such a big deal. It helps us understand what we're reading so we can understand what He's saying to us. Only when we understand what He's saying can we apply it correctly to our lives.

We can't claim or stand on His promises if we don't understand them. Many people read a principle in the Scripture, genuinely think they are applying it to their lives, and are left utterly confused and disappointed when it doesn't work out as they thought it would—as they thought Scripture promised it would. Often people never realize the error lies in their understanding of Scripture, not in Scripture itself. This leaves them disappointed, confused, and sometimes ready to give up on God because they think He didn't come through. Such a tragedy. This is why the field of proper hermeneutics exists.

Understand this: everyone practices hermeneutics every time they read something, the Bible included. But many people exercise bad hermeneutics with Scripture on a daily basis. Most do this unknowingly, but the lack of proper knowledge isn't an excuse. Truth is truth, regardless of what we do with it. We need to learn together how to conduct proper and appropriate hermeneutics so we can understand and apply His word correctly to our lives.

We're about to embark on this journey so we can know how to

discover the truth of Scripture. We learn the truth so we can stand on His promises and submit to His will with all we are. Hermeneutics ushers us into that point with confidence that we understand His truth as He intended, not merely hoping we've come up with the right conclusion. God compiled Scripture to be known and understood as truth—"These *things I have written to* you who believe in the name of the Son of God, *so that you may know* that you have eternal life" (1 John 5:13, *emphasis mine*).

Ready to get started?

THE GOAL REVISITED

We've just learned the definition of hermeneutics; now let's review its ultimate goal once again. Then we'll see how the Holy Spirit helps with the process, and we'll conclude with some hermeneutical rules to remember.

The general goal of hermeneutics, as mentioned above, is to read, interpret, and apply Scripture correctly and accurately to our lives. The more specific goal, however, is to grasp the meaning of a biblical text (a.k.a. the theological principle) and apply it to our lives so we are transformed by His truth and into His image. The theological principle composes the main point of any given passage. We'll learn all about that later, but for right now, remember that finding the theological principle of the passage is our goal (the goal of hermeneutics), so we can appropriately apply it to our lives.

This is also a good time to introduce our theme verse for this study:

> Be diligent to present yourself approved to God as a workman who does not need to be ashamed, accurately handling the word of truth.[3]

---

[3] 2 Timothy 2:15

This verse is what we're all about, folks! We yearn to be men and women after God's own heart. We need to know His truth so we can handle and apply it correctly in a way that brings a smile to our heavenly Father. That's the goal. Now let's turn our attention to how the Holy Spirit helps us in this holy endeavor.

THE HOLY SPIRIT'S ROLE IN THE PROCESS

Ephesians 1:13 states, "In Him, you also, after listening to the message of truth, the gospel of your salvation—having also believed, you were sealed in Him with the Holy Spirit of promise." The moment we come to know Christ as our personal Lord and Savior, we receive the Holy Spirit—who guides and sanctifies us (sets us apart) as we continue to grow in our relationships with Him. We no longer find our identity in this world but now have Christ living in us—drawing us closer to God.

Paul emphasizes this point well:

> You are not in the flesh but in the Spirit, if indeed the Spirit of God dwells in you . . . and He who searches the heart knows what the mind of the Spirit is, because He intercedes for the saints according to the will of God.[4]

This is amazing to think about, isn't it? When we accept Christ, the Father commissions the Holy Spirit to intercede for us and help us know and understand the will of God.

Knowing and understanding God's ways is a process best accomplished through His Word. The Spirit initiates and fuels the process. "Now we have received, not the spirit of the world, but the Spirit who is from God, so that we may know the things freely given to

---

[4] Romans 8:9, 27.

us by God."⁵ One of those things is His Word. God appoints His Spirit to help us understand His Word. What a precious gift!

But before getting too carried away in our giddy thankfulness, we must address a couple of *howevers* worth mentioning. The first is that "having the Holy Spirit does not mean that the Spirit is all you need. . . . The Holy Spirit does not make valid interpretation automatic."⁶ The Holy Spirit's dwelling within us doesn't render us infallible.

How many of us become perfect after accepting Christ? (If you're nodding in confirmation, congratulations! You just joined the rest of us with that little lie!) We are still far from perfect after we accept Christ, though we make every effort to pursue Him and righteousness over the world and its evil desires. Though the Spirit helps us interpret and understand the Bible, He does not do it for us. We are responsible for using our brains. Even then, we potentially err in misunderstanding His Word if we're not careful.

The second *however* worth noting is that the Spirit does not create new meaning or provide any new information through reading Scripture.⁷ The original words of Scripture remain available to us today. The Spirit, while going deeper in study, may help us realize the truths already present in Scripture, but He does not reveal new truths. This may step on some toes, but it's the way it is.

We won't get into the "are there modern-day prophets" debate, but we'll address one point for our friends who believe new truths are revealed through the Spirit today. Deuteronomy 18:20 clearly states that any "prophet" who is not of the Lord (tells a lie or gives a false prophecy), should be put to death. That's a heavy and serious law because it's a heavy and serious issue.

Prophets must be 100 percent accurate in everything they prophesy because prophecies originate from God, who is never wrong. We don't put false prophets to death in the good ol' US of A today, but the

---

⁵ 1 Corinthians 2:12
⁶ Duvall and Hays, *Grasping God's Word*, 208.
⁷ Duvall and Hays, *Grasping God's Word*, 208.

point remains. If someone today gives a false prophecy, he should be discredited and never listened to again in that capacity.

The bottom line, whether or not you believe in modern-day prophets, is that nothing spoken or revealed today is new revelation from God, nor should it ever be placed on par with Scripture. Scripture is complete, period. In Revelation, John says this (primarily about Revelation, but most believe it applies to all of Scripture):

> I testify to everyone who hears the words of the prophecy of this book: if anyone adds to them, God will add to him the plagues which are written in this book; and if anyone takes away from the words of the book of prophecy, God will take away his part from the tree of life and from the holy city, which are written in this book.[8]

Don't mess with Scripture. Don't add to it, subtract from it, or dilly-dally around with it to suit your preferences. It is a holy book from the Holy God. Let His Word be His Word; don't try to compete with it or let someone else do so.

The final *however* to look at is that the Holy Spirit does not change the Bible to suit our purposes or match our circumstances. Rather, He brings the meaning of the Bible to bear on the reader (i.e. sanctification).[9]

Ever heard of popcorn reading? It's when someone prays, "Okay, God. I'll open up the Bible and assume that whatever verse I read first is what You're telling me to do in my situation." All of us bear guilt as popcorn-reading culprits at some point in our lives, but that does not make it right. The Spirit's role with us and Scripture is to help us understand it on His terms, not our own.

Scripture was written at a particular time, in a particular place, to a particular people. This point is crucial because Scripture was not

---
[8] Revelation 22:18-19.
[9] Duvall and Hays, *Grasping God's Word*, 210.

written originally to us. It was written to a particular people going through a particular situation at a particular time in history. Our job is to realize who they were and what they were facing, glean the principle from their encounter with God, and apply to our situation.

We do not automatically take a verse like Psalm 92:9: "For behold, Your enemies, O Lord, for behold Your enemies will perish; all who do iniquity will be scattered," and claim that His enemies are our annoying coworkers. God does not (at least, with all serious probability) consider your annoying coworkers His enemy, nor will He make them perish or go away. Get the point? The Spirit helps us understand what God was saying to the original audiences of Scripture. Our job is to learn what that is and apply it to our lives only when it is appropriately applicable.

To review, the Holy Spirit serves a crucial role in our hermeneutic journey because He helps us understand God's truth accurately. He does not make valid interpretation automatic; we have to be responsible stewards of His truth. Nor does He create new meaning for us. Rather, He reveals the truths already present so we can apply them to our lives. He also doesn't change the meaning of the text to fit our current situations. The text speaks for itself, and it's our job to find out what it says and how it applies correctly to our lives.

The Rules

Now that we understand the goal of hermeneutics and the Holy Spirit's role in it, let's discover some important general hermeneutical rules. These rules will guide everything we do in hermeneutics, so pay attention!

RULE #1: THE LITERAL, GRAMMATICAL, HISTORICAL METHOD

If we were taking bets, most of the money would be placed on the idea that this rule is going to be boring. Academic blah-blah-blah, right? Nope! Call off the bets! Though this content may not be as spicy as a mouth-watering taco from Guadalajara, it is super-important to understand and remember as our hermeneutic journey begins. (But it actually is quite interesting, so don't tune out yet!)

Deduction VS Induction

First things first. We approach interpreting Scripture (or any work of literature, for that matter) in one of two ways: deduction or induction.

Deduction simply means to start with a broad generalization and use it to determine something specific. For example,

> *God gives gifts to those He loves. Molly got a new car, so He must love her. Sarah lost her job, so He must not love her.*

See the problem? Broad principles should not determine the circumstances of particular situations (without other support, anyway). Does God love Molly? Yes. Does Molly's new car directly represent God's love for her? Probably not, but who's to say?

No one can answer that because we're not God. That's the problem with deductive reasoning. We assume things that may or may not be true, and then we use them to draw specific conclusions. Can Molly's new car be a direct result of God's love for her? Sure. But that may not be the case for Sarah, or anyone else, for that matter. Scripture affirms that God gives His children gifts. However, when something bad happens to us, we should never assume that He doesn't love us anymore.[1] Deductive reasoning is subjective and gives the reader far too much authority over what he reads.

Using deductive reasoning when reading and interpreting Scripture is not a good idea. Deduction allows the reader, rather than the author, to determine the meaning of the text. Scripture is God's Word, not ours. Thus, our job is to let it speak for itself, not the other way around.

Induction, however, is the other and most sound way to read and interpret Scripture. With inductive reasoning, we observe specific situations/stories/facts, collect them, and determine the general point or truth from them. It's like a puzzle—getting the big picture after we make sure we know all the details and have them in place. Details determine the broad/general truth, not vice versa.

Let's pause for another analogy. Put on a fashionable English cap, pick up a pocket watch, and start speaking succinctly, my dear

---
[1] Matthew 7:11

The Rules

Watson! Detectives, (whether in fun, fictional stories or in real life), master the art of inductive reasoning. When they enter a crime scene, they notice details. They know that observations and facts don't lie. They trust details and piece them together one at a time until a big picture forms.

Assumptions based from deductive reasoning, on the other hand, equate to big trouble in a detective's field because assumptions often lie and throw people off course. Detectives strive to avoid making assumptions or drawing conclusions based on what they see at first. It would be ridiculous to assume all the details of a crime with one glance at the crime scene!

You see where this is headed. Induction stands as the more objective of the two approaches. It focuses on discovering what God is communicating by observing His Words rather than starting with our point and trying to make Scripture back it up. See the difference? We must understand this before we continue. God's Word is *His*. We, as the readers, try to determine (and should be more concerned about) what He is saying rather than what we think He is saying. We come to the whole truth by observing all the details we can. We should not start with generalizations and then use them to filter our interpretation of the details.

After choosing inductive study over deductive study, we must determine how we will go about our inductive study. Contrary to what some believe, God never tells us how to read Scripture. Nowhere in the Bible will you find step-by-step instructions for reading, interpreting, and applying it to our lives.

He did, however, equip us with functioning brains and common sense! We will tap into them when we choose a method for our inductive studies. There may not be a verse we can point to as foolproof truth (wow, try saying that three times fast), but we can use our fully functional minds and determine the best by laying out our options.

Three Types of Induction

Option 1: Textual Criticism

Textual criticism determines what the autographs of Scripture said. If you remember from our previous study, Bibles today are copies of the autographs. Textual critics work to determine the exact verbiage of those autographs. They practice this using one of three approaches: textus receptus, majority text, and the critical method.[2] We're not going to get into those individually, because it gets complicated and time-consuming, but this approach as a whole pursues a worthy goal. Discovering the truth of His Word is what we're all about, right?

However, most textual critics focus too much on the text. Consumed with the individual words and characters of the manuscripts, they often neglect to move from reading to interpreting and then applying. There's certainly nothing wrong with exploring textual criticism, as long as we move beyond it and get to the actual interpretation and application of Scripture. Textual criticism fails as a hermeneutical method because it leaves out two of its three components! Not a good thing to do, friends! If used as a *part* of hermeneutics, it's fine and dandy, but as a complete hermeneutical method, it comes up short.

Option 2: Allegorical

Unlike textual criticism, which merits some redeeming value if kept in check, the Allegorical Method of hermeneutics is deeply and irreconcilably flawed. This method assumes the Bible is figurative and should not be taken literally. Adherents of this method believe parts of it can be literal, but it's left to the individual reader to distinguish the literal from the allegorical.

---

[2] For more information on each of these, visit http://www.gotquestions.org/textual-criticism.html.

Red flags and caution signs should flash in your mind as if it's the Fourth of July. This has "bad" written all over it. The irredeemable flaw of this method is that it puts the reader in authority over the Author of Scripture.

Pause for a moment. The Bible does contain allegories as figures of speech, helping communicate truth by relating it to something we can understand. But a significant difference exists between an allegory *in* Scripture and allegorical Scripture. An allegory in Scripture is a specific figure of speech used to make a point. Allegorical Scripture, on the other hand, is a broad-sweeping gesture claiming Scripture as allegorical in general, and readers determine when to make exceptions for literal interpretation.

In other words, fallible, fallen, sinful, and debilitated people have the right to determine when the infallible, perfect, holy and true God is being literal or not, when He Himself makes no such distinction. It's at once laughable and utterly disheartening. Oh, yeah, and wrong!

Readers never get to place themselves in an authoritative position over what they're reading, especially when the book in question is the only God-inspired book in existence. We're not at liberty to determine when God says this but really means that in His Word. Such distinctions are highly subjective and downright dangerous to anyone upholding the sanctity of Scripture.

Consider this: when do you ever pick up a book, let's say a biography on George Washington, and not read it at face value? That would be like saying, "Well, it says Mr. Washington was the first president of the United States, but what it really means is that he was a strong leader who fought for America, made lots of friends, and is well-known today."

Well, sure, but with that definition, a thousand others would qualify as the president of the United States as well. See how ridiculous the entire concept of allegorical interpretation is? We do not have the right, privilege, or authority to devalue Scripture by inserting our opinions in lieu of its truth.

The moment we place ourselves in authority over Scripture is the moment Scripture loses all its authority. The divine hierarchy is this: God, then His Word, then us. Never God, then us, then His Word, or us, then His Word, then God, which is what happens when we practice the allegorical method. We submit to Him and His Word totally or not at all. If He is not above us, then we are above Him. There's no in between. We cannot pick and choose parts of the whole. It's all or nothing. It's Him and His Word entirely or none at all.

The allegorical method blurs that line and makes proper hermeneutics a passing sentiment. There's no point in pursuing the truth of Scripture if we are ultimately the ones who decide what truth is. Bottom line: Scripture stands on its own and has authority over every person in existence. Even Jesus submitted to it! To argue is to assert yourself over its authority and the authority of God. Good luck on that one.

Option #3: The Literal, Grammatical, Historical Method

Ah, now this is more like it. This method upholds three rules. First, Scripture was written literally and should be read as such. Second, normal, traditional rules of grammar apply when reading it, and third, it is based in history with specific contexts that cannot be separated from the text.

Let's explore these three rules.

Literal

Scripture stands unique among books, yet is like any other in that we should read it literally. When we pick up a novel, we don't read hidden meanings into the words, nor do we infuse them with diatribes about what we think the author is trying to get across. We read novels like any other literature except maybe some poetry, in the normal, plain, everyday sense of the words in which they are written. Well, surprise, surprise. We must interpret passages of Scripture the same way—in the normal, plain, everyday sense of the words. If it makes sense the way it was written, there's certainly no need to "spiritualize" it or make it allegorical. When God says "you shall have no other gods before Me," it is not a suggestion for us to comply with only when we feel like it. There are no exceptions, nor does the statement contain any *buts* or *yets*, *unlesses* or *howevers*. He literally means that we are not to place anything before Him. He is always number one! We should always take the Bible literally, unless the context demands otherwise. In those situations, it often becomes clear that a figure of speech is being used.

Grammatical

The grammatical aspect of our preferred method of interpretation now comes into play. God utilizes figures of speech throughout Scripture to communicate a point. In these instances, we are called to use our brains (that common sense we referred to earlier) to recognize that they are figures of speech and adjust our interpretation accordingly. In 1 Peter 5:8 Peter writes, "Your adversary, the devil, prowls around like a roaring lion, seeking someone to devour." Does he mean that Satan is literally a lion on the hunt for us? Does he have a mane and a tail and weigh 400 pounds? Is he the king of the jungle? No. Though he would be easier to handle if he were. Anyway, you get the point. Do you see why God chose to use that metaphor to communicate what He wants us to understand about that verse—that Satan is not dead or dormant, but actively seeking to destroy us?

As we learned before, Scripture is not monotone, routine, or mundane. It's exciting and comprised of lots of different literary styles and techniques. These techniques communicate a truth and help our minds grasp the truth God is extending through His Word. We as the readers don't decide what is literal and what is not. God does that by giving us clear literary patterns we can recognize and adjust our interpretations to. Thus, we always interpret Scripture literally unless the context itself demands that we consider otherwise, namely, that we're reading a figure of speech.

Historical

Now that we understand the importance of reading and interpreting Scripture literally, yet with sensitivity to certain figures of speech, we can move into the third component of our hermeneutical method: the historical. What do we mean when we say we should interpret the Bible historically? First, if you'll recall from previous sections, we learned that Scripture was written at a particular time, in a particular place, to a particular people, for a particular purpose. In other words, it has historical context. The context in which each book was written cannot be separated from the text that comes with it. For example, when reading the apostle Paul's first letter to Timothy, we cannot forget or neglect to consider the fact that we are reading a letter from someone (the apostle Paul) to another specific someone (his disciple in the faith, Timothy).

Historical details like that transform our understanding of passages from black and white to dazzlingly vibrant and radiant color. If you turn on the TV in the middle of a news story in which an anchor is reading a portion of a letter, it might recount interesting material and leave you mildly curious. But when you find out that the letter was written by Abraham Lincoln to one of his trusted advisors back in the day, the letter suddenly has much more significance. Why? Because you understand the context in which it was written. Context is a vital component in our hermeneutic journey. We must interpret Scripture historically because it was written within specific historical contexts that we should always try to understand.

The second reason we should interpret Scripture historically compliments the first one. We read through historical lenses in order to achieve a thorough interpretation of any given passage. Forming a conclusion on the Lincoln letter in our last example before discovering its author would be ridiculous. Yet people hastily draw conclusions from one item/story/fact all the time. That's why discovering a passage's historical context aids our effort in drawing proper and well-informed conclusions of what we're reading.

Scripture is no exception to this point. Read Paul's encouragement to the Philippian church:

> For to you it has been granted for Christ's sake, not only to believe in Him, but also to suffer for His sake, experiencing the same conflict which you saw in me, and now hear to be in me.[3]

What does it mean? You can glean a couple of things. Maybe they were experiencing persecution for their faith and are now called to join with Paul in his conflict. But what conflict? And what kind of persecution did they face? To typical Americans, religious persecution means enduring snide remarks from peers or coworkers. In extreme cases, they may be forced out of social circles or jobs. But in third-world countries, persecution often means torture, imprisonment, and ultimately, martyrdom. What did it mean to the Philippian church?

If you conduct some background research on the church, you'll discover that Philippi was primarily a Roman colony with so few Jews (if any), there wasn't even a synagogue. Paul founded it when he received the famous Macedonian Call in Acts 16, and they were a church dear to his heart—likely his favorite of all the churches he wrote to. Paul wrote from prison, and the believers of Philippi experienced resistance to the faith among their Roman peers. This resistance led to full-blown persecution, because the Philippian believers were forced

---

[3] Philippians 1:29-30.

to choose which was more important to them: being citizens of Rome or citizens of heaven through Jesus Christ. They could not actively and forthrightly be both.

Paul personalized it by saying that the persecution is something he already endures. He gave them an example to follow, for he already publically identified with Christ over Roman citizenship—the most highly esteemed citizenship of the day. This certainly wasn't intended to be a Philippians Bible study, but do you get, or at least catch a glimpse of, how much we miss if we don't read the Bible historically? We miss far more than we could ever imagine! We can easily avoid this simply by digging deeper and reading the Word in the context in which it was written.

We must read and interpret Scripture literally, grammatically, and historically in order to apply it correctly. The literal, grammatical, and historical method is the best way to approach Scripture because it keeps us "big-picture" focused (unlike the textual criticism method), and keeps us objective and in submission to God's Word (unlike the allegorical method).

We've said it before and will say it again: Scripture is God's inerrant, infallible, inspired, living Word. It should be read as such—with His intentions and priorities in mind, not ours. Our job as readers and believers in Christ is to take Him at His Word—literally, grammatically, and within its proper historical context—and let the Holy Spirit use it to give us an application that will transform our hearts and lives for His glory. That's what it's all about, folks; and it's also a mighty fine segue to Rule #2.

RULE #2: SCRIPTURE IS THE ULTIMATE AUTHORITY

We must constantly remind ourselves that Scripture is our authority; we are not its authority. This is of utmost importance as we embark on our hermeneutical journey. One question to pose with this rule is, "Who controls the meaning of a text—the reader or the author?" You've probably guessed the correct answer, but still, many of us would probably initially say it's the reader.

How many of us have heard or asked the following question: "What does this passage mean to you?" Though it sounds insightful and as if we care what other people think, this question is all wrong. It assumes that our opinion, not the passage itself, is what matters. Instead, the question should be, "What does this passage mean? And how then should you apply it to your life?"

See the difference? It's huge! The emphasis in the first question is on the reader. After all, the reader's opinion is the one that matters, right? With some literature, sure. With the Bible? Surely not. Why? Again, because it's *God's* Word written to *His* people to communicate *His* truth and message to a lost and dying world.

We have no business placing our commentary and our opinions on the same level as God's. That's why it doesn't matter what a passage may or may not mean to you. Your opinion of a passage isn't worth much of anything in comparison to what God is saying, friends! Now, if your opinion happens to coincide with God's after you have taken our hermeneutic journey, then we're all just peachy. But even then, you're agreeing with God's opinion. He's not agreeing with yours.

Since God's opinion is the only one that matters, our goal is to discover exactly what that opinion is! Of course, we accomplish this by engaging in proper hermeneutics (which we're getting to, I promise). But another little spot to note here is that we are seeking to discover the meaning that He has already placed in His Word. We touched on this when we talked about the Holy Spirit's role in hermeneutics, but because it's important, we'll elaborate some more.

We, the fallible, fallen, sinful, roughly inept readers, do not create meaning. It is not our job to put words in God's mouth. He doesn't need our help. Rather, it is our duty, joy, privilege, and great responsibility to determine the meaning that's already there.

We inevitably come to Scripture with certain biases, beliefs, and/or persuasions that we've either been taught our whole lives or have formed on our own. These have no place in the world of hermeneutics. In fact, we should check them at the door. When we come to Scripture, when we sit down and open the well-worn and beautiful pages of the Bible, we are to come humbly and with as few presuppositions as possible. We come with great expectation and minute opinions. We come to be filled, not to fill. It's full on its own, thank you very much!

Eisegesis VS Exegesis

This is a grand time to introduce two new vocabulary words! The first is eisegesis (pronounced eye-si-jee-sis. That'll impress the friends!). Eisegesis means to read meaning into a text. Or, as the dictionary defines it, "an interpretation, especially of Scripture, that expresses the interpreter's own ideas, bias, or the like, rather than the meaning of the text."[4] This, as you can imagine, is bad. Eisegesis happens when someone picks and chooses certain verses of Scripture to support her opinion, which backs up her beliefs, rather than letting Scripture determine those beliefs. Case in point: feminism.

It may be a sore subject for many and undoubtedly entices a broad spectrum of reactions. But did you know that the feminist movement uses Galatians 3:28 as their signature verse? It states, "There is neither Jew nor Greek, there is neither slave nor free man, there is neither male nor female; for you are all one in Christ Jesus." With resounding voices, feminists claim this verse. It holds a few gregarious titles: "the golden text" by evangelical feminism, "the Magna Carta of Humanity" by Paul King Jewett, "the feminist credo of equality" by Beverly Allen, and one feminist group actually calls themselves "Galatians 3:28 Press."

With little study, we realize the point of this verse has nothing to do with promoting feministic ideals, yet an entire movement has

---

[4] http://dictionary.reference.com/browse/eisegesis.

based its cause on it. Why? Because the feminist movement (in relation to this verse specifically) is guilty of eisegesis. They read their own incorrect and erroneous meaning into the text. They let their bias and agenda get in the way of properly observing, interpreting, and applying Scripture. This is a perfect example of what not to do.

Eisegesis occurs more often than we'd like to admit, which is why we must exercise extreme caution and perform frequent self-analyses when we embark on our hermeneutic journeys. Our goal is to discover God's truth, not twist His Words to back up our agendas, biases, and personal beliefs.

The other vocabulary word for this rule is exegesis (pronounced ex-eh-jee-sis), and is the antonym of eisegesis. Exegesis means to discover the meaning already in the text. The dictionary defines it as a "critical explanation or interpretation of a text or portion of a text, especially the Bible."[5]

This is exactly what we are supposed to do. When we approach Scripture, we come as humble students who greatly anticipate discovering its truth. We long to meet with God and let His Word wash over our hearts, transform us into the image of Christ, and sanctify us—set us apart for His glory on Earth! None of that is possible if we're too busy reading our own meanings into it. You can't fill a bucket that's already full!

People who practice exegesis of Scripture come humbly before the Lord with full understanding that His Word, not their own opinions and biases, is their authority. Exegetes thrive on discovering His truth, not reading their own ideas into it. They choose to get out of the way so the Bible has all the room it needs in order to be absorbed into their hearts. They're not looking to prove anything; they're looking to learn everything. See the difference?

As believers and students of the Word, our goal is to let the text speak for itself (without our commentary) and discover what it's saying so we can apply it to our lives. What a beautiful and magnificent process!

---

[5] http://dictionary.reference.com/browse/exegesis

Yet it works only when we submit to it and realize that Scripture is our ultimate authority. We may question, stumble, doubt, and fall, but God's Word remains standing and shines even brighter when our perspectives conform to His. Let's be exegetes, yes? Let's discover the meaning already there, not read our own into it!

A closely related topic of exegesis is that of the truth (no shocker there). To discover the meaning in a text is one thing; yet with Scripture, the meaning we're getting at is truth. It's not an opinion, idea, theory, or hypothesis. It is certifiable, non-negotiable truth straight from the Truth Himself—God. God is Truth, so it makes sense that He gives us His truth in His Word. His Word is filled with truth—the whole truth and nothing but the truth! We're given all we need (though maybe not necessarily all we want), and it's always enough.

PROBLEMS PEOPLE HAVE WITH TRUTH

"Relative" Truth

People today believe in "relative truth," which means they determine their own truth based on personal opinions. It's subjective and varies from person to person. You often hear something like, "What's true for her isn't true for me." That's acceptable in our culture. It's also known as being "tolerant." Americans pride themselves as advocates of tolerance and political correctness. In fear of being labeled "politically incorrect," we shy away from defending our beliefs and absolute truth. We're content to let people do what they want as long as they don't impose their opinions, ideas, or beliefs on us, and vice versa. No need to upset the flow, right? Wrong!

Relative truth could be labeled "irrelevant truth" for all it's worth (which isn't much). Truth that varies from person to person isn't truth. It's a worldview. Worldviews change from person to person, but truth—the truth—is constant and does not change.

Consider this: Sally believes the sky is orange. Not the sun, mind you, the sky. Sue hears Sally say that and calls her crazy (understandably so) because the sky is blue. Sally doesn't flinch an inch at Sue's accusation. She merely replies, "Well, I've decided that blue and orange should be rearranged. Blue is orange, and orange is blue."

Ridiculous, right? This is a simplistic example, but you know people advocate the same argument (albeit different topic) all over the place in this little world of ours. Sad, but true. Sallies of the world are people who believe in relative truth—that truth is dependent on people and is not absolute. From our example, you can see how insane this world would be without absolute truth!

Unfortunately, a lot of people believe in relative truth. They don't want absolute truth—a standard by which life, morals, ideals, and beliefs are measured—because then they would have to submit and be accountable to something. Instead, they fool themselves into believing their opinion is the only one that matters and their personal truth is the only thing that counts.

Let's bring Scripture into the discussion. People who practice relative truth fall under our eisegesis category above. When they look at Scripture, they see golden opportunities to twist its verses to support their views. They like the fact that Scripture is truth but concern themselves only with making its truth agree with them. Folks, this approach isn't concerned with truth at all because it doesn't recognize that there's an absolute truth to begin with. It's completely pointless.

One last point will always pause a relative truth-ist (like that term? Thanks . . . I made it up). Relative truth-ists claim that *there is no absolute truth*. Read that last sentence again. In that single sentence, they betray their own position. By saying "there is no," they mean they know for a fact that something is not true. How can they know something is not true if they don't believe in truth? Beats me!

Remember our earlier reference to using our God-given and

functional brains in the hermeneutic process? I'm calling you to use yours here. Relative truth isn't truth at all. It's self-defeating and meaningless. There is absolute truth out there, and it is found within the pages of Scripture.

The Whole Truth and Nothing But the Truth? Nah, Just Give Me Part of It

The second problem people have with the truth of Scripture is they refuse to accept the whole truth, only the parts that make them feel good. People don't readily embrace the command to deny themselves, take up their cross, and follow Jesus daily. However, they like being told they can ask God for whatever they want and He will give it to them. Our second-problem people often overlook the hard, uncomfortable, and/or misunderstood passages of Scripture because they don't like them. Often, it boils down to laziness. But that's beside the point. We can't pay attention to the bits and pieces of the Bible that make us feel good and neglect the parts that step on our toes.

Truth is not always convenient and filled with bubbly emotions. We must accept it for what it is as a whole—the easy, the tough, the warm and fuzzy feelings, and the gut-wrenching convictions. All this we must face head-on, without compromise. Truth invokes many reactions, yet with God's Word, it's still all or nothing. We don't get to pick and choose. We either accept Scripture (completely) and experience a life with Him beyond our most astounding imaginations or reject it and face the bleak eternal consequences. It's completely our choice, as is believing in relative truth.

Truth itself doesn't change or go away depending on what we choose. It remains steadfast within the pages of your Bible. It doesn't need us; it's fine and content on its own. But God wants us to know it! That's why He gave it to us in written form. We're left to accept it on His terms or reject it. There's no middle ground.

Both relative truth and the bits-and-pieces approach fall short in the end and are completely incompatible with Scripture. Truth, on the other hand, is what Scripture is all about. In fact, it's the only book ever written that contains zero errors (as originally written), because it's the only one that God—the Truth—has written! So what will it be? Faux truth, incomplete truth, or the whole truth, His truth, and nothing but the truth?

Should you accept the third option mentioned above (one that comes highly recommended, by the way), we can then turn our attention to some final thoughts for our rule number two: Scripture as the Ultimate Authority.

We Cannot Impose our Thoughts, Ideas, or Beliefs Upon Scripture; Rather, Scripture Dictates our Thoughts, Beliefs, and Ideas

Because our personal opinions, ideas, and beliefs are irrelevant apart from Scripture, we should be careful not to impose them upon Scripture. We go to Scripture to get our thoughts, beliefs, and ideas, not the other way around. Scripture does not need our input or faulty opinions It's fine on its own.

Remember it's the inerrant, infallible, inspired, living Word of God. We, on the other hand, are none of those things (except living, I suppose). Thus, our responsibility when coming to God's Word is to let His truth take its rightful place in our lives and hearts—far above us. We should derive our opinions, worldviews, ideas, and beliefs from it, rather than letting our opinions, worldviews, ideas, and beliefs dictate what it means to us. Bottom line: Scripture is it, the final word, the ultimate truth.

We Must Approach Scripture Humbly and With as Few Assumptions and Presuppositions as Possible

We covered this point thoroughly in our eisegesis/exegesis conversation, but it's worth mentioning again . . . this time with a little slant. We know we should approach Scripture to find the meaning (truth), not to give it meaning. Now we must recognize that just as Scripture is our ultimate authority, truth within its pages is our ultimate concern.

Truth is what we seek, and we must be willing to accept it regardless of any preexisting opinions, ideas, or beliefs. If in our hermeneutic journey, we come to a passage of Scripture that, after careful and thoughtful study, teaches something that contradicts what we previously thought, we must accept the truth of Scripture. This is a scary thought for most of us.

Many of us grew up in Christian homes, have attended church our whole lives, and have been injected with lots of traditions over the years. Unfortunately, most traditions were taught to us as truths dictated by God, not traditions crafted by man. We don't think of our traditions as traditions; we think of them as truths. Thus, when we come to Scripture and learn something that contradicts something we have believed our whole lives, we feel attacked. It pains us to discover that something we thought was truth is actually a tradition/opinion. No one made the difference clear, and we have believed incorrectly for years . . . sometimes our whole lives.

If you are new to your relationship with Jesus Christ and are just beginning your journey of figuring all this out, you are at an advantage. You come to Scripture with a clean slate and can approach it much more objectively than others who have been familiar with it their whole lives. You're starting fresh, and that's a great place to be!

Well-seasoned Christians and newbies alike pursue one thing: truth—His truth. Sometimes truth is easy to accept because it's clear, obvious, and already being practiced in our lives. Other times, however, it will be difficult because it flies in the face of everything we've known—and may require significant change in our lives. How do we discover truth within the pages of Scripture? How do we avoid falling into eisegesis and reading our own thoughts into it, rather than letting our thoughts be dictated by it? Glad you asked! That's what Rule #3 addresses.

RULE #3: CONTEXT, CONTEXT, CONTEXT!

And again we say, "context!" Context is one of the most important steps in the hermeneutic journey. Without placing Scripture (each chapter, passage, verse, and word) within its proper context, we cannot interpret and apply Scripture correctly. Serious statement? Why, yes it is. Serious rule? Even more so.

The only way to ensure that we don't misuse Scripture or impose ourselves above its authority is to pay attention to the context of the verse or passage we are observing. We must never separate meaning from context. Think about it. When you read a novel, you don't start by opening it to the middle and going from there. That would be ridiculous, and you would have no idea what was going on. Why, then, do we often do that very thing with Scripture?

Granted, certain passages are straightforward and require little context in order to understand them. For instance, "Be kind to one another, tender-hearted, forgiving each other, just as God in Christ also has forgiven you."[6] This verse is easy to understand and get an application from. But what about verses like:

> For since in the wisdom of God the world through its wisdom did not come to know God, God was well-pleased through the foolishness of the message preached to save those who believe.[7]

---
[6] Ephesians 4:32
[7] 1 Corinthians 1:21

What does all that about foolishness and wisdom mean? And how do we apply that to our lives?

Most passages in Scripture (and any other works of literature, for that matter) require our understanding of context before we can understand what is being said and draw a proper application from it. Regardless of how easily understood a verse seems, we need to place it within its context before we draw a conclusion from it. If we don't, we're looking at a black-and-white photo when we could be looking at intoxicating colors exploding before our eyes. Grasping a passage's context is key to both interpreting and applying it to our lives.

One other key point to note with this rule: never study one singular verse. Studying one verse is like reading one sentence in the middle of a novel. It won't make sense. What a lot of people don't realize about Scripture is that the autographs didn't contain the convenient little chapter and verse sections organizing our Bibles today. They were written like letters—continual and without pause. Remember, real people were writing to other real people about real situations. How many of us divide our letters into mini-sections, with labels and titles to boot? Do we then number our sentences? That would be bizarre. But aren't you glad we have Scripture broken up like that today? Sword-drills would be complicated without those divisions! Anyway, sometime between 300-400AD, translators inserted nifty little breaks in the text, which is where our chapters and verses come from.

The downside to these niceties is that we are tempted to read bits and pieces at a time. Then we fail to understand the context of what we're reading. Never in this book will you be discouraged from reading Scripture. One verse is always better than no verse at all. But your study, understanding, and application of Scripture will be limited if you read only one verse. You can spend hours poring over one particular verse, dissecting the intricacies of the grammatical structure and observing every dot and tittle of every letter, but you will probably miss the point God is trying to communicate in the passage. Reading one verse doesn't do much good without placing it within sufficient context.

So what's a good rule of thumb? How many verses should we study at a time? There is no magic number, but study a passage—usually around ten verses but never less than three. This will vary depending on where you're reading, but never focus on less than three verses. Sometimes five will be plenty; other times it will take up to fifteen before you grasp the principle at hand. But never read only one verse and draw application from it. Remember to put it in its context. Context, context, context, people!

RULE #4: SCRIPTURE INTERPRETS SCRIPTURE

The topic of context yields quite nicely to our fourth and final rule: Scripture interprets Scripture. It sounds funny, but it's a simple concept. Scripture must be interpreted in light of itself. If you come to a conclusion from a passage and it blatantly contradicts another passage, something is off, and it's most likely your conclusion. However, most of the time all that's required is a little more study. Let's consider an example, shall we?

James writes, "You see that a man is justified by works and not by faith alone."[8] That seems straightforward, right? You think you can draw your application from that and call it a day. But what about Paul's instruction to the Galatian church:

> Nevertheless knowing that a man is not justified by the works of the Law but through faith in Christ Jesus, even we have believed in Christ Jesus, so that we may be justified by faith in Christ and not by works of the Law; since by the works of the Law no flesh will be justified.[9]

---

[8] James 2:24.
[9] Galatians 2:16.

This poses a quandary when compared with Mr. James, doesn't it? This is why we have to make sure any conclusion we draw from a passage is represented and confirmed in other passages of Scripture.

Here's another reason why this is so important. If you remember from our earlier study of the human authors of Scripture, each man was influenced by his character, background, personality, and experiences when penning Scripture. Each author makes a point, and different men choose different aspects of the truth to emphasize according to the leading and inspiration of the Holy Spirit. Why does this matter in Rule #4? If we limit ourselves to one particular passage's conclusion, we're getting only a one-dimensional view of the truth being conveyed.

James states his case one way, and Paul does another. We get solid conclusions from both individually, but how much fuller is the picture when we weave them together? Suddenly, a one-dimensional square becomes a two-dimensional box! Add another view given in another context, and you get the full three-dimensional picture. Get the idea? The more we expand the truth we're discovering within a particular passage in light of other Scripture, the more brilliant and complete the truth shines.

As you can see, interpreting Scripture in light of itself is crucial in our hermeneutic journey because it broadens our perspective and makes it more like God's. Remember, it's His Word we're reading, interpreting, and applying. Let's make sure we get the whole picture, and not just portions!

REFLECT

We have now fully examined the four basic rules of hermeneutics. The first is to understand and implement the literal, grammatical, and historical method rather than the textual criticism or the allegorical method. Scripture must be taken literally like any other written document, not allegorically, leaving the reader to determine a "hidden meaning" of the text. There are no hidden meanings in Scripture. The Holy Spirit does reveal the depths of its truth as we continue to mature in our faith and study, but we never discover something that wasn't already present.

Scripture also must be read within the universal grammatical rules that apply to any other body of literature. There's nothing bland or boring in Scripture. It has figures of speech like similes, metaphors, and hyperboles that we are to look out for. God chose to communicate His truth to us using terminology and examples that we understand (the devil is a "roaring lion"), but we need to interpret it correctly, adjusting our interpretations in light of figures of speech and varying literary genres.[10]

Scripture also has a historical context. It was written at a particular time, in a particular place, to a particular people. We must research before forming an interpretation of a passage because background information may impact our interpretation significantly. We can usually derive a black-and-white interpretation of a passage by simply reading the text, but how much more exciting and grand it is when we see it in full color and in 3-D! That's what background information accomplishes. We have to know where it's coming from before we understand what it means and how it impacts our lives.

After applying the first rule—the literal, grammatical, and historical method—we must apply Rule #2, which states that Scripture is our ultimate authority. God controls the meaning of the text; we do not. He's the Author; we're not. We cannot impose or let our opinions cloud what He is trying to communicate. We always take a back seat to His truth and seek to discover it over anything and everything else.

We discover truth through proper exegesis, which includes serious context time—Rule #3. We must pay attention to context, because the meaning of a text cannot be separated from it. Also, one verse is never enough to study on its own. Three to ten verses suffice

---

[10] The next chapter is devoted entirely to genres, and how to interpret each to its own.

a study, because only when we look outside of one verse can we put it into its proper context.

Context yields to our final rule because it emphasizes that Scripture must interpret Scripture—Rule #4. Before we make any kind of interpretation or application, we must explore the main concepts and/or theme elsewhere in Scripture to make sure we have an accurate understanding of it. Remember, Scripture speaks for itself. Our job is to find out what it's saying!

6

Old Testament Genres

It would be an injustice to explain all these wonderful descriptions and rules of hermeneutics without pausing to note the different literary styles (more specifically, genres) of Scripture. Yes, we've talked about this before. But we haven't yet discussed how to interpret each genre on its own terms. All the principles and rules of hermeneutics apply to every genre, but we need to appreciate and explore the quirks of each genre individually. This is not a foreign concept when you think about it. You read love letters from your spouse differently than you read than a memo from your boss. Scripture is no different.

Scripture contains many different genres of writing: historical narrative, law, poetry, wisdom, prophecy, the Gospels, parables, letters, and Acts and Revelation (genres unto themselves).[1] It seems like a lot, but in addition to what you've just learned about hermeneutics, you'll need to note only a couple tips for each. This chapter will cover the genres found primarily in the Old Testament (historical narrative, law, poetry, wisdom literature, and prophecy), and the next chapter will cover those of the New Testament (the Gospels, Parables, Acts, the Letters, and Revelation). Let's get started!

---

[1] Duvall and Hays, *Grasping God's Word*, 27.

Historical Narrative

Narrative, of course, simply refers to the telling of a story. Add *historical* in front of it, and you find yourself with a story that happened in the past. Nothing complicated about that! We find historical narratives all over Scripture, from Genesis to Revelation. The first good hint about them is that they are *true*. A lot of stories we hear today either aren't true (they're bedtime stories we read to our children), or they follow our telephone-game scheme in the way they're told. What started as true morphs into some other creature rarely resembling the original. Not so with the historical narratives of Scripture.

Scripture's stories record real-life events captured by the real flesh-and-blood people who experienced them. Are you thinking about our Canon discussion from earlier? We've mentioned it before: Scripture was written mostly (as far as human authors go) by men who experienced firsthand the events they wrote about. No one knows exactly how much time passed between each story and when it was penned in Scripture, but we can be certain the Holy Spirit kept them accurate!

God apparently enjoys narratives, because they comprise over 40 percent of the Old Testament and a substantial chunk of the New Testament as well.[2] Historical narrative portions of Scripture, like any other narrative, follow a certain order of reading so we can fully grasp what's going on in the story.

---

[2] Fee, Douglas and Gordon Stuart. *How to Read the Bible for All it's Worth*. Grand Rapids, Mich: Zondervan, 2003, 78.

SOME TIPS TO THINK ABOUT [3]

Pay Attention to Context

Woot-woot for Rule #3 again! Sure, narratives are stories that can be understood on their own. But since when is mere understanding our goal? Our first goal in hermeneutics is understanding, which is followed closely by interpretation, application, and life transformation. In Scripture, most narratives tie into another narrative told somewhere else in Scripture.

Let's consider the narrative of Abraham, recorded in Genesis 11. This is the first mention of Abraham (then called Abram). It begins by explaining his genealogy and then tells of God placing a special calling on Abraham's life. That is a historical narrative—a story about God calling Abram to be the father of His people.

But how sad would it be to stop there! That narrative can stand alone, but if we don't pursue it further we miss out on a lot! Abraham's life story continues for fourteen more chapters, and he is mentioned in twenty-six books of the Bible. For those of you who are mathematically challenged, like me, that's almost 40 percent of the Bible. Shame on us if we stop at Genesis 11! Now, this doesn't mean we have to include all the other chapters and stories in our direct hermeneutical study. It simply means we become aware of them to help give us a greater understanding of the people we're reading about.[4]

That's the beauty of historical narrative accounts in Scripture. They have context outside themselves. Many repeat elsewhere in Scripture, and since each author tells the story in a slightly different way, based on individual perspectives, we get a fuller version of the account with every version we read. This also directly corresponds to Rule #4—

---

[3] Much of this information is gleaned from *Grasping God's Word*, which is highly recommended for anyone wishing to pursue this study further.
[4] We'll get into this more when we introduce the steps of hermeneutics.

Scripture in light of Scripture. No rule or principle of hermeneutics exists in a silo; it's a beautiful tapestry woven by its magnificent author!

Next we'll get into the components of narratives and discover what makes a story a story.

Plot

Historical narratives, like any other stories worth reading, contain a plot. Something happens in the story—a beginning, a middle, and an end. The plot weaves the whole story together. Each part plays an important role, and paying attention to the plot helps us understand what the story is about. Ask questions like, "What's going on?" "What's the conflict in the story?" "How is the conflict resolved, if it is at all?" All these and more help us see the progression of events occurring in our narrative. Giving these events a name and a face does wonders for our comprehension of the story!

Setting

Every plot and/or storyline comes with its own setting. Dorothy finds herself far from Kansas in the magical Land of Oz. The Titanic wouldn't be much of a story without an iceberg-infested ocean. *Law & Order* wouldn't cut it on a prairie in the middle of Montana. Get the idea? The setting of the narrative is crucial because it tells us where the story takes place. It gives our brain the picture to put the plot into.

A narrative's setting comprises of much more than its physical location. And not all stories remain in one physical location. In our Abraham example, God's first words to Abraham (when his name was still Abram) were about the setting. Let's take a look:

> Now the Lord said to Abram, "Go forth from your country, and from your relatives and from your father's house, to the land which I will show you.[5]

God makes no small demand. Imagine this for a minute. Here's Abram, nice and cozy in a land in which he and his ancestors have lived for many years. He's married, doesn't have any children, and lives with his extended family (they tended to do that back then). God shows up and says, "Leave your country and your family. Go, and keep going, and keep going some more until you get to a land I'll eventually show you."

Most of us wouldn't respond well to this kind of instruction. God is telling Abram to sell his house, quit his job, pack up, and start driving, leaving behind everyone except his wife, nephew, and some hired help.

"To where?"

"You'll see."

"How long will we travel?"

"I'll let you know."

So much for planning! Can you imagine receiving instructions to leave the comfortable, known, and established for the risky, unknown, and insecure?

What does knowing the setting accomplish? It makes us think. It forces us to engage the story and put ourselves into it. The setting encompasses far more than the geographical location of a particular story. This, of course, all depends on our willingness to look beyond the surface of the narrative. The setting benefits us only if we observe it and think about it. We must engage the story rather than skimming over the facts. Skimming works when we read a newspaper, but not when we read God's Word. God's Word is worth far more than any newspaper, so we should give it more of our time and attention. Pay attention to the setting of a narrative and you automatically have

---

[5] Genesis 12:1

an inside scoop. You'll know what's going on and will be in a better position to understand, interpret, and apply it to your life. Don't skimp on setting!

Characters

The plot is the ribbon, and the setting is the package. Now we get to look at the characters—the people who give the package its dimension. We all know and are thankful that no two people are exactly alike. This means we must understand the characters of any given story before we can proceed in understanding the narrative.

People possess a range of backgrounds, passions, emotions, personality quirks, and character traits. No combination of these are exactly alike in any two people. Some are shy, quiet, sensitive, kind, and merciful; others are brash, rigid, logical, daring, and strong. Some struggle with finances, planning ahead, and being organized; others can't seem to define the word "fun." Yet all of us are the same in more ways than we can imagine—we all have strengths, we all have weaknesses, and we've all fallen. We're all stumbling, trying to find our way.

The commonalities among us make reading narratives interesting. Regardless of origin (Bible or not), people are interesting to read about because we can relate to them. Many of us don't have much in common with thieves. However, if we read about a thief who stole only to feed his starving family, we connect with him in providing for and protecting his family. You don't have a family? Then you can relate by thinking of your friends. We all have people in our lives who need our protection and provision. Therefore, although the thief's unfortunate choices make it difficult for us to connect with him on an intellectual level, we're challenged to see things through his perspective when we consider his heart and motives. We do not live in a silo where everyone around us is incompatible and totally different. We can find something to relate to in most everyone.

Understanding the similarities and differences we have with others fuels our draw toward people. We like to be around people because they challenge us and make us grow. Even the most hermit-like of folks enjoys people, sometimes without realizing it. They enjoy reading, watching TV, working on projects—all of which were created or influenced in some way by people. You don't have to have a conversation with someone in order to enjoy the fruits of community. We learn from each other in a myriad of ways, which is probably a big reason God chose to use humans to pen His Word.

As we've said, Scripture was written by real people who experienced real events, which God inspired them to write about. It would be difficult to read a strict rulebook and obey it without any explanation or examples. God knew this and chose to give us a book containing rules yet concentrating more on His interaction with humanity than His dictation of them. He wants us to see that although He is holy, powerful, mighty, and awesome, He remains personal, intimate, and bent on saving us when we don't deserve it. The people or characters of the stories recounted in Scripture display this beautiful balance of His characteristics and qualities because they are living proof of God at work.

They are people just like us, whom God uses to communicate His truth—something we would find incomprehensible had it not been told to us by a source we trust: other people. God spoke to us through people we can relate to—the good, the bad, and the ugly. Our goal is to learn as much as we can about them so we can develop a connection, a relationship of sorts with them. The more we know about those people, the better chance we have of understanding the full story.

Conflict/Tension

Every interesting story exposes some conflict or tension. Stories aren't interesting without them. A story about two women walking and talking in a park isn't exactly thrilling. But our interest heightens if we add some conflict—if the two women were walking in a park in the middle of the night, planning a jewelry heist, the FBI hot on their trail.

We're not saying people aren't interesting or that life is boring without drama or tragedy. But good, intriguing, and engaging stories all possess some sort of conflict that must be worked through, overcome, and/or resolved.

Think of it this way: most interesting stories offer a good-versus-evil scenario. There's a good guy and a bad guy, a hero and a villain, or a bully and an enforcer. Bad guys cause trouble; good guys catch the bad guys and bring justice to the situation. That's the conflict we're talking about.

In all fairness, some stories, like romances, don't necessarily have a bad guy. They do, however, have conflict and tension because something always goes wrong, or miscommunication comes on the scene to make things difficult. There's also the tension of the unknown. A budding romance or prospective job interview might not have direct conflict or a bad guy, but it has tension because the outcome is never guaranteed. This tension leaves the readers/audience engaged because they relate to the tension of the unknown.

The tension of tragedy is also a good example of this conflict in narratives. Tragedy is a part of life, and it may not be brought on by a bad guy. In everyday life, we face accidents, health failures, and unstable economies. These make for relatable and realistic stories.

Scripture doesn't isolate itself among literature by remaining conflict-free. Though some may think everything should always be good in a holy book, this would fail to engage an audience. How could we relate to a story that didn't address conflict or tension—trials, hardships, losses, and sin? Hardships punctuate the path of every life. No one is immune, and no one lives without conflict.

God addresses conflict head-on in His Word. He recognizes that conflict and tension are unavoidable parts of life, thanks to the Fall. It would be mere fantasy and utter naivety to think this world is peachy all the time, so God doesn't pretend it is. He doesn't give us a book that ignores the tough questions, nor does He claim that reading His word will prevent every problem you will face. He doesn't promise that once you decide to follow Him, your life becomes perfect or carefree. That would be ludicrous, and no one would follow that kind of teaching. People might try it, but they wouldn't make it very long without realizing that it was a bunch of nonsense!

Few religions deal with the concept of pain, suffering, and conflict. Buddhism reigns as one notorious worldview that addresses this topic. Buddhism claims that life is suffering, and the only way to diminish it is to separate yourself from anything that could cause you pain and/or let you down. That translates to cutting out pretty much everything and everyone in your life. Buddhism teaches you to be a recluse from society, family, friends, work—all aspects of life—because only when you're not dependent on and don't expect anything from anyone can you truly be happy. It's about adjusting your desires to the idea that the only person who can make you happy is yourself.[6] This is not a very uplifting worldview. But it does address conflict and struggles in this world.

A better source of understanding such conflict is, of course, Scripture. It confronts this topic without hesitation. Historical narratives reveal real men and women who struggled with real issues and were really met by God. These narratives show how God responds to the conflict His children face on a daily basis.

Continuing with our Abraham example, we see that he experienced several conflicts. A little further along in his story, God promised Abraham that he would not only have a son but would be the father of

---

[6] Brian White, "BuddhaNet" http://www.buddhanet.net/elearning/5minbud. htm. 1993.

many people—more than the stars in the sky. Abraham means "father of a multitude."[7] The area of conflict/tension Abraham experienced was that he was seventy-five years old and hadn't fathered any children because his wife, Sarah, was barren. Reaching a certain age makes having children a little difficult!

The plot thickens when Abraham takes the situation in his own hands and fathers a child out of wedlock with Sarah's maidservant (with Sarah's blessing, strangely enough). Thirteen years later, when he's ninety-nine years old, God appears after years of silence and repeats his promise: Abraham will have a child via his wife, Sarah.

Can you feel the tension? Put yourself in Abraham's shoes. He's way past the age of childbearing and has waited for years for God's promise to come to fruition.

This is an example of conflict. The process of overcoming and working through difficulties like this certainly isn't easy, and the Bible doesn't pretend otherwise. Scripture doesn't suggest Abraham remained stress-free with God's promise as he waited twenty-five years for it to be fulfilled. He struggled a lot. I have yet to meet or hear of someone with that kind of faith! We're all working toward it, but we'd be lying to ourselves if we didn't admit to struggling from time to time. Scripture's narratives embrace conflict and tension because they are real issues that we face (as believers or not) every day.

Narratives require us to observe more than just the plot and the setting. We must engage with the characters and their struggles, conflict, and tension. These issues are included in the narration so we can relate to them and learn how to deal with them. By observing how characters worked through issues and how God interacted with them through the process, we can then learn how to work through them ourselves. Conflict and tension are a part of every story, and we have the privilege of observing and learning from them.

---

[7] http://www.blueletterbible.org/lang/lexicon/lexicon.cfm?Strongs=H85&t =NASB

The Narrator

Logically, a narrative must have a narrator, right? We won't get too deep into this because we've already touched on it with the "author" section in our Canon chapter. But when you read a narrative, ask yourself whether the author is narrating in first person (the author using personal pronouns: "I," "we," "ours," "us," etc.), third person (no personal pronouns), or from an omniscient perspective (knowing the thoughts of other people in the story. The Holy Spirit helps a lot with that kind!).

Recognizing the type of narrator helps us grasp the story because we learn from what perspective the story is being told. The historical narrative of Abraham is told from an omniscient perspective. Moses authored the Pentateuch, which includes the book of Genesis. Moses wasn't born until the beginning of Exodus, so there's no way he could write this story in first or third person since the events took place several hundred years before his birth. Thus, through the inspiration of the Spirit, Moses penned these words and narratives.

One important fact to understand about ancient Middle Eastern culture is the value they placed on oral traditions. Writing was not the primary mode of communication or preservation of history in that day. They passed down stories, history, truths, family genealogies, etc. from one generation to the next through verbal means, not written. This culture held repetition and memorization in high regard back then, which differs greatly from the telephone game we referenced back in chapter two.

Today, if information is not written down, it carries little weight. Without printing and signing documents, words hold no real significance. (I'm talking in a general and legal sense—how it is, not how it should be). Because of this, we don't encourage or promote memorization. That's why we play the game of Telephone so poorly. Society neglects to condition us as memory people like it did back in the days of the Old Testament. In their day, stories and a people's history were as valid and accurate when passed down orally as they are on notarized paper today.

Moses probably knew much of what he wrote about Abraham and Israel's history before he began to write. He may not have known intricate details, but the Holy Spirit guided and inspired him to write exactly as He wanted him to. For example, Genesis 18:12-15 recounts Sarah's reaction to hearing that she would become pregnant at the ripe old age of eighty-nine:

> Sarah laughed to herself, saying, "After I have become old, shall I have pleasure, my lord being old also?" And the Lord said to Abraham, "Why did Sarah laugh, saying, 'Shall I indeed bear a child, when I am so old?" Is anything too difficult for the Lord? . . . Sarah denied it however, saying, "I did not laugh."

God, of course, called her out on her lie. But the point is that God (and the human author, Moses) knew Sarah had laughed to herself. Abraham didn't know she had laughed, but God did. And He chose to include this little moment of weakness in His Word. There's no way Moses could have known what Sarah was thinking when he penned these verses. But through the guidance and inspiration of the Spirit he executed an omniscient perspective, which gives us considerable insight into the story and characters.

Cueing into the narrator's perspective gives us an edge on the story. Another interesting fact about the historical narratives of Scripture is that the narrator often remains morally neutral in his telling of the story. Meaning what, exactly? The narrator sparingly provides a moral commentary on the actions of certain individuals. We are not always told that this particular character is doing something right or wrong; we're simply told what he is doing.[8]

For example, when Sarah encouraged Abraham to sleep with

---

[8] Duvall and Hays, *Grasping God's Word*, 321.

her maidservant so they could have an heir, the narrator doesn't add anything that would indicate the wisdom, or lack thereof, of that decision. Granted, most of us know, from surrounding circumstances and what we know about the nature of God, whether something is right or wrong. Sarah and Abraham obviously decided to do something wrong. They took the situation into their own hands without waiting on the Lord. Yet the author doesn't say this in so many words. We have to research the passage and learn through observation.

Unfortunately, it's not always easy to determine whether a character's action qualifies as right or wrong. For instance, in Genesis 14, we read of a war that resulted in the capture of Abraham's nephew, Lot. Abraham heard of it, took 318 trained men by night and attacked the forces that held Lot, presumably killing several as he defeated them. Was this right or wrong? Did Abraham consult God before doing this? We're simply not told. This is one example of a blurred line. We're told only that it happened, not whether it was of the Lord or an example for us to follow today.

With narratives like this that don't provide a clear moral line, we've got to fight the temptation to analyze it to death, because if we do, we run the risk of missing the bigger picture. We are finite, limited, and fallen people. Even as children of God we are limited in our understanding and will never be able to grasp the entire dynamic truth of God's Word. He revealed much in His Word, but has not revealed all. We wouldn't be able to understand it all, partly because the created cannot completely understand the Creator. We must do our best to understand and interpret His Word to the best of our ability, which observing the components of a narrative, like the narrator's perspective, helps us to do.

Throughout the process we must understand that certain tensions will always exist, and we may never find answers to specific questions this side of heaven. If you've observed, researched, studied, prayed, obtained wise counsel, and still don't have an answer, don't worry about it. Start a list of things you'd like to ask God when you meet

Him face to face. He's given us much Scripture that we can understand thoroughly. Let those truths and doctrines take up most of your time, energy, and effort.

The "Levels" of the Story

We've covered plot, setting, conflict/tension, and narrator within historical narratives; let's now finish with one more element of narratives worth noting. Narratives often contain many dimensions. Dimensions decrease or increase with the amount of details presented in a story and how many new mini-plots arise as the story progresses.

Few one-dimensional stories exist. A one-dimensional story (as I'm calling it) would be something like a man taking a walk down a random street. There's not a lot going on, and the character is not affecting anyone or anything. Two-dimensional stories provide some give-and-take between characters or objects. This time, our man runs into a friend and has a brief conversation with him. Both men are affected by this interaction, though it still may not be an earth-shattering or exciting experience.

A three-dimensional story goes one step further by adding another nugget to the plot. Our two men have a brief conversation when a woman they both know (and secretly adore) appears. When she leaves, the men talk about her and remain pleasant to each other, all the while secretly scheming how they can be the first to ask her for a date. Most stories have several dimensions, and as the narrative progresses, more dimensions are realized, and the plot thickens.

Scripture, especially the historical narratives recorded in it, are multi-dimensional. Scripture is one book composed of many, yet a common thread weaves throughout its entire composition. Genesis mentions Abraham first, followed by twenty-seven other books throughout Scripture. New Testament authors build theological doctrines around Abraham and his faith— adding significant dimensions to the narratives recorded about him in Genesis.

Like you, I am a student and readily admit when someone else can explain something more elaborately than I. Gordon Fee and Douglas Stewart compiled a wonderful way of helping us understand the different dimensions or "levels" of narrative in the Bible.[9] They explain that narratives (particularly in the Old Testament) have three levels. The first is the bottom level, which refers to the specific story at hand. With Abraham, this level includes the story itself—the basic details of the plot, setting, characters, conflict, etc.

The second (middle) level expands on the individual story of the bottom level by focusing on Abraham and his relationship with Israel. Abraham is the father of Israel—God's chosen people—in two ways. First, he is the physical father through whom a nation was born. His physical descendants are the Jews, whom God chose to be His representatives to the world. Abraham also fathers Israel spiritually. His faith in God is regarded as most important, and it is the reason anyone of any race can be called a child of Abraham and a child of God. To be Abraham's child in faith means you follow and emulate his faith in God.

These two ways—physical and spiritual—make up this middle level. It goes beyond the mere story and moves into another realm of Abraham and his relationship with God's people. The middle level takes the story a step further by placing it within its broader context of the book and Testament it is written in (Abraham—Israel—Old Testament).

The final or top level steps outside the box completely by discovering how the particular story (level one) combines with the broader story of God's people (level two) and how both fit within God's universal plan of redemption for all the world (level three). With each new level, several dimensions are added that help us understand God's Word as more than just a book or story. It builds on itself and

---

[9] Fee and Stuart, *Reading the Bible for All It's Worth*, 79.

More Than Words

allows us to understand a fuller and more elaborate picture of His truth and plan of redemption for humanity (the Gospel). The Bible is more than worldly history; it's theological and doctrinal history that we'd never know otherwise.

LEVEL 3 ... THE GOSPEL

LEVEL 2 ... ISRAEL / OLD TESTAMENT

LEVEL 1 ... SPECIFIC STORY

With our Abraham example, we observe the specific story first. Second, we see how it fits within the middle level of Israel and its relationship with God as His chosen people. Third, we understand how both of those fit within the universal plan of God. Few modern-day narratives carry that much depth and multi-dimensional goodness, huh?

We could say much more about historical narratives, but this will get you started. Remember, we find them all over Scripture—both Old and New Testament. Read them for what they are (stories) and keep in mind all the different components we talked about—they are true, they have a plot, setting, characters, conflict/tension, narrator, and three different levels with multiple dimensions that we should read them in light of. Narratives are straightforward and easy to relate to because we're in the habit of reading stories all the time in our modern day. But in Scripture, these narratives go much further than being just stories with lessons we can learn from; they are God's truth and exhibit how He interacts with us through a glorious display of His gospel! Definitely not something to take lightly.

Law

The Law, similar to historical narratives, is a genre we relate easily with today in some aspects. We're familiar with laws—our government, society, and culture are governed by many laws designed to keep people, businesses, and families in order. Without laws, chaos would reign. William Pitt states it well, "Where the law ends, tyranny begins."[10] This is true because mankind is depraved at its core. We are all sinners. Left to ourselves, we create nothing short of turmoil and anarchy.

Laws and rules are good. They govern society and give us boundaries and lines we don't dare to cross, unless we'd like to be punished. Laws have permeated society since the beginning of time—since God announced the first law to Adam and Eve in the Garden of Eden.

> The Lord God commanded the man, saying, "From any tree of the garden you may eat freely; but from the tree of the knowledge of good and evil you shall not eat, for in the day that you eat from it you will surely die.[11]

Before sin entered the picture, God established laws to help Adam and Eve keep on track of knowing God and pursuing Him over and above all else. Laws regulate action and behavior; breaking regulation results in punishment. When Adam and Eve broke the law, punishment ensued. The same happens today. When we break the law—by going 50 m.p.h. in a 40-m.p.h. zone or by committing fraud or lots of other crimes—we get punished.

Laws keep our behavior in check because we're accountable to them. If you don't think that's true, consider this: How many of you drive differently when there's a police officer behind you? Even

---

[10] http://www.allgreatquotes.com/law_quotes.shtml
[11] Genesis 2:15-16.

More Than Words

if you're an excellent driver, you are more cautious with a patrol car following you, right? We may not be thieves or murderers, but we push and stretch the law and the rules more often than we'd like to admit. If there were no laws or rules, we'd make a mess of things. That's human nature. We're fallen, and we need rules and guidelines in order to keep ourselves under control.

No one understood this principle more than the Israelites in the Old Testament. They were accomplished sinners and needed serious guidance in the behavior department. So God gave them laws, the most well-known of which are the Ten Commandments. These commandments are the backbone of all law, yet God provides many other rules to clarify what He expects from His people.

The Torah (the first five books of the Old Testament) contains most of the Law as we know it. Here's the scene: Abraham's gone to heaven, and the covenant God made with him passes down to his son Isaac, then Jacob, and then Joseph until Moses arrives on the scene in Exodus. Moses leads Israel out of slavery in Egypt and into the wilderness for forty long years—a direct result of their continuous rebellion against God. During this time, God provides Moses with the Ten Commandments to govern Israel. The Ten Commandments are accompanied by another 600 or so ordinances and commandments, which get specific and cover many different aspects of Jewish life with sundry laws, moral laws, sacrificial laws, and more.

Many people don't realize this, but Israel at this point is a baby nation. They were about a million strong (600,000 men plus an uncounted number of women and children) but had never been on their own as a nation before. Jacob and his sons moved to Egypt during a famine 430 years prior to the Exodus, and numbered only 70 at that time. But God promised He would make Jacob a great nation during their time in Egypt, and that's exactly what He did. In 430 years, Israel grew from 70 to around 1,000,000 people!

Still, they abided by Egyptian law because they were not a nation unto their own. They remained distinct from the Egyptians in their traditions, heritage, and practices but were still immersed in Egyptian culture. They'd never governed themselves, so when they were on their own for the first time in the wilderness, they had a lot to figure out! As time went on, they proved incapable of figuring out much of anything on their own, so God did it for them. He did so by establishing and solidifying His law.

Most of us would probably agree that sitting down to read hundreds and hundreds of laws isn't a super-appealing plan. Few people leap for joy at the prospect of doing their personal devotions in books like Leviticus and Deuteronomy. That is one reason this genre is little-understood and little-read. It's easier to skip these books and head for Psalms or the New Testament. Those are at least applicable to our lives!

Ah, but the Law is too. A lot of people don't recognize it. They give up trying to understand the point of the Law because some laws seem inapplicable to them.

For example, in Leviticus we read laws like, "When a woman gives birth and bears a male child, then she shall be unclean for seven days, as in the days of her menstruation she shall be unclean." Huh? How on earth are we supposed to read, understand, interpret, and apply that to our lives? Present-day Americans get a perplexed look on their faces and scratch their heads when reading it. This reaction is understandable, yet we shouldn't let that deter us from our studies in the Word—which includes this genre!

Here's lesson number one for this genre (though it's applicable for all biblical genres as well). Just because something may not appear applicable or valuable for our lives, that doesn't mean it isn't. Not understanding the relevance of something at first glance does not mean it's not relevant. It simply means we need to look a bit harder or research it a bit more before finding the nugget of truth that's present.

This genre gets us up close and personal with ancient Israel, which grows our intimacy in understanding how God related to them and used them in His plan of redemption for the world. If for no other reason, the revelation of the gospel through Israel proves valuable for us to understand. It enables us to get in their shoes and see what it was like to live under the Old Covenant. How did they relate to God? What did they have to do to get into the (manifest) presence of the Holy One? For those who don't know, it was different than the way we communicate and relate with God today—through Jesus Christ.

Christ had yet to come when the law was written. The Israelites knew their Savior was coming, but they had no idea when. Since it wasn't time for Him to arrive, God established boundaries and guidelines to follow in their pursuit of holiness until His arrival. Only when we understand the Law and its purpose can we appreciate the depth of the New Covenant available to us now through Christ.

So let's explore this mysterious yet fabulous genre, shall we? For quite some time it was (and still is) believed that the Old Testament Law was divided into three categories of laws: moral, civil, and ceremonial. (For the purpose of this conversation, we'll refer to this as the tri-category theory).[12] This theory is popular and claims each law we read in Scripture can be classified based on its type, and from there we determine whether it applies to our lives. The underlying assumption with this theory, though, is that not every category is applicable to our lives. This would mean that some aspects of Scripture are applicable while others aren't. If that's the case, we determine which parts are or aren't applicable (a direct contradiction to our inductive method). The logic of this theory takes us to a sour place hermeneutically. In an effort to avoid such a destination, let's arm ourselves with some specifics.

The moral-law category appeals to moral behavior—the innate values we're all born with acting as an ethical gauge. Morals tell us it's good to share with others and bad to harm them. When we hear a story about a man who molested a little girl, we don't react well. A pit forms in the bottom of our stomachs, followed by clenched fists and a jolt of adrenaline that makes us want to deal with the scumbag. If we

---
[12] Duvall and Hays, *Grasping God's Word*, 329.

saw him that moment, many of us would lunge at him and not relent until he begs for mercy.

People react this way—Christian and non-Christian alike—because of the moral compass God imbeds in us. We may disagree with what the exact punishment should be for evil like this, but nobody (with the exception of psychological sociopaths) denies that it's evil.

Ernest Hemingway observed, "About morals, I know only that what is moral is what you feel good after and what is immoral is what you feel bad after."[13] The enlightening aspect of this quote is that people act both in accordance with and against their own moral standards. If that's the case, how do we monitor our actions and make sure they're keeping in line with our morals? The law. Laws exist to solidify and make certain the guide already present in our hearts. Abiding by the law helps us stay on track and gives us that extra cushion in maintaining moral excellence.

It's a merry-go-round indeed! God endows us with morals; yet He gives us laws to keep those morals in check because we often act outside of them. The Law of the Old Covenant is given for the same purpose—to give boundaries and guidelines to a people who needed them. According to the tri-category theory of the Law, moral laws include "Love your neighbor as yourself." This, under the tri-category assumption, still directly applies to us today because moral laws aren't culturally bound, and time doesn't change God's moral standards.

Laws that do change, however, fall under the civil category—those dealing directly with legality and a justice system. An example of this law in the Torah is:

> If an ox gores a man or woman to death, the ox shall surely be stoned and its flesh shall not be eaten; but the owner of that ox shall go unpunished. If, however, an ox was previously in the habit of goring and its owner has been warned, yet he does not confine it and it kills a man or a

---

[13] http://www.brainyquote.com/quotes/keywords/moral.html

woman, the ox shall be stoned and its owner also shall be put to death.[14]

This law is considered civil because it deals with civil matters—ordinances common to the general public of the day. Tri-category adherents assume that since laws (like this one) have changed since then, the ones found in the Torah are not directly applicable to modern-day Christians. Hardly anyone argues that the ox law directly applies to most in American society. It did, however, apply to the Israelites living in the Old Testament because they were an agricultural society—they owned oxen and ran into this problem far more often than we do today.

What are we to do with this discrepancy? The tri-category view expects little from us because civil laws aren't applicable today. Just read it and move on. An interesting perspective, but definitely not hermeneutically responsible.

The third category—ceremonial—remains free from direct application to us too (according to tri-category) because these laws regard the Old Covenant ways of relating to God. Old Testament believers progressed through a strict process to attain purity and acceptance before God and His Temple. Believers today live in the New Covenant ordained by Christ, so we don't need to bother with such laws. This is partially accurate; but if that's the whole case, we wouldn't have much need for the Old Testament at all, would we? Why not just throw out the whole thing?

We don't disregard the Old Testament because it is *all* still valuable and applicable to our lives today. The tri-category theory is appealing. It distinguishes between the laws to determine which ones still apply today. This makes it easy and convenient for us when reading the Law because we can determine which category a particular law belongs to, then adhere to its category to see if it applies to our lives.

This theory makes the genre of Law convenient, and if it stopped

---

[14] Exodus 21:28-29.

at classifying the laws into these three categories, it would be fine. Its main problem, though, is that it uses the categories to determine whether a particular law is relevant for us today. Moral laws are; civil and ceremonial ones aren't. At this point, problems arise.

First, Scripture does not distinguish any of these categories within the Law directly, nor does it adhere to them anywhere throughout the rest of Scripture. Rule #2 in hermeneutics proclaims Scripture as the ultimate authority. Scripture makes the rules; our job is to learn and obey them. We don't declare one sentence relevant and another not so much. But that's exactly what the tri-category theory suggests. It claims that because a law falls into one made-up category, it's relevant. But when another one falls into some other category we made up, it's not relevant. Scripture cannot be dissected into parts in which some are relevant and others aren't, based on man-made categories. Since Scripture doesn't make categorical distinctions between the laws, neither can we.

Here's an example of a moral law being referenced right in the middle of civil and ceremonial ones without any distinction being made. Consider the following:

> If any man has a stubborn and rebellious son who will not obey his father or his mother, and when they chastise him, he will not even listen to them, then his father and his mother shall seize him, and bring him out to the elders of his city at the gateway of his hometown. They shall say to the elders of his city, "This son of ours is stubborn and rebellious, he will not obey us, he is a glutton and a drunkard." Then all the men of his city shall stone him to death; so you shall remove the evil from your midst, and all Israel will hear of it and fear. If a man has committed a sin worthy of death and he is put to death, and you hang him on a tree, his corpse shall not hang all night on the tree, but you shall surely bury him on the same day (for he

who is hanged is accursed from God), so that you do not defile your land which the Lord your God gives you as an inheritance.[15]

All three categories of law are present within this passage, yet the passage itself makes no distinction between them. It addresses the moral law of obeying father and mother, along with the civil law of how to handle a child who deliberately rebels and refuses to listen, much less repent. It also refers to a ceremonial law regarding the proper way to care for the deceased. All three categories are represented; yet they are man-made categories, not dictated by or classified in Scripture.

If Scripture doesn't make a distinction, then we certainly don't have a right to! Every verse of Scripture is relevant to us today. Not all, however, hold us accountable because they represent the first covenant God established with His people, not the covenant we're under in Christ. The New Testament introduces the guarantor of a new covenant—Jesus Christ. Christ ushered in a new covenant, making the old one (the Law that fleshes out over 600 commandments) obsolete. The Law remains important and still merits our time and study as Holy Scripture, but our relationship with it has changed through the redemption of Christ. How, then, do we go about understanding, interpreting, and applying such a difficult genre? Carefully!

HERE ARE SOME TIPS

No Law is Given Without Context

Context is the heartbeat of everything we do in hermeneutics, and understanding the tricky genre of Law is no exception. Laws weren't written in a vacuum. Before and after each blurb of laws flows a

---
[15] Deuteronomy 21:18-23.

narrative in which it is placed. In our aforementioned example, God speaks with Moses, giving him all the commandments so he can, in turn, give them to the Israelites. Remember, at this point in Israel's history, they were just being established as their own nation. God distributed laws and rules to govern them for quite some time as they became a nation and established a land. Understand the context! It helps the interpretative process tremendously.

What the Law is Really About

God isn't some scary dictator who annihilates humanity if they break one of hundreds of laws. Why, then, does God articulate so many laws in the Old Testament? That question, my friends, is flawed. It's not about the amount; it's about their purpose.

A key question to ask in this genre is, "Why is the law being given?" Though it's not always possible, if we understand the reason, we can glean its importance and purpose. Remember the "level" analogy from the narrative genre? We can apply that to the Law too. The bottom level is the specific law—God commanding how Israel should punish a continuously rebellious child. This law fits within the Law as a whole, which reflects the middle level of our analogy—how God relates to His chosen people through it. This second level plays a huge role in the Law genre yet even bigger in the top level as we look at how the Law fits into God's universal plan of redemption.

The Law is a permanent reaction and a temporary solution to the Fall. It's a permanent reaction because it provides the strict requirements that must be observed in order to approach God. It remains permanent today because through it we learn that we can never approach or be right with God on our own. The Law serves as a mirror. We look into it to see how far we fall short of God's standards.

It's a temporary solution as well, setting up guidelines for Old Testament believers to maintain their relationships with God.

Understand this: the Law was never intended to *establish* Israel's relationships with God. It was never intended for their salvation, but for their sanctification—teaching them how to be righteous and holy. Justification comes by faith apart from the Law.[16]

Do you see the difference? The Law shows how to live, not how to come to a saving relationship with God. The Law assumes the relationship already exists. We must maintain this perspective when reading and studying the Law in order to remain good exegetes of Scripture.

Keep the Law in Perspective through the Covenants

When reading a Law passage, we must determine what covenant it falls under. Why? Because covenants change as the gospel progresses throughout Scripture. A covenant is "a usually formal, solemn, and binding agreement; a written agreement or promise under seal between two or more parties especially for the performance of some action."[17] In Scripture, covenants represent how God relates to His people at a given time.

Much debate exists regarding the number of covenants there have been, but to keep it simple, we'll narrow it down to the main six. The first covenant was with Adam in the Garden of Eden, broken with sin. The Noahic covenant arrived when God started over through Noah's family, destroying by flood every other living thing on earth. God chose Abraham for the third covenant, followed by Moses with the fourth. This is the most detailed covenant under which most of the Law genre falls. The fifth covenant is that of David, which looks forward to the sixth covenant—the New Covenant God installed through Christ.

Why is determining the covenant so important? When we see what covenant a particular Law passage is under, we can focus on

---

[16] Romans 3:28 (But don't stop there; read all of Romans for some great study of the Law and our relationship with it today)
[17] http://www.merriam-webster.com/dictionary/covenant

the interpretation and application portions of our study. First, we glean facts from each specific law by observing what covenant it is under. Our Deuteronomy passage from above resides under the Mosaic covenant. We observe Israel's deliverance from over 400 years of slavery in Egypt, revealing God's faithfulness to His promises. We also see Israel wandering in the desert at the time, punished for their lack of devotion to God. God, through the Law, establishes the order of conduct He expects His children to follow in order to protect them (the sanitary and dietary laws) and be pleasing and acceptable to Him.

Along with gleaning facts, knowing what covenant a certain passage of Law falls under helps us understand whether it is directly applicable and authoritative to us today. The passage in Deuteronomy we read isn't directly applicable for us today because we are not under the Mosaic covenant. Christ fulfilled that covenant, and those who belong to Him stand free from the Law of sin and death.

Now, this doesn't mean the Deuteronomy law isn't *relevant* for us today. We're not held accountable to it on a judicial level, but we can't ignore it. It's still valuable for our faith and comprehension of the gospel. We must observe its context and covenant and use both to determine the principle of the passage. The principle is what we apply to our lives directly. (No worries; we'll find out how to discover the theological principle of the passage when we get to our steps!)

We could make many more observations, but you get the gist. Understanding the covenant helps us place the particular law we're looking at into context. Why is God giving that law? Has it changed since then? If so, how? These are all questions answered when we interpret and apply the genre of Law to our lives.

This will help you get started. The Law is not the last step in this covenant deal. Those who confess Jesus Christ as their personal Lord and Savior are under the New Covenant, not the covenants of the Old Testament. The specific laws under the five previous covenants no longer apply to us as laws we're governed by. Why? Because the covenant of Christ completed the laws of Abraham, Moses, David, etc. Jesus mediates a new covenant, one that trumps the old ones in comparison.[18]

We, as children of God through Christ, are no longer bound by the Law, but rather by the Spirit. This is a subject Paul harps on many times in his New Testament letters. For now, realize that though appreciating and understanding the Law is of utter significance in our understanding of Scripture, it is not the end. Christ completed what humanity was incapable of keeping on its own. Never forget that, folks!

The genre of Law requires research, context, and awareness of its purpose and covenant in order to be properly and thoroughly understood. It may never be a hot topic among the modern-day body of Christ, but that doesn't mean for a second that it's not important! Our understanding of God and His plan of redemption through the different covenants and laws therein is monumental in grasping His Word. The Law genre is part of the canon, and we can't afford to miss or ignore it!

Poetry

"How do I love thee? Let me count the ways. . . ."[19] Oh, poetry. From children's books to the famous works of Shakespeare and even modern-day rap, poetry saturates our culture. We're familiar with it, but familiarity can hinder us when we interpret poems in Scripture because Bible poetry differs slightly from the poems we have today.

The Psalms contain most of the poetry found in Scripture, but several other books include it as well. Psalms are poems put to music, so they're technically not poems to be read out loud in a coffee bar on talent night. Hebrew poetry differs vastly from modern-day poetry (it doesn't rhyme in English), and we need to observe a few key points to ensure we interpret soundly.

---

[18] For a more thorough study of the new covenant, read Hebrews. It does a far better job than I could ever do!

[19] Browning, Elizabeth. "How Do I Love Thee?" (Sonnet 43).

TIPS FOR INTERPRETING POETRY

Hebrew Poetry Entices Emotions

Hebrew poetry is not known for its objective reasoning and logical theological processing. Rather, it appeals to the reader's heart and emotions, which is why we must exercise extreme caution in the interpretive process. The Psalms should not be your first stop when studying theology!

When David wrote, "Arise, O Lord; save me, O my God! For You have smitten all my enemies on the cheek; You have shattered the teeth of the wicked,"[20] he was not implementing objective theological reasoning. He's not declaring that God literally shattered all of his enemies' teeth. That would be silly. He is, however, speaking from his heart—the seat of his emotions. We must interpret poetry with that in mind.

We cannot read something like the above verse and pray, "Lord, You smote all David's enemies and shattered their teeth. Do the same with my super-annoying colleague!" That misses the point entirely. David far from endorses an all-of-my-enemies-are-God's-enemies-so-He-has-to-get-rid-of-them theology.

Rather, if you look at the context, you realize David wrote this Psalm when he was fleeing his son, Absalom, who was trying to take over the kingdom. David, utterly distressed, decided to share his emotions transparently with God, who understands, can comfort, and will take action on David's behalf. Further observation shows that in the past, David experienced God's salvation from his enemies. This Psalm cries for Him to do it again. We must not jump to quick conclusions of application when reading biblical poetry. Psalms entice our hearts and are:

> Intended to appeal to the emotions, to evoke feelings rather than propositional thinking, and to stimulate a response on

---

[20] Psalm 3:7

the part of the individual that goes beyond a mere cognitive understanding of certain facts.[21]

They are not to be read in the same way as a narrative or exposition. Psalms and biblical poetry appeal to the heart and emotions; consequently, we must look beyond the specific words into their context to determine what the author is trying to get across.

Word Usage

The emotional appeal of the Psalms expresses primarily through figurative language, not the strict teaching of facts and literal word usage. Metaphor, hyperbole, simile, personification, and other literary devices comprise the figurative language found in Psalms to detail graphic word pictures to emphasize the feeling of the author. This forces us to move beyond figures of speech in our interpretation to discover what the author is communiting through them. For example, Psalm 83:13-15 states,

> O my God, make them like the whirling dust, like chaff before the wind. Like fire that burns the forest and like a flame that sets the mountains on fire, so pursue them with Your tempest and terrify them with Your storm.

So much figurative language! Whirling dust, chaff before the wind, fire burning the forest, and on and on. The author employs five figures of speech in these three verses and gets the point across. He yearns for God to avenge His people against their enemies, and he embraces vivid language in asking Him to do so!

On a side note, do you think God wants us to do the same when we pray? What do you think He appreciates more: when we

---

[21] Fee and Stuart, *How to Read the Bible for All It's Worth*, 190.

recite prayers we've been praying verbatim for years, or when we pour our hearts and souls into what we're talking to Him about?

Don't hear this wrong; it's not bad or wrong to recite prayers or pray the same thing all the time, as long as your heart is in it and you're engaged. Prayer can quickly become a mundane ritual we go through before every meal rather than passionate communication He desires us to share with Him. Just read the Psalms. How many boring and monotone verses do you find? Not many!

Back to the point. When we interpret Psalms or other biblical poetry, we must take the figures of speech for what they are: ways to communicate the principle of the Psalm to us. Conveying strict theology doctrine into figures of speech is hardly the authors' goal; their speech is used to usher us into the larger, more important point at hand.

Psalms and other forms of biblical poetry stand unique because their primary function shows us how to talk to, worship, and meditate on God and His Word. They are not designed to teach us doctrine or moral behavior.[22] Unlike the majority of Scripture, which reflects God speaking to us, Psalms reflect people speaking to God.[23] So again, use caution in your interpretation of biblical poetry, understanding that it appeals to emotions, uses ample figurative language to get the point across, and is not written to give us guidelines of theology and/or how to live.

Wisdom Literature

Wisdom literature resembles poetry in a couple of ways. First it distinguishes itself from the majority of the other writings of Scripture. Therefore, it requires a closer look if we aspire to understand and interpret it correctly. Second, wisdom literature most often expresses

---

[22] Fee, Douglas and Gordon Stuart, *How to Read the Bible*. Grand Rapids, Mich: Zondervan, 2002. 205.
[23] Ibid, 205.

itself in poetry as opposed to a narrative or other biblical genre. Poetry and wisdom literature complement each other well yet remain distinct from each other. Let's learn how!

We find wisdom literature primarily in Job, Proverbs, Song of Solomon, and Ecclesiastes—three of the four written by King Solomon, the wisest man who ever lived (not a bad dude to take advice from!).

Unlike narrative and law, which are comprised of a lot of instruction for us to believe and obey, wisdom literature encourages readers to use their brains—to *think*.[24] This genre offers lots of practical advice and principles. Let's look at some helpful hints for wisdom literature. We'll use Proverbs as our running example, but we'll address some special notes about the other books as we conclude.

SOME TIPS

Principles, Not Promises

Many people mistake interpreting Proverbs and other wisdom literature as *promises*, not general life *principles*. Take Proverbs 12:14 as an example: "A man will be satisfied with good by the fruit of his words, and the deeds of a man's hands will return to him." This principle is generally regarded as true in life—you reap what you sow. If you're good, you will be content. If you're honest, kind, encouraging, and spend your time investing in good things, you will be satisfied and rewarded.

However, this is not always true. Sometimes life throws you curve balls, and you reap lots of bad for the good you sowed. Job's life provides us with an excellent example. The guy did everything right. God even called him blameless and upright. He prayed for his family, feared God, and turned away from evil. But we all know the story. He

---

[24] Duvall and Hays, *Grasping God's Word*, 390.

endured quite the testing period, in which he lost everything except his wife.

Does Job's story reflect Proverbs 12:14 from above? Not quite. But it also doesn't mean Proverbs 12:14 lies and should be cut out of the pages of Scripture. Wisdom literature is not a bunch of promises from God. They are principles that cause us to think about how we live, think, act, etc., so we can exercise wisdom in our daily lives.

Literary Structure

We didn't breach literary structure with poetry because it would've taken a whole additional chapter. But it's worth noting, at least briefly, in the genre of wisdom literature. First, we'll look at comparisons/contrasts (or parallelism) in this genre, then the rhythm of the structure.

As mentioned before, wisdom literature frequently mirrors poetry, having lines, stanzas, groupings, and more. Oh, and lots of comparisons and contrasts! Comparisons/contrasts closely link with parallelism in wisdom literature because they often *parallel* or piggyback off each other.

> He who shuts his ear to the cry of the poor
> Will also cry himself and not be answered.

Proverbs 21:13 exemplifies many verses we could use in this discussion. Read it again. Where are the comparisons and/or contrasts? Are they paralleled? Those who ignore the cries of the poor are contrasted with the poor (an obvious distinction). If they ignore the poor, it's safe to assume they're not poor themselves. The contrast progresses in irony because those who ignored the poor then find themselves ignored. Ode to the parallel. In this case, the ignorers are compared to and paralleled with the poor/ignored

More Than Words

because now they're in the same boat. The overall point? You reap what you sow.

Wisdom literature is full of comparisons, contrasts, and parallels just waiting for us to explore! Look for them in every verse you read. Noticing them enhances our understanding of the text and highlights the drama of the author's lessons. In Proverbs 21:13, the author, Solomon, did a fine job of pointing out the foolishness of those who ignore the poor but then expect to be treated better than they are. Comparisons and contrasts . . . good stuff!

The other structure signature worth noting in wisdom literature is rhythm. "In Hebrew, many of the proverbs have some sort of rhythm, sound repetition, or vocabulary qualities that make them particularly easy to learn."[25] This is the signature stamp of wisdom literature. Even in wisdom literature God avoids a long, detailed monologue of everything-wise-in-everyday-life. He rather chooses to give us short, pithy, easy-to-remember slogans.

English advocates its own proverbs: "A chain is only as strong as its weakest link," "A friend in need is a friend indeed," "A penny saved is a penny earned." All these are proverbs available in tasty fortune cookies. God knows we enjoy and easily memorize short, catchy phrases. I'm not saying that's the reason He gave us the proverbs-style wisdom literature (I'm not God!), but it wouldn't surprise me a bit!

Wisdom literature provides us with good food for thought and is easy to remember and apply to our lives. But we can't apply what we don't know, so read it, learn it, dwell on it, and apply it!

Now to the special notes for the wisdom books that contain more than proverbial sayings: Job, Song of Songs, and Ecclesiastes.

Duvall and Hays (we've mentioned them before) capture the unity of all four wisdom books and their relationship to one another remarkably.[26] They observe that Proverbs represents wisdom literature as the basic approach to life, with general principles and guidelines

---

[25] Fee and Stuart, *How to Read the Bible for All It's Worth*, 218.
[26] Duvall and Hays, *Grasping God's Word*, 390-391.

that will steer you clear of unnecessary hardship and consequences if you heed them. The rest of the wisdom literature books pose as exceptions to the Proverbs rule.

Job is exception number one, for he lived a righteous life and still found himself in a terrible predicament. He lost his home, children, wealth, and health, despite being righteous (so much for the health and wealth gospel that's being preached today!). His life stands as an exception to the Proverbs rule that "wise, righteous, hardworking people can expect a blessed, prosperous life while foolish, sinful, lazy people can expect a hard life."[27] In Job's case, he must rely on God when life throws chaos at him, trusting that He'll get him through it (which He did).

Exception number two to the Proverbs rule is Ecclesiastes, arguably the most philosophical book in all of Scripture. In this book, Solomon articulated his search for the meaning of life. He accumulated everything anyone could possibly hope to attain yet found it all meaningless. He ultimately discovered that only a relationship with God can give meaning and/or worth to life. This is an exception to the Proverbs rule because you can spend your whole life following all the practical advice of Proverbs, but without God, it's meaningless and a waste of time.

The third and last exception to the Proverbs rule is Song of Songs—a spicy and passionate book detailing the romance between a husband and wife. This one always throws people for a loop! Definitely smashes the sex-is-bad-and-never-supposed-to-be-talked-about-among-Christians taboo to pieces! Song of Songs gets graphic and is an exception to the Proverbs rule because it shows the irrationality of love. Proverbs prides itself on its rational, thought-out approach to life, which Song of Songs quashes. It advocates intensely passionate love as a qualified exception to mere objective reasoning.

We've only scratched the surface of wisdom literature, but I hope this overview helped shape your understanding of it. Remember,

---

[27] Duvall and Hays, *Grasping God's Word*, 390-391.

Proverbs contains general principles addressing practical life issues. They do not promise everything will turn out hunky-dory if we practice them. Job, Ecclesiastes, and Song of Songs provide three excellent exceptions to that rule, which makes our study of Scripture far more interesting! Our fascinating God offers us a mesmerizing method of communication, folks!

Prophecy

This is a touchy subject, especially for those who get wrapped up in the end-of-the-world-is-happening-now prophecies recently creating stirs among Christians. Harold Camping gained fame for his prophesies, the most recent declaring the end of the world on May 21, 2011. He, of course, was wrong, like every other person who's claimed to know "the day"—or year for that matter. Thank goodness biblical prophecy provides a lot more sustenance than a bunch of know-it-alls guessing when Christ is coming back.

What is biblical prophecy, and how do we know who to trust and what to look for? We will explore that and more with this genre overview. We will first discover where prophecy is found in Scripture and who the prophets were. We'll then define it, discover the general message of prophets, discuss the three major time periods/events prophesied about, and conclude with tips for interpreting it properly in Scripture.

Where is Prophecy Found?

The prophetic books of the Old Testamant house most of the prophecy in Scripture. We read of five Major Prophets (Ezekiel, Daniel, Isaiah, Jeremiah, and Lamentations, which was written by Jeremiah), and twelve minor ones (Hosea, Joel, Amos, Obadiah, Jonah, Micah,

Nahum, Habakkuk, Zephaniah, Haggai, Zechariah, and Malachi). Christ's teachings in the gospels also contain prophecy, along with some New Testament letters, and, of course, the mystifying book of Revelation.

Who were the Prophets?

The prophets were men chosen by God as His spokespeople to the world, particularly to believers. God called them at a particular time to deliver a particular message to a particular people. Many prophets infuse the Old Testament, but the most prominent ones are recognized by the books that bear their name (like Jeremiah, who wrote Jeremiah).

We find prophets in the New Testament as well, just not as neatly bunched together with books attributed to each of them. Jesus was a Prophet (*the* Prophet). The apostles are also considered prophets since the books they wrote contain prophecy, especially Revelation, which we'll get to later.

Whether in the Old or New Testament, prophets were men with a mission—to declare God's prophetic word to people. As mentioned before in our studies, prophets who claimed to be of God but were wrong about their prophecies were killed.[28] Prophecy—especially if it invokes God's name—is incredibly serious. True prophets were chosen individually to carry specific messages to specific people for a specific time ordained by God.

Consider Jonah, who was called to bring a harsh warning of repentance to Nineveh. Or Ezekiel, who endured serious hardships in order to give Israel visual examples of the atrociousness of their sin. God commanded Hosea to marry a prostitute, have children with her, and buy her back when she continued practicing harlotry (to show how Israel was acting as a harlot with God). Many prophets were ignored, abused, outcast, and lonely. Being a prophet in the Old

---

[28] Deuteronomy 18:22

Testament was not a cup of tea! As God's representatives, prophets endured difficult lives and callings and were held at a high standard as God's chosen messengers.

Though their missions often proved difficult, the Old Testament prophets were (initially or later on) faithful to their callings. Some ranked high socially and in class, while others worked as mere shepherds. God chose prophets based on His knowledge of their fitness for the task, not their societal status. (Whether or not they knew it is an entirely different matter.) Nonetheless, prophets were generally loyal and steadfast servants of God amidst a generation that strayed far from Him.

What Is Prophecy?

Biblical prophecy pertains to the foretelling of future events. Modern-day readers mistakingly think prophecy in Scripture is about events in *our* future. Though some prophecy addresses an event in our future, most prophecy in Scripture has already been fulfilled. Check out these statistics:

> Less than 2 percent of Old Testament prophecy is messianic. Less than 5 percent specifically describes the New Covenant age. Less than 1 percent concerns events yet to come.[29]

Pretty crazy, huh? That means over 90 percent of prophecy in Scripture refers to an event already fulfilled. Prophets did proclaim the future, but most of it was *their* future, not ours!

This leads to another awesome point. Ninety percent of biblical prophecy *has been fulfilled!* How's that to substantiate the accuracy Scripture's prophecy, and as a genre to be taken seriously? We'd settle for 90 percent of weather predictions being fulfilled! But ninety percent

---

[29] Fee and Stuart, *How to Read the Bible for All It's Worth*, 166.

of Scripture's prophecies? That brings the concept of trustworthiness (and inerrancy) to a whole new level!

Prophecies recorded in Scripture are a big deal because of Who they come from. The prophets who spoke them were not ancient psychics who got lucky in their predictions. They did not read tarot cards or inspect palms in order to receive visions of the fture. They served as God's mouthpieces.

They spoke only when He gave them something to speak. We're not sure how God communicated His message to them. We know some received visions, others dreamed, while others received direct word from God. But exactly *how* all this happened remains a mystery and something we can ask the Lord when we meet Him face to face. Regardless of how the process happened, it was a serious endeavor to speak on God's behalf, and God treated it as such in His Word.

The Prophets' Messages

The prophets' messages varied in details but remained consistent in the main emphases. They warned people (most often Israel) about the impending consequences of their wicked behavior (the incessant sin-repent-forgiven-sin-again cycle we mentioned before). Prophets often lived as social outcasts because of this. Their warnings brought light and the truth of God into the dark places of Israel's hearts. Most didn't want to repent. They preferred listening to false prophets who praised their idolatry and promised that life would be grand. Sounds like a familiar trend with some preachers today, doesn't it?

We'll avoid that tangent, but we must remember that even the darkest days Israel faced with exile, banishment, persecution, etc., were not the end. That's where the second part of the prophets' messages comes in. Their warnings of repentance paired with God's promises of comfort, healing, and restoration, should they repent and return to Him. God never abandoned them, a fact woven throughout all the prophetic books of Scripture. He sometimes corrects His children through difficult means, but always for the purpose of restoration and displaying His glory through them.

Three Time Periods

Now that we understand their messages in general, let's step outside the box and look at the timeline of prophecy—how great a span they covered when they originally prophesied. Another quick side note: prophets did not necessarily know when their prophecies would come true. They trusted God to take care of those details and simply obeyed what they were told.

Prophesies are generally categorized into three time periods—three main points in time that believers looked forward to for fulfillment. We've already noted how little prophecy applies to us directly; now we'll learn why!

Imminent

The first time period is one *imminent* to the original audience. These prophecies targeted Israel and *their* near future in the Old Testament (this is the 90 percent category mentioned before). This is tricky for us because when reading Old Testament prophets, we're required to go back and place ourselves in their shoes. Old Testament believers relied on the Law and the prophets' word as God's instruction to them. They couldn't access the completed Bible—not even the Old Testament. They literally lived out the Old Testament!

The Assyrian exile exemplifies the imminent time period well. Old Testament prophecies overflow with references of this exile (as well as the Babylonian one several years later). These exiles served as punishment for Israel because they refused to repent of their sins and turn to God.[30] The Assyrian exile represents imminent prophecy well because the same people who heard it experienced it coming true later in their lives. If they didn't, their children did. Amos prophesied that exile was coming around 750 BC, and it came around 725 BC. *Imminent* may not have meant twenty-four hours, but it certainly was in the near future for Israel in the Old Testament.

Coming of the Messiah

The second time period prophesied about is the *coming of the Messiah*—Jesus Christ—who would redeem Israel and restore her relationship with God. This time period impacts Old and New Testament believers, as well as believers living today. If you've been skimming pages until this point, now would be a fabulous time to slow down and tune in.

Since the moment Adam and Eve sinned in the Garden of Eden, creation groans for redemption—reconciliation to the God it longs to be restored with.[31] How did God decide to reconcile the earth to Himself? Through His Son, the Messiah, the One who would save the world by living a sinless life, dying on the cross for our sin, and rising again on the third day. Every Old Testament believer dreamed about and prayed for Jesus—the Promised One Who would save them from their turmoil of sin and set them right with God again.

Jesus Christ is the Messiah they were waiting for—the One whom the prophets testified about repeatedly in Part Two of their messages (hope, encouragement, comfort, etc.). Prophecies about the Messiah infiltrate the Old Testament abundantly, and Jesus Christ fulfilled over *three hundred* of them. There's not one direct prophecy about the Messiah left unfulfilled. That's a lot of prophecies to fulfill in one lifetime! And it gets better. According to Dr. Charles Ryrie, it would:

---

[30] Amos 5:27 is just one example of God's warning of sending His people into exile because of their idolatry and constant sin.
[31] Romans 8 is an awesome chapter to read further on this point.

More Than Words

> Require two hundred billion earths, populated with four billion people each, to come up with one person whose life could fulfill one hundred accurate prophecies without any errors in sequence. Yet the Scriptures record not one hundred, but over three hundred prophecies that were fulfilled in Christ's first coming alone.[32]

Wow! That's why time period number two is crucial. The Old Testament prophets spoke about the Messiah arriving about *four hundred* years later, and He fulfilled every one of those prophecies! Isn't that amazing? He changed the world radically and set the tone for the third and final time period—the end times.

The End Times

Our discussion comes back to where it began—the end times. This marks the final time period the prophets, both Old and New Testament, testified about. From Ezekiel to the apostle John, the end times are described in graphic detail and have been dissected, argued over, and brutally theorized since the prophecies were penned. A deep discussion of the end times would distract us from our journey, but we'll address it briefly because Scripture does, and God most certainly will usher it into fruition in His perfect timing.

This is the only time period not yet fulfilled. Ironically, it's also the one people spend the most time on and go mad trying to figure out. People hypothesize endlessly about seeing present-day connections to end-time passages in Matthew 24 and so on, but the truth is, we will never know exactly when these things will take place.

People speculate about mathematical evidence and other nonsense they claim predict Christ's return, a big event of the end times. But no

---

[32] Ryrie, Charles. *Today in the World*. MBI, December, 1989, p. 7.

one except God the Father hopes to know when Jesus will come again. Christ makes this explicitly clear: "The Son of Man is coming at an hour when you do not think He will,"[33] and "Of that day and hour no one knows, not even the angels of heaven, nor the Son, but the Father alone."[34] Pretty straightforward. No one knows, so anyone claiming to know isn't worth listening to.

Remember that the next time a Harold Camping comes around. If someone says he knows when Jesus is coming back, he claims to know more than Jesus. That is at once ludicrous and laughable. Be careful what you listen to, friends. Use discernment!

Back to time period number three. The end times is definitely the most mysterious of the periods—one to be respected and studied, but not to the point of causing dissention among believers.

We could spend our entire lives on this subject and still remain mystified about specifics. Scripture tells us all God wanted us to know, folks. If He wanted us to know every detail of what would happen, He would've given it to us in His Word. He didn't, so we shouldn't try to piece together every detail on an unrevealed timeline.

TIPS FOR INTERPRETING PROPHECY

Context, Context, Context!

Yes, we're fans of Rule #3! With the genre of prophecy, however, understanding the context is even more crucial when determining the meaning of a passage. Why? Because when you read prophecy, you're reading a message from God through a particular prophet to a particular people addressing a particular point. If you don't understand the context surrounding the message, you can't fully grasp its meaning.

Also keep in mind that most biblical prophecy has already been

---

[33] Matthew 24:44b
[34] Matthew 24:26

fulfilled. If you happen to read such a passage, exercise Rule #4 (Scripture in Light of Scripture) and find where it has been fulfilled. It's a lot of fun! If you're reading an unfulfilled prophecy (in Ezekiel, Daniel, or the New Testament, perhaps), then pay close attention to its context. What is the main point the author is trying to communicate with his audience? What teachings surround the prophecy? How do those teachings shape what's being prophesied about? Don't be afraid to ask questions! Doing so is healthy and beneficial.

Stay Focused on the Main Point

After making sure we understand the context, we must stay focused on the main point. This is difficult with prophecy, especially prophecy yet to be fulfilled, because there's much we don't understand.

Complicating matters is the fact that prophets often use a variety of figurative language when they describe the visions God gives them. They use word pictures because they aren't certain what they're seeing. Some witnessed objects, events and scenes foreign to their minds and ears. They described what they saw to the best of their ability, leaving us at a loss more often than not.

An example? Good ol' Ezekiel. Early in his vision he describes,

> Figures resembling four living beings. And this was their appearance: they had human form. Each of them had four faces and four wings. Their legs were straight and their feet were like a calf's hoof, and they gleamed like burnished bronze. Under their wings on their four sides were human hands. As for the faces and wings of the four of them, their wings touched one another; their faces did not turn when they moved, each went straight forward…[35]

---

[35] Ezekiel 1:5-9

Old Testament Genres

The longer the description progresses, the stranger it gets. Really, Ezekiel? What in the world was going on, and what are we supposed to do with that information if we ever figure it out? That's precisely why it's crucial to understand the context and stay focused on the main issue. Ezekiel writes because the hand of God came upon him and he saw visions of God, who commissioned him to preach to His rebellious children. He recorded what he saw and heard as clearly and as detailed as possible.

Yet even with mesmerizing details, our focus shouldn't be on dissecting what the "calf's hoof" comment could mean. That is a part of the description, not the point of the account. We should instead focus on the overall picture Ezekiel tried to communicate (awesomeness beyond our wildest dreams) and the point he made—that all these fascinating and powerful creatures became completely still when God spoke. God's presence commands the utmost attention and worship from creatures that blew Ezekiel's mind? Ezekiel reacted by falling on his face. Wouldn't that be our reaction too? Is that what we do when we pick up His Word or pray, knowing we're in His presence? Just some food for thought.

When we get sidetracked and start fussing over supporting details (like the extras in a movie scene), we miss the whole point (what's going on in the movie). And that's certainly not our goal! So when reading prophecy, learn the context and stay focused on what the author is trying to say. That's the nugget of gold we're looking for!

You now have a better understanding of prophecy. We've looked at its position in Scripture, who the prophets were, what prophecy is, what the prophets' messages were, three different time periods prophecy in Scripture addressed, and finally, some tips for interpreting prophecy today.

We must be as careful and diligent (maybe more so) in interpreting prophecy as we are with all the other genres. Reading, understanding, and applying prophecy requires us to understand the context of the prophet's message—both his immediate situation and the situation he prophesied about. Anything less significantly disappoints and shames this great genre. Don't skimp when practicing hermeneutics on prophecy or any other genre. It's well worth the effort, I promise!

The genres we've just explored are most often (though not always) found in the Old Testament. They each tend to concentrate in one particular place in Scripture, but they are certainly not restricted to it. Now that we've explored the genres typically found in the Old Testament, let's turn our attention to those of the New.

New Testament Genres

THE GOSPELS

The Gospels don't sound as if they should be their own genre, but we're about to discover all kinds of wonderful reasons why they are! We'll look at what they are, their unique time in history (when Christ walked the earth), how they bridge the covenants (the old and the new), and finally, hints to remain aware of when interpreting them today.

What are They?

The Gospels are the first four books of the New Testament—Matthew, Mark, Luke, and John. Did you know that only two of these authors were among Christ's original twelve disciples? Or that the books are not written chronologically? We're about to learn all about that and more!

All four Gospels are written accounts of Jesus' life on earth. They record His birth, baptism, ministry experiences, teachings, death, resurrection, and ascension. However, they probe deeper than just His physical life on earth. Christ's life reached way beyond the physical into eternity. He was the Messiah—the Promised Savior of the world. Each Gospel emphasizes its own dominant theme, yet they each capture Christ's humanity and deity as He comes to redeem the world from its sin.

The first three Gospels (Matthew, Mark, and Luke) are known as the Synoptic Gospels. Synoptic means taking or presenting a similar or common view. Each book was written by the man who bears its name—Matthew, Mark, and Luke. These three men presented similar accounts of Christ's life—event to event from their own perspectives. The structure of each book is similar, but their themes and emphases range significantly.

For instance, Matthew's theme exalts Christ as the Messiah and King. Matthew wrote to a primarily Jewish audience to convince them that Jesus Christ is the Messiah they have been waiting for. He used lots of Old Testament Scripture and showed Christ as fulfilling many Old Testament prophecies in hopes that his fellow Jews would recognize Christ as their long-awaited Messiah.

Mark, on the other hand, lived fast-paced. He wrote the shortest of all the Gospels and used the word "immediately" forty-one times, more than all the other New Testament books combined. He portrayed Christ as active and dedicated to His ministry and mission on earth. Mark wasn't concerned with chronology. He also wasn't one of Jesus' original twelve disciples. Many scholars believe that he wrote as Peter's shadow since, among other reasons, he mentioned Peter often in his book. Mark's spunky, action-oriented Gospel recounts Christ's life in an interesting read.

Luke's Gospel is the one most concerned with chronology. Luke was a doctor, and his gospel reflects a doctor's precision and attention to detail. We find the most well-read nativity story in Luke, who gave a descriptive account of Jesus' birth and the events surrounding it. Luke, also not one of the original twelve, wrote a detailed, chronological account of Christ's life, filling it in with fascinating details the other gospels don't mention.

John is a Gospel unto itself. John forgoes much of the content that the other Gospel authors contain; hence, it isn't considered one of the Synoptic Gospels. He took a theological position in recounting Christ's life and ministry and left out events the other gospels include, such as narrative parables, the institution of the Lord's Supper, the transfiguration account, the casting out of demons, or any of Jesus' temptations.[1] However, he included the "I AM" statements of Christ, and he strives to show Christ's deity as the divine and holy Son of God. John emphasized Jesus' divinity most.

Parables

We can't study the Gospels without pausing for a few words about parables. Parables are brief, fictional stories that illustrate a moral point or value. Jesus used lots of them to communicate the point He wanted to make with His disciples and followers. He chose to use parables instead of direct language because the people weren't yet able to comprehend His truth.[2]

Most of us are familiar with parables—the wise man who built his house on the rock, the shepherd who left his ninety-nine sheep to find the missing one, the rich man who sold everything he had in order to buy a piece of land with hidden value, the Good Samaritan. All these and more comprise the sub-genre of parables in the Gospels.

Parables are valuable communication tools because they liken a spiritual truth to a real-life analogy. The parable of the Good Samaritan, for instance, reminds us that righteousness involves far more than race or rank and is revealed by our actions.

---

[1] Carson, D.A.. *The Gospel According to John*. Grand Rapids: Wm. B. Eerdmans, 1990, 21.
[2] There are many examples of this point—how the disciples weren't yet ready to hear the direct truths that Jesus was sharing with them. Read the story of Jesus' warning of the Pharisees and Sadducees in Matthew 16 (particularly verse 11) for one such example.

The most important point in studying parables is acknowledging that they communicate a limited amount of truth. Typically, there is "one main point for each main character or group of characters."[3]

With parables, people get into a lot of trouble by dissecting details never meant to be the main point (as with prophecy). When studying the parable of the Good Samaritan, we would be foolish to investigate the specific type or amount of money the Samaritan paid to care for the injured man. That is a supporting detail; it bears no significance to the point of the story. Yet some people spend hours, days, weeks, and months picking apart parables, looking for hidden meaning. It's not there, folks.

The entire purpose of parables is to communicate simple truths in ways people can comprehend. Why would Christ go to great lengths to bury secrets deep within fictional stories when He was having a hard enough time getting people to understand the simplest of truths? He wouldn't. He didn't. Parables have one main point for each character or group of characters, not a point for every detail mentioned in the story.

We must also consider the original audience to correctly understand the meaning of a parable.[4] When we dig too deeply into the details of parables and create meaning that's not there, we miss the point. The point has to be one that the original audience would have understood. Otherwise, it wouldn't have had much value.

Here's a parable recap. 1) Parables are fictitious stories used by Christ to communicate a moral truth or value to His followers. 2) There is typically only one main point for each character or group of characters present in a parable. 3) Whatever points you derive from your interpretation must have been understood by the original audience.

Now back to John and a review of the Gospels.

Known as the "Beloved Disciple," John communicated Christ's

---

[3] Duvall and Hays, *Grasping God's Word*. 261.
[4] Duvall and Hays, *Grasping God's Word*. 261.

life on an intimate level. He started at the beginning (actually, before the beginning of the world) by announcing that Christ (the Word) was the beginning, was God, was with God, and all of creation was formed through Him and by Him. John started with a lofty image of Christ, which he carried through to the end of his Gospel.

Matthew, Mark, Luke, and John give personal accounts of Christ's life and ministry. If they didn't witness an event first-hand, they heard a detailed description of it from one of the original twelve disciples and recorded it accordingly. One characteristic of the Gospels that we must take into account is that they are four different perspectives of the same man, Jesus Christ, and His ministry on earth. Though a story such as the feeding of the five thousand may appear in each gospel, it is not repeated in the same verbiage or fashion each time. Why? The Gospel authors (like all other Scripture writers) wrote in ways that expressed their own minds, personalities, styles, and experiences. They were unique men with different perspectives, and their accounts reflect that.

Let's pause for clarification. Each Gospel author wrote his account differently and from a unique perspective, but each is true. They do not contradict each other. (If some seem to contradict, go deeper in your study of them, and the contradiction will fade). Remember the diamond analogy from a while back? If there's one diamond in a roomful of people, each individual will describe the diamond differently.

It's the same with the Gospel authors. They experience the same event but communicate it differently to us. Some notice a particular detail or two that the others don't. Others choose to emphasize a particular part of the story over another. They tell the same true story, using different ways of expressing it. The Gospels accurately and distinctively narrate Christ's life from four unique perspectives. Praise God for enhancing His Word and revealing so many dimensions of Christ's life to us!

Unique Time in History

Now that we've discovered what the Gospels are, let's look at their unique time in history. About four hundred years separate the end of the Old Testament from the beginning of the New. Why is that significant? Because the absence of written Scripture means there was no obvious, ongoing communication between God and His people. They received the Law and the prophets but no more direct word from God. These years stood silent as Israel waited for God's promises to come true.

All that changed when Christ arrived! Christ answered all the promises God repeatedly spoke to His people. He was and still is the fulfillment of God's redemptive plan. The Gospels are the four unique books of Scripture that capture their name, the gospel, coming to fruition in God's plan. Christ is the fulfillment, yes. But He also turned the people's expectation on its heels!

The people awaited a magnificent show of political restitution and kingdom reestablishment; they got a baby in a manger. They wanted a captivating king who would militarily subject all nations to Israel; they received the son of a carpenter, who lived quietly for much of His life. They anticipated a dazzling display of prestige and power; they got a Man who hung out with sinners, lepers, the lame, and the poor. They desired Him to initiate a new Davidic reign establishing Israel as the world's ruling nation; they got a Savior who was brutally crucified on a cross.

Jesus was nothing Israel expected or wanted, but He was everything they needed. The Gospels capture this unique transitional time in history, when Christ was here, but the church had yet to be established. Christ closed the Old Testament way of relating to God (namely, the old covenants) by establishing the New Covenant—one of redemption and final forgiveness of sins.

The Bridge Between the Old and New Covenants

Christ established the New Covenant through His coming, death, and resurrection. We need a working knowledge of covenants in order to understand the Gospels. Read this closely: as the events of the Gospels happened, the people experiencing them were under the Old Covenant, or the Law. By the time the Gospels were completed, their readers were subject to the New Covenant. This is why the Gospels are tricky to read, interpret, and understand.

As the Gospel accounts unfolded in real-time, while Christ was living on earth, people were still under the Law. They knew only the Law, that Israel was still God's chosen people, and that He would send a Messiah at some point. The people living during the time of the Gospels were Old Testament people. Christ and God's redemptive plan eluded them. Even if they knew and believed in Christ as the Messiah, they didn't completely understand how believing in Him would change their relationship with God.

Christ ushered in a whole new era, a whole New Covenant that wouldn't be entirely understood until decades after He ascended back into heaven, as the Gospels were written and distributed. By the time the Gospels were written, the authors and believers who would read them were under the New Covenant. Christ completed His work, fulfilled the Law, and invited Gentiles into the New Covenant.

Tips for Interpreting the Gospels

Knowing the Gospels bridge the two covenants helps us to read, interpret, and apply their passages to our lives. Our first tip in understanding the Gospels is to become aware of each passage's context. If you're reading a passage in Matthew, you must understand that the people it's talking *about*, the people in the story, are under the Old Covenant; but the people it's talking *to*, those the author of the

Gospel addresses in his writing, live under the New Covenant. The Gospels have two contexts. Explore both fully when reading them.

The second tip to remember when studying the Gospels is to refer to all four of them when studying a passage. We mentioned in Rule #4 that Scripture must be read, studied, and applied in light of itself. The Gospels give us opportunity to do this because many of the accounts are repeated in two, three, or all four of them. Not every account is represented in each Gospel, but it's rare to have one all by itself! So look for it in the other Gospels to get a fuller, more complete picture.

The Gospels comprise a fascinating part of Scripture, for they bridge the Old and the New Covenants. They describe Jesus and also provide us with special insight into His life and teachings. This benefits us greatly in our reading and studies. Each Gospel author provides his perspective of Christ's life and ministry, giving particular emphasis to different characteristics of the Messiah. Christ, along with Scripture, is multi-dimensional and difficult to grasp within the confines of words on a page! Yet, with the help of the Gospels, we can know Him on a personal and intimate level and see how radically His life impacted the world.

ACTS

A single book, Acts stands alone as its own genre because there's nothing like it in the rest of Scripture. We've learned that the Gospels are a bridge between the Old and the New Testaments and Covenants. Well, the New Covenant is first realized in Acts for believers—for the church. In this genre study, we will conduct a mini-history lesson of Judaism and its role in God's redemptive plan, learn how Christ significantly impacted that plan, discover how Acts begins where the Gospels leave off, and discuss some major turning points that occur in

Acts. Then we'll wrap up with another shout-out to the importance of understanding context!

Mini-History Lesson

The title Christian ("little Christ") makes its debut in Acts. Here the church is brought together as an official entity. Remember, in the Old Testament, Jews were the only chosen people of God. He always desired the whole world to come to faith in Him, but He chose the Jews to be the instruments through which that happened. The Old Testament reveals their failure of being His witnesses to the world. But with Christ on the scene and His establishment of a New Covenant, that opportunity extends to everyone, not just Jews.

This was a hard concept for early Christians to grasp because most Christians were converted Jews. Think about this for a minute: Christ's original twelve disciples were Jews. They observed the Law as best they could, went to the synagogue on the Sabbath, obeyed the Ten Commandments, listened to their rabbis—all in an effort to be good Jews. When they came to faith in Christ, they (not surprisingly) thought Christianity *was* Judaism. They were under the impression that Judaism simply progressed with Christ, their Messiah.

They were right, to an extent. Christ should have been accepted by all the Jews as their long-awaited Messiah. But that's not what happened. Instead, only a few accepted Him at first—mostly His eleven disciples (minus Judas by this point), along with others who followed Christ before He ascended. They eventually grew in number and became an entirely different faith entity than Judaism, because Judaism, as a whole, rejected Christ. Thus, believers in Christ became known as Christians and the Church.

A Continuation of the Gospels

Acts picks up the story where the Gospels leave off. It begins precisely where the Gospel of Luke ends, because both Acts and Luke were written by Luke. Acts begins with a recap of Christ's last days on earth—His visit to several hundred people over a period of forty days, a commission to His disciples, the promise of the Holy Spirit, instructions for the time of waiting until He came, and His ascension back into heaven.[5] After His ascension, Acts records the beginning of the church age—the one we live in today.

We cannot understand church history without founding our studies in Acts. It is a historical documentary, a timeline, a biography of one of the greatest apostles who ever lived (Paul), an account of the Holy Spirit's role with believers in the New Covenant, a story of how the church overcame overwhelming odds (persecution) to proclaim the gospel all over the known world, the record of how the gospel spread through several missionary journeys . . . it's the Genesis of the Church as we know it. It is the true story of how the Church grew to thousands from a mere 120 scared and nervous men and women crowded in an upper room, awaiting Pentecost. In it God reveals one of the last installments of His redemptive plan for the world, and it tells us how our faith came to be.

Turning Points of Faith

The book of Acts records some major turning points of the faith. We've already mentioned that faith in Christ was now freely offered to Gentiles (non-Jews)—as to the Jews. But in Acts we also learn that the Law is no longer the final word regarding lifestyle and behavior. In the Old Testament, in order to worship God properly, a Gentile had

---

[5] See Acts 1:1-9

to become a proselyte, a convert to Judaism, in order to be acceptable and presentable to God.

Not anymore. God accepted Gentiles as they were, without requiring them to change their customs (unless said customs were idolatrous or displeasing to God in some other way). They could live as Gentile while being as acceptable to God as Jews were.

Paul explains this new way beautifully in Romans 2.

> For all who have sinned without the Law will also perish without the Law, and all who have sinned under the Law will be judged by the Law; for it is not the hearers of the Law who are just before God, but the doers of the Law will be justified. For when Gentiles who do not have the Law do instinctively the things of the Law, these, not having the Law, are a law to themselves, in that they show the work of the Law written in their hearts, their conscience bearing witness and their thoughts alternately accusing or else defending them, on the day when, according to my gospel, God will judge the secrets of men through Christ Jesus.[6]

Jews were convinced that living by the letter of the Jewish Law was the only way to please the Lord. They didn't think for a second that Gentiles could please the Lord without first converting to Judaism and placing themselves under subjection to the Hebrew Law. Ironically, the Jews neglected to understand the heart and intent of the Law — that God wanted their hearts and love more than He wanted their observation of a bunch of rules.

That's why Paul referenced the Gentiles bearing fruit of the Law — the one written on their hearts, the one that honors and glorifies God. They were unfamiliar with the Jews' customs and practices, but the Gentiles who followed Christ as their personal Savior made Him Lord of their lives and hearts. The Law was always meant to do the same for

---

[6] Romans 2:12-16.

the Jews. Yet few Jews understood this concept. They were territorial of their religion and status as God's chosen people, and they hesitated to let Gentiles into their inner circle without putting them through the "proper" Jewish channels.

Christ rendered "proper" channels obsolete. However, the Jew/Gentile friction didn't catch on for quite some time in the church. Understanding this friction is essential for any study in Acts because it infiltrates its pages. For example, in Acts 6 we read about a conflict between the Hellenistic Jews and the native Hebrews because their widows were overlooked when food was served. (Christians at this point, though increasing in number, still remained a relatively small group that lived together, shared everything, and devoted themselves to each other and the spread of the gospel. Pretty cool, huh?)

The apostles told them to "select from among you seven men of good reputation, full of the Spirit and of wisdom, whom we may put in charge of" distributing the food.[7] The remarkable part is found not in the plan, but in whom they chose—seven *Gentile* men. Had we not understood the history between Jews and Gentiles at this point, the story remains facile. Acts delivers dozens of stories of Gentiles coming to Christ and serving Him, even to the point of martyrdom. In fact, the first recorded martyr was Stephen, a Gentile.

Context!

Do you see how a little historical context goes a long way in illuminating our understanding of Scripture? It is particularly so in Acts. As you go further in your studies, you'll discover even more. You'll see how churches were started, by whom, and on what journey. This also enhances studies we conduct in New Testament Letters to the churches (the letters that follow the book of Acts). Acts records the beginning of the church and its remarkable growth—all a part of

---

[7] Acts 6:3

God's plan to spread His Word and gospel to the ends of the earth. What a story, indeed!

In the brief survey of Acts we just strolled through, we learned how vital a role the book plays within the canon of Scripture. Without it, we would move from the Gospels to the New Testament Letters without understanding what happened in the time between them. Acts serves as a crucial foundation of church history, which gives us lots of context for understanding how the church (and churches today) came to be.

NEW TESTAMENT LETTERS

The Letters of the New Testament is often a favorite genre among Scripture, probably because it's the most straightforward and easiest to apply to our lives. In this genre overview, we will review some facts about the New Testament Letters, dig into their history a bit, and then conclude with a hint or two to help you interpret them correctly.

Some Facts

New Testament Letters include the books of Romans, 1 & 2 Corinthians, Galatians, Ephesians, Philippians, Colossians, 1 & 2 Thessalonians, 1 & 2 Timothy, Titus, Philemon, Hebrews, James, 1 & 2 Peter, 1, 2 & 3 John, and Jude. Whew. That's all but six books of the New Testament! Over half of them were written by the apostle Paul (thirteen of the twenty-one). The others were named after their authors, with the exception of Hebrews with its mystery author.

New Testament Letters were actual hand-written letters sent to the early churches by the apostles. The apostles founded many of the churches they wrote to, and they used the letters to check in with, encourage, correct, praise, and comfort them, along with a host of other reasons.

More Than Words

Though similar, these aren't entirely like the letters we receive (or perhaps *used* to receive) via snail mail today. They similarly follow the universal pattern of letters we see today—a greeting, main content, and concluding remarks. But differences arise when we probe a bit deeper.

For instance, New Testament Letters, though personal, were not written to a particular person (usually). Rather, apostles address them to an entire church. The apostles cared greatly about the people they wrote to but knew full well that the letters would travel far beyond an individual recipient. In fact, they wanted them to. The letters were meant to be distributed to the churches and were done so through *verbal* readings (another difference). They were not often read by one person and then passed to another and so forth. The church designated one person to read the letter aloud to a congregation, and then it was passed along to another house church in that region.

Another difference we observe between letters then and letters now is the fact that New Testament Letters were considered authoritative in the absence of their authors.[8] For example, Paul's letter rebuking the church of Galatia for falling away from the gospel is just as authoritative and weighty as if he were preaching to them face to face.

Some History

So why letters? Didn't the churches have pastors to help them along? Why did they need apostolic authority at all? The book of Acts helps us understand the answers to these questions. In Acts we learn that the church wasn't organized as it is today. The "Bible Belt" didn't exist with a church on every Middle Eastern corner. The gospel was a new entity. It spread quickly and mightily, but the organization and establishment of churches evolved as time went on.

The apostles traveled the known world to preach the gospel and

---

[8] Duvall and Hays, *Grasping God's Word*, 229.

set up groups of believers. Once established, they left for another region and did the same there. But they didn't forget about the new churches. As they traveled, they prayed for the churches and received reports about them from their peers and fellow servants of Christ. The apostles often followed these reports with letters to the churches, providing them with instruction, wisdom, advice, and counsel.

Again, the letters were situational. They were not generic, impersonal mass mailings the apostles wrote out of obligation. Rather, they were personal letters, written carefully and through much prayer as the apostle communicated the truth God revealed to him. Though not physically present, the apostles exercised authority over the churches, and their letters carried that authority. They still do today.

Along that line, both the apostles and churches recognized the letters as God's Word. Let's look at 2 Peter 3:14-16 as an example:

> Therefore, beloved, since you look for these things, be diligent to be found by Him in peace, spotless and blameless, and regard the patience of our Lord as salvation; just as also our beloved brother Paul, according to the wisdom given him, wrote to you, as also in all his letters, speaking in them of these things, in which some things hard to understand which the untaught and unstable distort, as they do also the rest of the Scriptures to their own destruction.

Peter considered Paul's letters authoritative and called them Scripture. The apostles knew they had been ordained to write God's truth to the churches, and that's precisely what they did. Can you imagine being in their shoes? Wouldn't it have been sobering to know the letter you were writing would be considered God's Word and included in His holy canon?

God used the letters in huge ways. Because the apostles were mobile and traveled frequently, He spread His Word and teachings out to the various churches, establishing His Church on His truth.

More Than Words

Remember, the believers living in the time of the New Testament were just figuring out this New Covenant. They couldn't reference Scripture like we do, because it was all new.

Jews learned their relationship with the Old Testament Law was changing dramatically through Christ. Gentiles learned that Christ made salvation available to them just as they were. They didn't have to change their cultural practices in order to be accepted spiritually. Both Jew and Gentile could worship in Spirit and in truth, and it didn't matter when, where, or in what style that was done!

That brings us to another radical transition the early church experienced: the role of the Holy Spirit in and through their lives. The Holy Spirit invokes His new role with believers in Acts and is fleshed out with greater detail in the context of theology in the New Testament Letters. The Holy Spirit definitely shows Himself in the Old Testament, but in a different role.

In David's Psalm of repentance for committing adultery with Bathsheba, he wrote,

> Hide Your face from my sins and blot out my iniquities. Create in me a clean heart, O God, and renew a steadfast spirit within me. Do not cast me away from Your presence and do not take Your Holy Spirit from me.[9]

This passage cues us in to the role of the Holy Spirit in the Old Testament. He anointed and was with believers individually, but not permanently as a sign of salvation. His anointing presence wasn't guaranteed to remain with them, temporarily or for a whole life. God sanctified specific people with His Spirit for specific purposes, like Bezalel ordained as the craftsman for many elements of the Tabernacle.[10] The Holy Spirit ordained different people for different

---
[9] Psalm 51:9-11.
[10] Exodus 31:1-5.

purposes in the Old Testament, but many times that anointing was situational and temporary.

With the coming of Christ and His establishment of the New Covenant, however, the Holy Spirit embraced a much greater and intimate role with believers. The Spirit was active with Christ when He was on earth and is with those who make Him Lord of their lives today. Jesus promised that

> The Helper, the Holy Spirit, whom the Father will send in My name, He will teach you all things, and bring to your remembrance all that I said to you. . . . but when He, the Spirit of truth, comes, He will guide you in all the truth; for He will not speak on His own initiative, but whatever He hears, He will speak; and he will disclose to you what is to come. He will glorify Me, for He will take of Mine and will disclose it to you.[11]

After Jesus ascended and the Day of Pentecost came, the Holy Spirit sealed believers in salvation and enacted a permanent role with them. The Spirit indwells believers, equips us to live according to His truth, not the flesh, and testifies that we are children of God. He helps us in our weaknesses and in our prayers, sanctifies us, and demonstrates His power in and through us. He imparts spiritual gifts to us, reveals God's truth through His Word, teaches us, and gives us wisdom. He brings unity among believers, seals us, is given to us as a pledge, helps us exercise our freedom in Christ, and much more!

The Holy Spirit's ministry came to life, in a sense, with the dawn of the new covenant. The early church kept busy learning and experiencing everything He had to offer them! Through Him, God increased His intimacy with us through the redemption of Christ, and His ministry to believers is seen in real and personal ways within the book of Acts and the New Testament Letters.

---

[11] John 14:26 & 16:13-14.

This was an exciting time in church history, and the New Testament Letters were crucial for explaining the New Covenant, the new relationship between the Jews and Gentiles, and the new role of the Holy Spirit. They also served as the authoritative presence of those God was communicating directly with. What a treasure they were and still are today!

Some Tips for Interpretation

Despite the differences, New Testament Letters remain easy for modern-day readers to understand, interpret, and apply. Not much mystery is associated with them. The authors kept them simple and wrote directly about real-life issues the churches experienced at the time of their writing. They give advice, offer correction, and explain theology in ways easy for us to understand and follow. These letters are, for the most part, written in a straightforward fashion, which makes readers like us happy!

Yet (of course there's a *however!*), we must exert caution when reading them. The biggest caution worth noting (again) is to remember that they are, in fact, letters—written by a particular person to a particular group of people for particular reasons. You and I are not a part of that original group! Thus, when interpreting New Testament Letters, we must place ourselves in the original audiences' shoes, understanding the context of their situation in order to interpret correctly. Never forget or neglect to find the context, dear friends!

What a ride! New Testament Letters are a treasure, as much for us today as they were when originally penned. In them we learn that the church was never (and will never be this side of heaven) perfect. They struggled with issues, and the authors had no problem calling them on it! We also learn how the church was established in the transition of theology from the Old Testament to the New. It was a confusing time for first-century believers, and the New Testament letters were vital to the church and their understanding and application of God's truth.

The third item we learn is that, though we are similar to the early believers in the New Covenant, we still must utilize discernment when reading, interpreting, and applying New Testament Letters to our lives. We are not first-century Christians. Although we may go through similar experiences or hardships, the contexts in which we endure them are much different than those of the early church. The key is to understand the context, which is what we've just finished exploring in this beautiful genre!

Revelation

Like Acts, Revelation qualifies as its own genre because of its uniqueness among Scripture. A million thoughts probably fight for your attention when you think of Revelation. It tends to have that effect on people. Revelation is the most mysterious book of the Bible because it's prophetic and filled with intense word pictures and graphic descriptions of the author's vision. We'll get to that in a minute. In this mini-overview we are going to learn what Revelation is, discover a few things about apocalyptic literature, and explore some tips to keep in mind when reading it.

Revelation: What Is It?

Revelation is technically a letter. John (the same John who wrote the Gospel of John) wrote it to seven churches in Asia: Ephesus, Smyrna, Pergamum, Thyatira, Sardis, Philadelphia, and Laodicea. Like other New Testament letters, it circulated among the churches, not being confined to a single reader.

Also like other letters, it is situational. John receives a vision (revelation) from Jesus Christ to be communicated to the seven churches for a particular purpose. He obediently writes down what he sees, and the end product is the book of Revelation. By the way, it's Revela*tion* not Revela*tions*. One vision. One revelation. It may be a long vision, but it's still only one.

The first three chapters are quite normal, or at least familiar to us now that we're New Testament Letter experts! Christ addresses each church individually, including a rebuke and/or instruction He wants to impart to them. Problems are addressed, solutions are given, and warnings are administered. These were real churches experiencing real issues specifically addressed by Christ through John. Nothing foreign about that after our New Testament Letter overview!

In chapter four, the book's uniqueness picks up a bit. Now that the seven churches have been addressed, John began describing his vision. And what a vision it was! John was ushered into the presence of God (we're not quite sure how, and he probably wasn't sure himself), and experienced a glimse into the end times—during the Apocalypse.

Apocalyptic . . . what?

We've already discussed prophecy as a genre. Revelation is considered prophecy, yet with an even greater focus. It is apocalyptic. A formal definition of apocalyptic writing is:

> Apocalyptic literature is symbolic visionary prophetic literature, composed during oppressive conditions, consisting of visions whose events are recorded exactly as they were seen by the author and explained through a divine interpreter, and whose theological content is primarily eschatological.[12]

---

[12] Alexander, Ralph. Abstract of "Hermeneutics of Old Testament Apocalyptic Literature," doctor's dissertation, 1.

Quite the mouthful, huh? That one is for all our genius friends. As for the rest of us, who need it on simpler terms, here's another one:

> The term apocalyptic refers to a group of writings *(Revelation)* that include a divine revelation *(John's vision)*, usually through a heavenly intermediary *(at various points including: Jesus Christ, an elder, a living creature, etc.)*, to some well-known figure *(the apostle John)* in which God promises to intervene in human history and overthrow evil empires and establish his kingdom *(emphasis mine)*.[13]

So maybe that wasn't in laymen's terms, but you're tracking with me, right? Apocalyptic literature is ultimately about God promising that good overcomes evil in the end. However, the process of getting to that conclusion makes apocalyptic literature difficult, Revelation included.

Since the apostle John had never before seen most of what he wrote about, we expect that he would have a difficult time describing it. Imagine describing an iPad to a child living in the jungles of Tanzania. Would she understand what it was? If you don't have terms like electronic tablet, Internet, touch screen, pictures, and graphics to work with, you're limited in your description!

The apostle John finds himself in the same pickle. He knows what he saw, but his limited vocabulary makes it difficult to describe. He's forced to use word pictures and figures of speech to capture one dimensionally (1D) what he experienced in, like, 10D! I wouldn't volunteer for that task!

That's what we experience when we read Revelation. John uses lots of descriptions that don't make sense to us because we have no context to base them in and nothing to compare them with. When he describes strange creatures, our response is to scan the text, skip over it, and say, "Well, that's nice." Or we jump too deep and read our own

---

[13] Duvall and Hays, *Grasping God's Word*, 287 (emphasis mine).

interpretations into it, or try to determine what he's communicating. The last option is the preferred one, but that requires significant effort on behalf of the reader. So let's look at some tips that will help us get inside John's vision.

TIPS FOR INTERPRETING REVELATION

These tips will resemble the ones for prophecy, but there'll be a couple of twists to keep it interesting.

Give It Some More Context!

Shocking, right? But oh, so important! Any hope of interpreting or applying passages from Revelation to our lives requires some serious understanding of context. Research, explore, and delve into as many facts as you can glean about the passage itself and the ones surrounding it. Dig into background information and soak up all you can. The more you can describe the setting, characters, plot, and conflict, the better chance you will have of recognizing the point of the story!

Get Out of the Way

Interpreting Revelation leaves zero room for pride. Same goes for any other genre of Scripture, for that matter. But this applies to Revelation more than the rest of Scripture because it contains much that we'll never fully understand this side of heaven. We each need to come to terms with this fact personally and with the Lord before we begin a hermeneutical endeavor in Revelation. We must open our minds and admit when we're wrong. And if we are wrong, we must humble ourselves enough to change our views when the evidence provided in Scripture leads us to do so.[14]

Remember, this process is not about us! The moment we start thinking otherwise is the moment we forfeit our usefulness in hermeneutics. Get out of the way and leave room only for His Truth. He'll lead you to it if you remain humble, responsible, and eager for it!

Pay Attention to Clues

This is a helpful tip and one that may save you lots of unnecessary frustration. Pay attention to textual clues! For example, when John says, "And He who was sitting was like a jasper stone and a sardius in appearance," what word does he use to signal our metaphor alert? The word *like*! That one little word lets us know that John's vocabulary doesn't contain an exact word to describe God's appearance, so he says the next best thing—what He looked *like*. Many such clues are scattered throughout Revelation, so pay attention to them!

Always Serious, Not Always Literal[15]

A big difference exists between taking something seriously and taking something literally. We learned in our hermeneutics introduction to interpret Scripture with the Literal, Grammatical, and Historical Method. We do so with Revelation too. Yet with Revelation we realize that significant portions of the book are not meant to be taken literally. This is where tip #3 comes in handy. Look for clues to determine what John is saying.

Regardless of whether or not we ever figure out what he's trying to say, we are always expected to take the writing seriously. Don't write something off as fiction or a waste of time because you don't understand

---

[14] Duvall and Hays, *Grasping God's Word*, 289.
[15] Duvall and Hays, *Grasping God's Word*, 291.

it. Let your limited understanding confirm your appreciation for a God unlimited in His understanding. We serve a holy, mighty, and powerful God! We do the best we can when interpreting His Word, and if we get stuck on a point after exhausting all our efforts, we trust that He knows what He's doing and add it to our "heaven list!"

You have now been introduced to Revelation and some of its mysteries. We learned what Revelation is, some interesting facts about apocalyptic literature, and some fabulous tips to keep in mind when reading and interpreting this fascinating book. Great job!

Genre Recap

That was quite the adventure, right? We've just walked through each of the major genres of Scripture. We started with historical narrative, then continued with Law, wisdom literature, prophecy, the Gospels, Acts, New Testament letters, and ended with Revelation. What a trip! You are now equipped to begin your hermeneutical journey on any passage from any genre you wish. We're about to work through one together, practicing the steps of hermeneutics on a passage of Scripture. Get on board, buckle in, and get ready to explore!

Step One—Meaning in its Day

A BRIEF OVERVIEW

The *what* questions are now answered: what the hermeneutical rules and interpretive principles of specific genres are. Now we move on to the *how* questions. How do we perform the process of hermeneutics on a passage? How do we use the principles and rules we learned and put them in practice on a passage of Scripture?

Numerous voices compete to answer this question. Many voices, of course, result in many different strategies and opinions. As mentioned before, everyone performs some kind of hermeneutic when reading a passage of Scripture. The question is whether you're performing a proper and accurate hermeneutic—one that glorifies God and results in a transformed heart and life.

Unfortunately, no perfect or magical process for hermeneutics exists. Again, Scripture never tells us directly how to do hermeneutics. It leaves us to use our God-gifted brains. Now there are correct ways and incorrect ways to conduct hermeneutics, and that's what we explored with our Literal, Grammatical, and Historical Method over and above the Textual Criticism and Allegorical Methods. We know the latter two are incorrect, but how are we to pursue our studies *within* the bounds of the Literal, Grammatical, and Historical Method?

The steps proposed in this book are ones I prefer and have practiced effectively in my hermeneutical endeavors. They hail from many sources including *Grasping God's Word* by Duvall and Hays and one significant college professor I studied under, Dr. David Croteau. They are succinct and straightforward with a balanced approach of observation, interpretation, and application. Others, like Kay Arthur, Rick Warren, James Kugel, and Gordon Fee, suggest slightly different ways to do the process, which are just as valid.

We've already learned the crucial, non-negotiable components of hermeneutics. The rest of this book will offer one way to put all those principles and rules into practice. But it's certainly not the only one. Explore different options. Read how others practice hermeneutics and see which process works best for you and your personal studies in the Word.

Remember all the while that no human author is inspired. Neither are our processes of hermeneutics, so be careful who you listen to. Most authors agree wholeheartedly with the rules and principles in chapters three and four of this book. I'm a student of the Word, and these are all principles I learned through practice and studies—some even written by the aforementioned authors. If, however, you read about a process that advocates or assumes rules contrary to those in this book, you may want to bypass that particular process. We must show caution in choosing our process, knowing it will impact our understanding of the truths of God's Word. So be careful!

Disclaimers out of the way, let's get into a thorough hermeneutical process that works well. There's no technical name for it, so let's call it Five Steps—yes, I'm super-creative. Imaginations are apparently overrated. Anyway, as you guessed there are five steps in this process. Each builds on the other to give us a comprehensive understanding of the passage at hand.

Five Steps is inspired by the process described in the book *Grasping*

God's Word. This is a marvelous book far more academic and elaborate than I could hope to achieve with this volume. However, Five Steps, though similar, takes slightly different perspectives and includes an additional step that *Grasping God's Word* does not include. Credit should go where credit is due. And *GGW* should receive the majority of any credit for Five Steps. That said, let's conduct a mini-overview of the steps together, and then get into them individually with further detail.

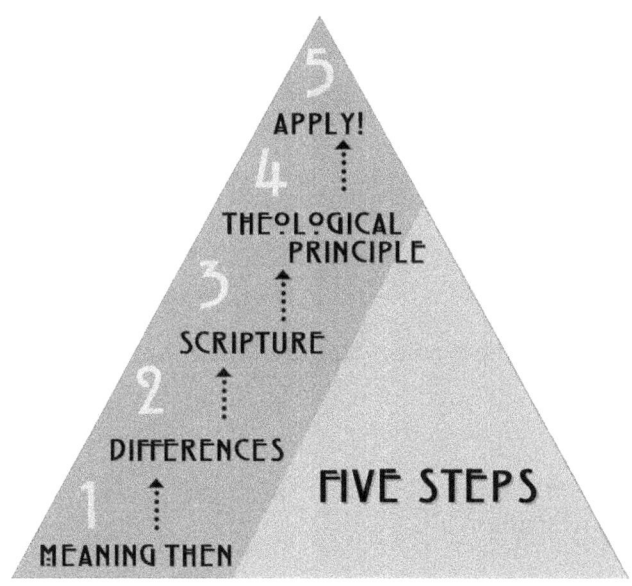

Step One—Meaning in its Day

You can probably already tell what this Step is about: discovering what the passage meant to the people it was written to. We need to place it in its context. Shout-out for Rule #3!

Step One has two mini-steps. The first researches the time period in which the passage was written. The second takes a hard look at the text itself, observing all we can about its grammatical structure so we can be confident in our understanding before we proceed to Step Two.

Step Two—Differences Between Then and Now

Because we don't live in the time that Scripture was written, we automatically face hurdles to overcome when interpreting it. Step Two is all about fleshing out those hurdles. For example, what differences exist between the original audience and us? This is where we put words to the differences so it helps us keep it in context (*their* context), and become aware of any of our biases or misunderstandings so they don't negatively impact our interpretation. Exposing differences remains critical for understanding the proper context and knowing where we stand relative to it.

Step Three—Scripture in Light of Scripture

I'll bet you can guess where this one came from—Rule #4! Scripture must be interpreted in light of itself. To do so, we need to discover the key themes in our passage and explore other passages in Scripture that have the same theme so we can get the full story of whatever theme we're working with.

Step Four—Determining the Theological Principle of the Passage

Once we've pointed out the background, context, differences, and themes, we're ready to explore the similarities between the original audience and ourselves so we can determine the theological principle of the passage. Pointing out the similarities is hardly a daunting task since we've already discovered the differences!

Once we articulate those, we move into the heart of hermeneutics—determining the theological principle. If you remember from our previous hermeneutics study, finding the theological principle is a major goal of hermeneutics. This principle answers the "What's the Point?" question for every passage. This allows us to apply it to our lives—the ultimate goal of hermeneutics. Step Three paves the way for finding the principle because the principle revolves around the main themes of the passage.

Step Five—Meaning for Today

Getting the theological principle is a huge step, but it's not worth much if we don't use it! This is where Step Five comes in. In Step Five, we think of a situation and/or story in which the theological principle would apply. This enables us to see the principle in action and then apply it to our lives.

Well, that was super-brief, but it's always nice to know where you're going! Now let's take a deeper look at each Step to see how it all works.

READ IT!

Technically, before we start Step One (Meaning in its Day), we need to pick a passage! Remember, a passage, not just a single verse! We read it once, twice, then again, and again, and again, and again. This passage will be your mission for the next bit of your life, so absorb it. Take it in. Get intimate with it!

Once we pick and read our passage of ten verses or so, we may begin Step One. Since working through a real-life example significantly helps us understand what we're reading, we're going to practice our steps on an actual passage, Philippians 2:1-10.

Let's follow our first advice: reading the passage!

> Therefore if there is any encouragement in Christ, if there is any consolation of love, if there is any fellowship of

the Spirit, if any affection and compassion, make my joy complete by being of the same mind, maintaining the same love, united in spirit, intent on one purpose. Do nothing from selfishness or empty conceit, but with humility of mind regard one another as more important than yourselves; do not merely look out for your own interests, but also for the interests of others. Have this attitude in you which was also in Christ Jesus, who, although He existed in the form of God, did not regard equality with God as something to be grasped, but emptied Himself, taking on the form of a bond-servant, and being made in the likeness of men. Being found in appearance as a man, He humbled Himself by becoming obedient to the point of death, even death on a cross. For this reason also, God highly exalted Him, and bestowed on Him the name which is above every name, so that at the name of Jesus every knee will bow of those who are in heaven and on earth and under the earth, and that every tongue will confess that Jesus Christ is Lord, to the glory of God the Father.

Does that not just give you goose bumps? If it didn't, read it again. And again. And again, until it does! We're not going anywhere. I promise we'll wait!

STEP ONE: MEANING IN ITS DAY

Step One seeks to discover what the passage meant to the original audience. To make this easier, we're going to phrase each Step as a question. The question for Step One is, "What did the text mean to the biblical audience?" We answer that first by backing up from the text and gathering as much information about it as possible, giving it some context.

Step One: Meaning In Its Day

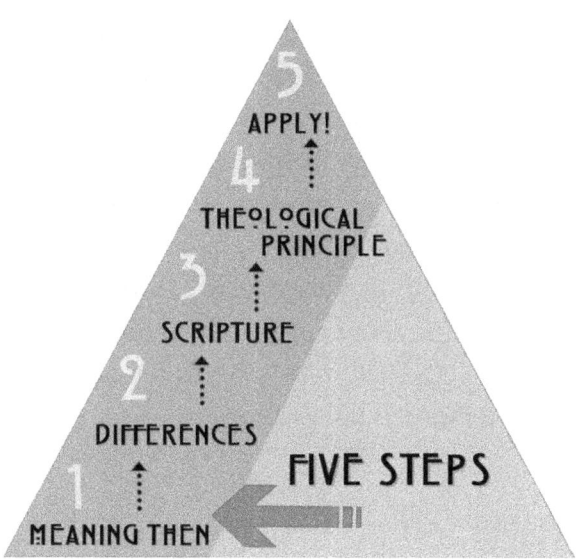

We must observe the big picture of the context surrounding the passage before zooming in to the narrow focus and understanding the passage itself. Remember, you don't open a novel to some random page and expect to know what's going on. Same with Scripture. Though we start by picking out a singular passage, we need to back up and figure out its context before we can understand what's going on.

Discovering the context involves two steps, duly named broad and narrow. The funnel concept best describes this whole broad/narrow step idea. We begin with a broad view of what's going on around the passage and then move toward the narrow, more focused-in view of the passage itself. This differs from the deduction/induction discussion we meandered through earlier. Deduction and induction deal with how to *interpret* Scripture, not how to *observe* it. Our goal in Step One is to observe, not interpret.

Alternative to the funnel, we would start by observating the passage itself, and then back up and re-work those observations because we didn't know the whole picture beforehand. Starting from the outside and working our way in is the best way to walk through Step One because it ensures we're not missing any key points along the way.

The broad step concentrates on the big picture. In it, we gather general information about the text itself as well as the book it's written in. We seek to discover the book's author, audience, time it was written, what was going on at that point in history, what's being said in the context surrounding the passage, etc. The more information we get about the book and the surrounding passages, the better foundation we have for understanding the context of our passage! The better foundation we have, the more apt we are to interpret and apply it to our lives correctly. Let's look into some different resources that will help us develop that foundation.

RESOURCES

Solid research depends upon solid resources. Every job requires tools of some sort. A painter needs paint brushes and rags, athletes need gear and training equipment, moms need cleaning products and patience, and teachers need curriculum and aides. Not surprisingly, Bible students need tools, and they benefit from them! We're about to investigate Bible study tools. We'll introduce each one, give a general description, tell you what it's used for, and then recommend an excellent example or two that will help us along this journey.

Study Bibles

We find study Bibles in any local bookstore or online. These Bibles provide extra descriptions and/or explanations that clarify the text of Scripture. In essence, they supplement Scripture by helping explain it. You've probably seen, heard of, or own lots of different study Bibles, ranging from women's study Bibles to life application and topical study Bibles. Study Bibles are great for basic information and explanations of Scripture. Most study Bibles preface individual books with information, such as its author, time of writing, major themes, and an outline.

This information proves most advantageous for those beginning their studying adventures in Scripture because it provides us with the basics without getting too technical. However, we must understand that study Bibles, like any other resource, have their limitations. For example, most of the supplemental information provided consists of the translator's opinions, not necessarily facts.

Consider this: in the introduction section, most study Bibles provide their readers with the major themes of each book. Every book of the Bible displays a theme, and usually more than one. Themes vary because different authors try to communicate their own points and emphases. Some are more obvious than others, but all biblical books revolve around a theme or set of themes. It's important that we understand themes when we interpret a book, which is why study Bibles include them.

Although themes are typically agreed upon by scholars and theologians, some leave wiggle room. A book's themes are negotiable in the sense that they can be worded or prioritized differently, depending on the person who's studying it. Perhaps a certain theme is generally agreed upon by scholars, yet the *emphasis* of the theme in the book is debated. In Philippians, one major theme is joy, yet scholars and pastors alike come to different conclusions about how that theme affects the book, what emphasis the book places on it, and so on.

This is what we mean when we say that the supplemental material in study Bibles is mostly opinion, not fact. Supplemental material is not inspired by God. It may be (and often is) true, but we cannot and should not assume so.

Study Bibles provide great basic information, but they should not be used as primary sources of information for those wanting to go deeper in their biblical studies. The information they provide remains limited and without substantial explanation as to why one opinion is chosen over another. Two excellent recommendations for study Bibles are the NASB Study Bible and the NIV Study Bible. The NET Bible is also a personal favorite because it offers far more information than one typically finds in a study Bible, including reasons the editors chose this translation over another one, etc.

Bible Concordances

Bible concordances are alphabetical listings of the words found in Scripture. Yes, every word. Having a "Doubting Thomas" moment? Surely we can't mean every single word in Scripture. But we do! *Young's Concordance* is popular among concordances and is quite the impressive composition. I'm not sure how long it took Mr. Young to tally, count, and place every word in its correct spot, but he managed to do it. This concordance totals 1,206 pages with itty-bitty print! Can you imagine how tedious that must have been? Be grateful that we can take full advantage of his work without having to look up all those words ourselves!

Concordances are available both in print and online. Online versions operate a bit quicker and are easier to work with (no flipping of pages and searching incessantly for a particular word). Using the Internet, we simply type it in and search.

How exactly are concordances useful? Many reasons exist, but it's mostly beneficial when conducting word studies. We'll get into the word-study process a bit later; but for now, it's enough to know that word studies look at particular words in Scripture and discover what they mean. Sounds simple, and in some cases it is. But it can also be quite challenging since we're looking at words in the original Hebrew and Greek languages.

Concordances help the process because through them we can find where a word is used elsewhere in Scripture and observe how it's used in those contexts in order to shed light on our passage. Concordances may not be used often, but they are certainly beneficial to the study process.

We mentioned *Young's Analytical Concordance* already—a fine, hard-copy book worth adding to your library. But as we said earlier, online concordances are also accessible, and they are free (examples of beneficial websites are listed in the Computer Software section coming up soon).

Bible Dictionaries

Another fabulous study help is the Bible dictionary. Bible dictionaries don't contain every word in the Bible as an English dictionary does, but they cover most, focusing on names, people, nations, places, etc. Bible dictionaries are excellent tools to have on hand because they provide historically accurate information about whatever topic, word, people, place, book, etc. you come across in Scripture.

Say you're reading our example passage (Philippians 2:1-10) and you are curious about the Philippian people. With a Bible dictionary, all you have to do is look up "Philippians," and it provides you with a brief summary of the book and the Philippian people. Some favorite dictionaries are the *New International Bible Dictionary* and the *Zondervan Illustrated Bible Dictionary*, complete with pictures.

Bible Encyclopedias

Bible encyclopedias stand similar to concordances and dictionaries, yet differ by focusing more on *defining* the original Hebrew and Greek words than telling us where they're used or their background information. The goal of encyclopedias is to help us understand the richness of the word we're researching, which is beneficial to our studies. A couple of solid Bible encyclopedias are the *New International Encyclopedia of Bible Words* and the *Zondervan Encyclopedia of the Bible*.

Bible Atlases

Bible atlases are important to any Bible study because they show us a map of our particular text. Visual learners particluarly love these. We can read all day long about the tribes of Israel or Jesus' travels through Jerusalem and Galilee, but without having a picture of those places, it's difficult to keep them all straight.

Imagine a friend returning from a month-long adventure in Europe and telling you all about it . . . without pictures. Hearing her astounding stories and descriptions of places goes only so far unless we have a picture to look at. Without pictures, it's hard to know where she went, what this museum looked like, how tall this statue was, etc.

Just like pictures and maps give us a face with a name, so to speak, Bible atlases enable us to see where a story or narrative takes place. It's hard to give a story context without knowing its geography. Scripture was written at a particular time, in a particular place, to a particular people. We need to know what the place looked like, otherwise we'll miss much of what's going on. A favorite Bible atlas is *Baker's Bible Atlas*, but some worthy runner-ups are the *Crossway ESV Bible Atlas* and the *Zondervan Atlas of the Bible*.

Bible Commentaries

Talk about great resources. As you can probably gather from their name, Bible Commentaries offer a commentary (go figure) of biblical books. They provide historical background information prior to and during the commentary of the text. The authors also incorporate interpretation of key words/phrases, along with practical application points for us to apply them to our lives.

However, as with all good things, we must use them with a grain of salt. Some authors are less sound in their theology than others and thus should be avoided. Some commentaries try to address the whole Bible in one or two volumes. Although we might find some nuggets of wisdom and insight, these types are probably not worth investing in because they remain shallow, not going into any measure of depth in their background, interpretation, and application.

Another caveat to note is that the process of writing a commentary is basically the process of hermeneutics. Sounds fabulous, right? It is, except when you're practicing hermeneutics on your own! If you're conducting a hermeneutics study on Philippians 2:1-10, and you read a commentary on that passage, there's little left for you to do! It has, in essence, done the work for you, which negates the entire premise of the exercise.

So, for hermeneutics purposes, use the beginning of commentaries for background information, then use the rest when you've completed your study. That way you can check your work with someone else's. Here are some wonderful and solid commentary series that would be worth adding to your personal library: The *NIV Application Commentary* Series, The *Pillar New Testament* Commentaries, and The *New International* Commentaries. Each can be purchased according to what book you're studying, but as your library expands, your theological and hermeneutical brain will too!

Bible Background Books

Bible background books are fascinating and immeasurably helpful. These books usually concentrate on one portion of Scripture and give the reader lots of intricate background information about them—equipping them with the ability to understand a passage's context to the nth degree! Hundreds of these books exist, but here are some fabulous recommendations: *Zondervan Illustrated Bible Background Commentary* Series, the *IVP Bible Background Commentary, The Greco-Roman World of the New Testament Era, Ancient Near Eastern Themes in Biblical Theology, A History of the Ancient Near East,* and *An Introduction to the Old Testament.* Each of these offers a wealth of information that will bump any one-dimensional study to 3-D in no time!

Bible Doctrine

Bible doctrine books serve more as a side-note than directly pertinent to hermeneutics but still remain a valuable tool. Bible doctrine books are theology books that help us process through and understand the key and significant doctrines of Christianity. Doctrines include subjects like the Trinity, Salvation, Sin, Redemption, the Holy Spirit, the Church, etc. Theology books walk us through each of these main doctrines of Christianity and provide the major views of each. They argue for the best one, based on Scripture and other factors.

They might not be necessary for hermeneutics studies, but if you come across a certain passage with a major theology doctrine represented, a theology book is a helpful resource. A couple of highly recommended ones are *Christian Theology* by Millard Erickson, and *Systematic Theology* by Wayne Grudem. You can't go wrong with these at your fingertips!

Recommended Publishers

We've delved into several different types of books, all of which are fabulous resources for our studies, but now we need to mention a warning before going further. Just because something is published does not mean it's accurate or worth reading. Crazy people permeate academia like every other venue, and some publishers publish just about anything to make some good old-fashioned dough. It's a tragedy, but it's true.

We need to find out which publishers are worth trusting and then limit our purchases (at least to use as resources) to them. Some publishers still take pride in what they're sponsoring, and we've got to capitalize on that and support them in their quest for quality material. Here are some recommendations: LifeWay, Zondervan, InterVarsity Press, Moody, Baker, Tyndale, Harvest House, and NavPress. Though not a comprehensive list by any means, it gives you a good head start!

Computer Software

Now that we've sufficiently covered in-print resources, let's get hip with technology and venture into the world of the Internet! The Internet is full of some great resources and information. However, it offers just as much nonsense that's not worth two seconds of our time. We must exercise extreme caution when choosing Web sites and software to use with our studies.

How do we know whether a Web site is doctrinally and theologically sound? We can look for and thoroughly dissect its statement of faith or doctrinal statement. Most worthwhile Web sites state one of those two things, so read it carefully. If it is accurate and biblically sound, you can proceed with fair certainty that the materials offered through the site are safe to use.

However, even sound Web sites have a couple of kinks in them, so use caution. This doesn't mean you must second-guess everything you come across. That would make study time dismal! But if you find yourself reading about a timeline, background information, etc., you can be fairly certain it's legit. Caution should be exercised when we venture into the commentary and/or application genre of literature.

The best way to keep your guard up in this department is to find the author's name, then look up that person. Google him, baby! Make sure he's qualified to run his mouth. Check to see whether he has credentials, preferably a degree or two in Bible. This is most important. Also, make sure the author is published by a solid publisher. Finally, look for qualified people or companies who support the author.

The above three points do not mean that anyone who doesn't have those qualifications should not be considered. However, use caution if an author has none of the qualifications listed.

We use so much caution because people are not God! They may accumulate a host of degrees from the most prestigious universities all over the world, but they are still fallible. That's why we use them for references, not for absolute truth. The Bible still remains our standard of measure for truth. As long as authors' opinions and words correspond with it, then we're good. Otherwise, move right past them to something else!

To get you started, here are some statement-of-faith-approved Web sites that offer lots of good, solid information: www.biblegateway.com, www.blueletterbible.org, www.bible.org, www.biblestudytools.com, www.biblos.com, and www.esword.net. E-Sword is a program you can download on your computer. It has different Bible translations, a place for note-taking, atlases, some commentaries, a concordance, and more. And the best part: it's free! Some additional downloads cost a few dollars, but you can get the program with lots of freebies to get you started.

You are now well-versed and equipped to tackle the world of biblical research. I hope you feel confident enough to get the ball rolling! Even if you're not quite there yet, take a deep breath and don't worry. We're going to work through it together! Let's continue our Step #1 discussion.

Step One: Meaning In Its Day

BROAD & NARROW OF STEP ONE

We discussed the broad focus of Step One. With the broad step, we focus on gathering general and historical background information about the book and chapters surrounding our passage. With it, we answer the main question of Step One: "What did the text mean to the original audience?" How were the autographs understood to those who originally received them? We find this out through observation.

This Step is all about observing the background, history, context, and actual text of the passage. We don't read anything into the text at this point (or ever), nor is this the time to draw conclusions. This is simply a time to observe. We do this best by answering questions like, "Who wrote the book?" "When was it written?" "To whom was it written?" "Why was the author writing?" "Where was it written?" "What was going on historically at the time?"

Since Philippians 2:1-10 is our example passage, let's work through the broad portion of Step One together.

STEP ONE OF PHILIPPIANS 2:1-10

Broad Focus/Big Picture

1. **Who is the author of the passage?**

    How to find it: Commentary or study Bible

    Answer: Paul

2. **What are some interesting facts about him?**
    How to find it: Commentary, study Bible, encyclopedia (in-print or online), Bible dictionary, or the Bible itself starting in Acts

Answer(s):
- Arguably the greatest man of God who ever lived
- Born around the same time as Christ
- "Saul" was his Hebrew name; "Paul" for the Gentile world (Acts 13:9)
- Converted on the road to Damascus (Acts 9), spent fourteen years training for ministry before going to Jerusalem (Galatians 2)
- Written during the two years Paul was imprisoned in Rome (over 700 miles from Philippi)

3. **To whom is this passage written?**

    How to find it: Commentary, study Bible, encyclopedia, Bible dictionary, or the first couple verses of Philippians itself

    Answer: The Philippian church

4. **What are some interesting details about the audience—the Philippian church?**

    How to find it: Bible encyclopedia, commentary, Scripture itself (Acts 16)

    Answer(s):[1]
    - The Philippians were the only church to help the apostle Paul with contributions, and did so four times (Phil 4:15, 2 Corinthians 8:1-5)
    - Seems the least Jewish of all the Pauline churches—no Jewish names mentioned

---

[1] Many of these answers (and the following) were learned from an accumulation of study from various resources (commentaries, encyclopedias, Bible dictionaries, etc.). Yet one great resource worth noting here that probably has all these answers and more is G. Walter, Hansen. *The Letter to the Philippians (Pillar New Testament Commentary).* Grand Rapids, Michigan: Wm. B. Eerdmans Publishing Company, 2009.

Step One: Meaning In Its Day

- Women seem prominent to a greater degree than other churches
- They were Roman citizens (all Philippians were)
- Ex-military and athletes were prominent, so Paul uses many appropriate figures of speech (life as a race toward the goal-3:14)
- There was no synagogue in Philippi, but there was a place of prayer (Acts 16:13)
- First European church founded by Paul, on his second missionary journey in AD 52

5. **What is the history of the audience's city/location?**

   How to find it: Bible encyclopedia, commentary, Bible dictionary, any kind of Bible background book/resource

   Answer(s):
   - A Macedonian town on the plain east of Mount Pangaeus
   - Founded by Philip II, father of Alexander the Great, in 358/7 BC
   - Amphipolis was the capital
   - Had a school of medicine connected with a guild of physicians, which the followers of early Greek medicine scattered through the Hellenistic world
   - Became a Roman colony in 42 BC and a home for discharged Roman army veterans
   - Since it was a Roman colony, it enjoyed all the privileges and benefits of Roman citizenship—exempt from taxes, governed under Roman law
   - Modeled after Rome—Roman arches, bathhouses, forums, and temples
   - Latin was the official language of Rome (and Philippi), although Greek was prominent too

- The imperial cult—worship of the emperor—was the most prominent religion in the city

6. **What was the author's relationship to the biblical audience?**

    How to find it: Bible encyclopedia, commentary, Bible dictionary, book of Philippians

   Answer(s):
   - Paul cared about them greatly
   - He was loyal and loving to them and never lost an opportunity to visit them
   - One of Paul's favorite churches, if not the favorite (Phil. 1:7-8; 1:25-26)
   - Paul and the Philippians were friends
   - Paul deliberately stayed away from a patron-protégé relationship with them, unlike with other letters to churches ("apostleship," "father," etc.)

7. **What was the audience's relationship with God? What were their strengths, struggles, etc.?**

    How to find: Book of Philippians, Bible commentary, encyclopedia, any backgrounds book/resource

   Answer(s):
   - They had a good relationship with God
   - Strengths:
     - Participated in the gospel with Paul from the beginning (1:5)
     - They prayed for him and the continued spread of the gospel (1:19)
     - They were progressing and joyous in their faith (1:25)

- God was at work in them (2:13)
- Many were "perfect" or mature, and Paul wanted them to continue living to the standard they had obtained (3:15)
  - Encouragements from Paul
    - To conduct themselves in a manner worthy of the gospel so they could stand firm in one spirit striving for faith (1:27)
    - To be of the same mind, maintain the same love, and be united and intent on one purpose, to consider others higher than themselves (2:1-2)
    - Not to grumble or complain (2:14)
    - To rejoice (3:1)
    - To work out their disputes (4:1)

8. **What is the predominant theme(s) of the book containing the passage?**

   How to find: Bible commentary, Bible encyclopedia, book of Philippians, online articles written about the book at www.bible.org, etc.

   Answer(s):
   - Unity, especially considering the diversity of cultures, religions, and citizenships of people comprising the church and the city of Philippi
   - Joy, no matter the circumstance, because we live for Christ, who is worth far more than anything on Earth
   - Humility and selflessness as Christ is/was
   - The gospel and community of Christ. The word gospel is used more in Philippians than any other letter

9. **What literary form did the author write in?**

    How to find: commentary, encyclopedia, Bible dictionary

    Answer:
    - A letter, not limited to a certain type
    - Written to be read aloud to the church in Philippi

10. **When was this passage written?**

    How to find: commentary, encyclopedia, dictionary, study Bible

    Answer: Traditionally AD 63 or 64, eleven or twelve years after he founded it in Acts 16.

11. **Is this passage in the Old or New Testament?**

    How to find: Bible index

    Answer: New Testament

12. **What covenant is this passage under?**

    How to find: Look at its placement in Scripture. If it's after Christ, it's the New Covenant that He established and that we live in today. If it's before Him, then observe exactly when it is—Abrahamic, Mosaic, etc.

    Answer: The New Covenant

13. **What is the historical context of this passage?** What was the audience going through when this passage was written?

    How to find it: commentary, encyclopedia, dictionary, study Bible, book of Philippians

Answer:
- The Philippians were steadfast, growing believers who supported Paul more than any other church
- Philippi itself "was an old Macedonian city which had been turned into a Roman colony. It was both Greek and Roman in its characteristics."[2]
- The church had sent Ephaphroditus to check on Paul and bring him supplies while he was in prison. Paul returned a letter to the Philippians through him
- They experienced disunity (4:2), suffering (1:12-26; 2:27-30), opponents of the faith (1:15-17, 28; 3:2), and saw Gentile Christians who were living as enemies of the cross (3:18-19)

You're now completed the "broad" portion of Step One! Congrats! All of that may seem overwhelming, but before you flip out, take note of a couple things:

You Do Not Need to Provide All This Information Every Time You Study Scripture

The beauty of hermeneutics is the freedom you have to go as deep as you want in your studies, but you don't have to go as deep as the example above. Keep in mind the hermeneutic principles and rules of chapters three and four. Think of the rules and principles of hermeneutics as food—the necessary but not-so-glamorous kind like carrots and broccoli. They contain the nutrients you need to stay alive (interpret Scripture correctly), but they may lack the glam you're going for sometimes. The Five Steps, however, are the scrumptious, five-star gourmet food like tiramisu that melts as soon as it hits your tongue.

---

[2] Jeffers, James S. *The Greco-Roman world of the New Testament era: exploring the background of early Christianity*. Downers Grove, Ill.: InterVarsity Press, 1999. Print.

Super yummy and delectable, it too has the nutrients that keep you kicking. However, you don't need to eat this kind of food all the time, nor will you necessarily want to since it's rich and heavy. But when you do, you enjoy it immensely, savoring it bite by bite.

That describes the relationship between the principles/rules and steps of hermeneutics. The principles and rules are the bare bones—crucial and non-negotiable to your studies. They give you the nutrients necessary to keep your biblical studies alive and healthy. Without them, you'll have a difficult time remaining true to what God is communicating through His Word. You will tend to put yourself above Scripture, not the other way around.

The Steps, on the other hand, are not vital. They are exquisite and teach you things that you won't learn by sticking strictly to the basics, but a proper study of Scripture does not depend on them. We reap what we sow in hermeneutics. The Five Steps of hermeneutics require work—a lot more work than the basics. You will spend more hours working on the Steps than you ever would in a basic study of the Word.

But all that work is worth it. You will learn much and will gain a greater understanding of the passage at hand than you ever would with the basics. The passage will illuminate before your eyes, and your mind will overflow with all the golden nuggets of information making the passage come alive in your heart and mind. And the best part is that you can start enjoying the fruit of your labor early in the process! Each answer you discover with the Steps contributes to your interpretation. It's exciting, yet it takes time, energy, focus, and dedication.

If you're in a season craving to go deep with God in His Word, the Steps are your best bet. If, however, you're not quite there, pore over the principles and general rules of hermeneutics based on each genre, and make sure your studies in Scripture align with them. Then, when things start settling down, dig into the Five Steps and get your study on!

As you can see, there's a lot of flexibility within the hermeneutic process. Through prayer, observe and assess where you are now and how deeply God may be prompting you to go in your biblical studies.

Step One: Meaning In Its Day

You have many options. Part of the fun is figuring out what works for you. Then get at it!

This Shouldn't All Be Done in One Sitting

If you decide you're ready for the Five Steps and want to get your hands dirty in this process, be sure you make time for it. The Five Steps should not be rushed. An exquisite meal from your favorite high-end restaurant is best enjoyed over the course of an hour or two or three. We don't cram it down our throats in five minutes. Where's the pleasure in that? You would hardly remember what it tasted like! And talk about a total waste of money. If you're going to gorge, do it with a one-dollar taco from Taco Bell, not a forty-dollar steak from Ruth's Chris.

The same principle applies to the Five Steps. We can't complete it in a half-hour. Depending on how deeply you go into your studies, you might complete it in an hour or two. But that's not the norm. Completing these steps thoroughly will usually take several hours— again, depending on the depth to which you want to take them. And though this may sound daunting, time will fly! You'll spend most of your time finding information and researching, but you can keep that in check by using the reliable resources in the section above.

We also have the freedom to decide *when* to conduct our studies. We all operate on different timetables. Some of us prefer early mornings, bundled up in our PJs and a blanket with a cup of joe. Night owls might consider setting aside some study time after dinner or before going to bed. If you're busy from sunup to sundown, squeeze it in whenever you can spare five or ten minutes. There's no perfect timeframe or schedule for study. Figure out what works best for you, then go for it!

You can practice hermeneutics in many different ways. There's no one-size-fits-all approach. The Five-Step process is good, but it can be used in entirety, picked apart, implemented in pieces, and/or ignored completely! What we can't ignore are the principles and rules we learned in chapters three and four. Those are the bedrock to the hermeneutic foundation—the cement and mortar, not the lattice and paint. The Steps complement and expand on the rules. They decorate and give them that little something extra. Okay, lots extra.

I pray you understand the relationship between the principles and Steps after having worked through the broad portion of Step One. This first portion of this Step gathers a wealth of information so we can answer the question, "What did it mean to the original audience?"[3] Always keep this question in the back of your mind when you read, whether or not you're working through the steps. We must always pay attention to context. But can you see how the principles and steps relate to each other? They complement each other extremely well, with the Steps giving us a guideline for putting the principles into practice.

The information of the broad portion of Step One keeps the passage in context (Rule #3). We use the general rule of hermeneutics we learned in chapter three. Step One then allows us to develop that rule and get a better understanding of the context surrounding our passage. We start understanding what the passage meant to the original audience, putting names and places to the text. When we understand the context, our understanding of the passage itself improves astronomically!

Yet we cannot stop at the broad focus of our passage/book. We must zoom in to the passage itself. The exercises may resemble assignments you did for your fifth-grade English class, but the more we observe, the more we learn, and the better we understand.

THE NARROW FOCUS

The narrow focus of Step One shifts from the big picture to the text itself. In this portion of Step One, we dissect the text and objectively observe everything we can about it. Drawing conclusions still isn't

---

[3] Paraphrased from Duvall and Hays, *Grasping God's Word*, 22.

our goal. We're not trying to determine what the passage means or could mean; our goal is simply to determine facts already present in the passage.

How do we go about this? I heartily recommend starting by printing out the passage on a sheet of paper, with the verses spread out from the top to the bottom of the page. This gives us lots of room to write our notes and observations. Then we return to our favorite point from above: read, read, read! Focus on the following questions:

- What sticks out? Words, phrases, names, titles, places, etc.
- Does the passage contain any lists?
- Is there a timeline or progression of events?
- Where does the story take place?
- What transitional words are used? (And, but, or, nor, for, yet, therefore, etc.) What do they connect?
- Are there any contrasts or comparisons?
- Who/what do the pronouns refer to?
- Are there any commands?
- Any questions?
- Any exclamatory statements?
- Are there any figures of speech? If so, what do they refer to?

I could list other questions here, but this gives you a good place to start. When answering these questions, mark up the paper! Get different colored pencils/pens and start circling, drawing, underlining, etc., so you can fully dissect the passage. In the following diagram, you'll see what the Philippians passage we're working on might look like after enduring the narrow portion of Step One.

More Than Words

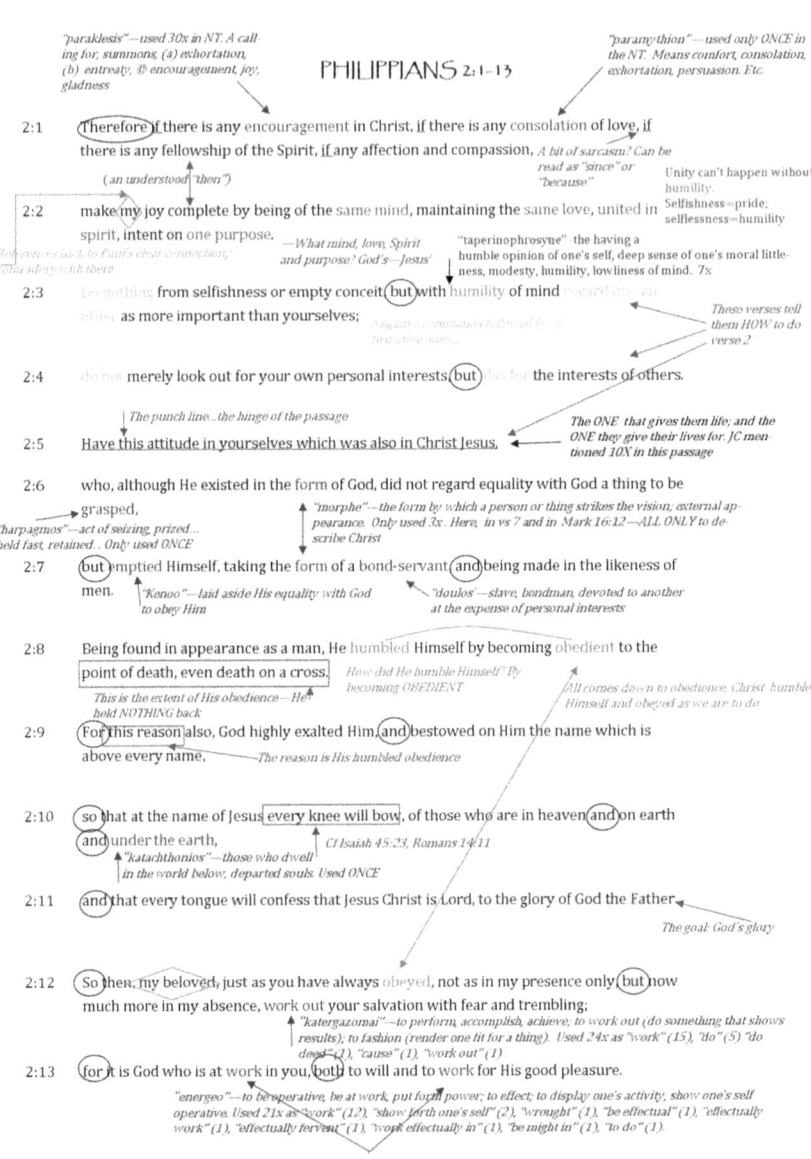

PHILIPPIANS 2:1-13

"*paraklesis*"—used 30x in NT. A calling for, summons, (a) exhortation, (b) entreaty, © encouragement, joy, gladness

"*paramythion*"—used only ONCE in the NT. Means comfort, consolation, exhortation, persuasion. Etc.

2:1 Therefore, if there is any encouragement in Christ, if there is any consolation of love, if there is any fellowship of the Spirit, if any affection and compassion, *A bit of sarcasm? Can be read as "since" or "because"*

(an understood "then")

Unity can't happen without humility.
Selfishness=pride; selflessness=humility

2:2 make my joy complete by being of the same mind, maintaining the same love, united in spirit, intent on one purpose. —What mind, love, Spirit and purpose? God's—Jesus'

References back to Paul's close connection; 'Y'all obey with them

"*tapeinophrosyne*"- the having a humble opinion of one's self, deep sense of one's moral littleness, modesty, humility, lowliness of mind. 7x

2:3 Do nothing from selfishness or empty conceit, but with humility of mind regard one another as more important than yourselves;

Again a command followed by 3 infinitive ones.

These verses tell them HOW to do verse 2

2:4 do not merely look out for your own personal interests, but also for the interests of others.

| The punch line...the hinge of the passage

The ONE that gives them life; and the ONE they give their lives for. JC mentioned 10X in this passage

2:5 Have this attitude in yourselves which was also in Christ Jesus,

2:6 who, although He existed in the form of God, did not regard equality with God a thing to be grasped,

"*harpagmos*"—act of seizing, prized... held fast, retained. . Only used ONCE

"*morphe*"—the form by which a person or thing strikes the vision; external appearance. Only used 3x. Here, in vs 7 and in Mark 16:12—ALL ONLY to describe Christ

2:7 but emptied Himself, taking the form of a bond-servant and being made in the likeness of men.

"*Kenoo*"—laid aside His equality with God to obey Him

"*doulos*"—slave, bondman, devoted to another at the expense of personal interests

2:8 Being found in appearance as a man, He humbled Himself by becoming obedient to the point of death, even death on a cross. *How did He humble Himself? By becoming OBEDIENT*

This is the extent of His obedience—He held NOTHING back

All comes down to obedience. Christ humbled Himself and obeyed as we are to do

2:9 For this reason also, God highly exalted Him, and bestowed on Him the name which is above every name, —*The reason is His humbled obedience*

2:10 so that at the name of Jesus every knee will bow, of those who are in heaven and on earth and under the earth, *Cf Isaiah 45:23, Romans 14:11*

"*katachthonios*"—those who dwell in the world below, departed souls. Used ONCE

2:11 and that every tongue will confess that Jesus Christ is Lord, to the glory of God the Father.

The goal: God's glory

2:12 So then, my beloved, just as you have always obeyed, not as in my presence only, but now much more in my absence, work out your salvation with fear and trembling;

"*katergazomai*"—to perform, accomplish, achieve, to work out (do something that shows results); to fashion (render one fit for a thing). Used 24x as "work" (15), "do" (5) "do deed" (1), "cause" (1), "work out" (1)

2:13 for it is God who is at work in you, both to will and to work for His good pleasure.

"*energeo*"—to be operative, be at work, put forth power; to effect; to display one's activity, show one's self operative. Used 21x as "work" (12), "show forth one's self" (2), "wrought" (1), "be effectual" (1), "effectually work" (1), "effectually fervent" (1), "work effectually in" (1), "be might in" (1), "to do" (1).

Try to get as close to and intimate with the passage as you can. Notice everything possible about the words, grammar, and what's going on in the passage. It is amazing how much you learn about a passage after doing the narrow Step!

Once you answer the aforementioned questions and observe all you can about the passage, summarize it in your own words. This forces us to engage the passage and own what it says. We're not trying to rewrite Scripture; we're simply showing that we understand it.

Word Studies

You may have noticed in our narrow-focus example that we defined several words of interest and placed some nifty little facts next to them. That information is derived from a process we call word studies. Word studies play a crucial role in hermeneutics, particularly in the narrow portion of Step One, because we get to explore particular words in more depth. Any words that stick out to you, are repeated, or seem at all interesting are worth conducting word studies on.

Word studies are segments of research pursued to discover a word's original meaning and how it was used in the original language. As we've mentioned in earlier studies, Hebrew and Greek are the original languages of Scripture. Whenever we find ourselves questioning the meaning or use of a particular word in our English Bibles, we can and should seek to discover what they meant and how they were used in the original languages.

Remember, English translations limit the originals words because languages differ from one another and can be complex. For example, in English we have one word for "love." We love our spouse, our children, our shoes, and pizza! Deep down we know that our affection for each of those things differs greatly from the others, yet only one word avails itself to us.

Not in Greek. Greeks use three words for love: agape, phileo, and eros. Agape refers to unconditional love, phileo is a love between friends; and eros evokes a passionate, sensual love. When we come across the word "love" in our New Testaments, it's helpful to find out which of the three "love" words was used.

How do we do this? First, get out your concordance! We need concordances when we conduct word studies because they contain every word written in Scripture, its definition(s), how many times it's used, and every time it's used.

Let's dig in! Our Philippians passage contains the word *grasped*. Let's study it. Here's how it's used in our passage:

> Have this attitude in yourselves which was also in Christ Jesus, who, although He existed in the form of God, did not regard equality with God a thing to be *grasped* (*emphasis mine*).

First, we look it up in our concordances. We need to determine what the word *could* mean before we determine what the word *does* mean.[4] Again, one word may have several different meanings. Because Scripture is our authority (we're not its authority), we don't get to determine which definition to assign to any given word. Rather, we observe the context of the word, how it's used in the verse, passage, then in the rest of the book.

The correct definition for some words will be fairly obvious, but not for all. When we struggle to determine the correct definition, we can look outside our current verse to other examples where the word was used in the same book, another book written by the same author, or another book in the same testament. Observing how the word was used in other contexts helps us understand how it was used in ours.

Back to our example of *grasped*. Since online concordances are faster and more convenient, for this example, we'll proceed that way.

---

[4] Duvall and Hays, *Grasping God's Word*, 139.

Here's a play-by-play instruction checklist, showing how to conduct a brief word study using an online concordance:

1. Look up www.blueletterbible.org in your internet browser.
2. Under "Bible/Dictionary Search," type the verse into the search box: "Philippians 2:5-6." (The default Bible version on this site is KJV. If you'd like to change it, simply choose another version by clicking the "Version" button next to the search box).
3. Hit "Search" and the passage will come up.
4. When it does, scroll down to verse 6 and click the "C" square (located to the left of the verse reference). This will give you the concordance entries for all the words in the verse.
5. Scroll down again to "grasped" and click on the middle column number for the word (this is the Strong's reference number).

Viola! Now you see the word in Greek, the transliteration in English, its possible definitions and the ways it is used every other time in Scripture.

The transliteration (or the English way to pronounce a word of another language), of *grasped* is *harpagmos*. Its definitions are "1) the act of seizing, robbery, 2) a thing seized or to be seized—a) booty, to deem anything a prize, b) a thing to be seized upon or to be held fast, retained." It's used only once in the entire Bible, which is rare. But that makes it easier for us to determine a definition, since the possibilities are limited.

The reason multiple definitions are provided refers back to the one-language-cannot-be-translated-verbatim-to-another-language concept. English words tend to be far less elaborate than Hebrew and Greek words, which is precisely the case with our word *grasped*. You can tell by observing the definitions from Blueletterbible.org that *harpagmos* carries more weight than our English word *grasped*. There's undoubtedly a sense of force and effort behind this word. Therefore, our verse can be paraphrased, "He did not consider equality with God a thing to be seized, held fast to, or retained." Boosts the imagery, doesn't it?

That's the beauty of word studies. We learn a lot through them, and our understanding of the text increases greatly when we take a few moments to go deeper. Word study away, dear friends! (P.S. That was obviously an abridged version of word-study methods. If you'd like a more in-depth walk-through of word studies, read pages 132-156 in *Grasping God's Word* by Duvall and Hays).

REFLECT

We are now in a position to complete Step One of hermeneutics (Meaning In Its Day). We've researched and discovered the broad focus of the book of our passage, dug into the passage itself, summarized it, and even thrown in a word study for good measure! Working through and completing Step One is important because it serves as the next part of our foundation for the rest of our hermeneutic Steps.

Step One builds on our solid foundation of principles and rules of hermeneutics. We're continuing in the journey! Again, going deeper and getting intimate with the Word requires effort, but I promise you this: it's worth it!

With Step One under our belts; let's move on to Step Two: Differences Between Then and Now. Now that we have observed, it's time to *think* and meditate upon those observations. Step One establishes our momentum. Step Two increases the momentum and begins putting all the pieces together. Ready?

Step Two—Differences Between Then and Now

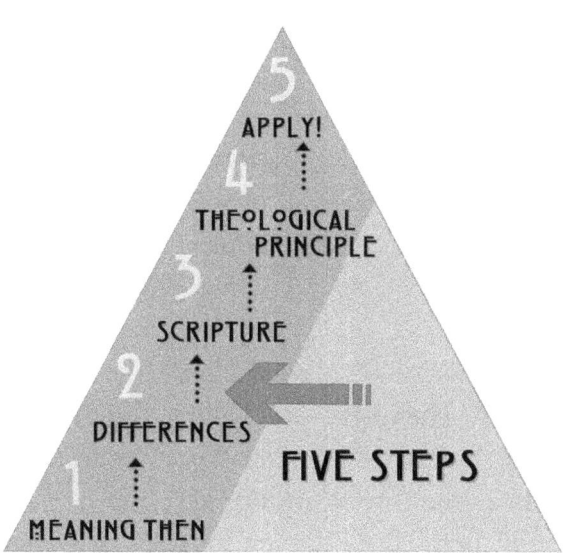

The key word of Step Two is *think,* which means we're going to get our hands even dirtier (like kids again—fun!). This Step is all about discovering the hurdles that hinder us from taking our passage as-is and applying it to our lives. Although we can apply some passages of Scripture by using minimal hermeneutic effort, we must place the majority of Scripture within its own original context before we can move on in our hermeneutic journey.

The main question to ask in this Step is, "What are the differences between the original audience and me?" If we don't recognize the differences, we will not be able to bridge the gap between us and move on in our interpretation and application processes. The differences between us and the original audience greatly impact the way Scripture applies to our lives. Therefore, we must be thorough to discern what those differences are!

Remember, Scripture was written at a particular time, in a particular place, to a particular people. We (Americans living today) are not included in that "particular people" category, at least, not directly. Knowing the differences that separate us will help us in the following ways:

1) We will become aware of any biases we bring to the table
2) We will understand the true context of the passage better
3) We will relate more to the original audience so we can move on to finding our theological principle and apply it to our lives

Think of it in terms of a relationship. Relationships are built on communication, chemistry, and learning more about the other person. If we don't understand someone, there's not much hope for developing a meaningful relationship with him. For example, if you are married, how long did it take you to realize that men and women are completely different in the brain-functioning department? Men and women do not process things the same way, nor do they express themselves or communicate in identical fashions. This often leads to frustrating moments between spouses!

Putting a man and woman together to cohabitate without explaining to either of them how the other operates is a recipe for disaster! Well, the same goes for our relationship with the original audiences of Scripture. We can never hope for a healthy relationship *with* them without knowing anything *about* them. We can't hope to bridge the enormous gap of differences between us without first realizing what those differences are. The goal of Step Two, then, is to begin a relationship of sorts with the audience of our passage by determining what barriers separate us.

How do we go about Step Two? It's similar to Step One in that we'll answer questions. But this time, we'll think our observations through more during our research. Some questions we'll answer are: "What nationality was the original audience?" "What nationality am I?" "What language did the original audience speak?" "What language(s) do I speak?" "What cultural differences are there between them and me?" "Are there any political/governmental differences?"

This is just a start, but a good one at that! So what do you say about getting at it with our passage?

Step Two for Philippians 2:1-10

1. **What nationality was the original audience? Me?**

    How do find: Commentary, Bible background book, encyclopedia

    Answer: Philippians—Roman citizens; American

2. **What language did the original audience speak? Me?**

    How to find: Commentary, Bible background book, encyclopedia

    Answer: Latin and Greek; English

3. What cultural differences are there between them and me?

How to find: Bible background book, encyclopedia, commentary, dictionary

Answer:[1]
- Slavery
    - Nearly every culture had its own form of slavery
- Marriage
    - Only marriages between Roman husbands and wives were protected and upheld by Roman law
    - Minimum ages: Twelve for girls (typically twelve to eighteen), fourteen for boys (typically much later, even thirty). There was usually a five-year age difference between husband and wife
    - Arranged by parents
- Infidelity:
    - Unfaithfulness in men didn't matter
    - If the wife was unfaithful, she was punished
    - It was a crime for unmarried or married men to commit fornication with unmarried "respectable" women
    - Caesar Augustus made adultery a crime in 18 BC
- Family Structure
    - The male head (paterfamilias) had absolute power. He alone could own property under Roman law, and his power was unbroken until death

---

[1] Many of the following answers are derived from *The Greco-Roman World* by Jeffers and *The International Standard Bible Encyclopedia*.

- *Fathers.* Showed love by imposing structure and desiring their children to be productive. More strict than mothers. Cherished children and showed affection and tenderness. Expected to teach their sons a trade or give them the means to make a living
- *Mothers.* Transmitter of traditional morality. Ideally a firm disciplinarian. Almost fully responsible for her daughters' education (which was comprised mostly of domestic skills.) Bond between mother and son was usually stronger than mother and daughter because daughters were married off at early ages and sons stayed around and were involved in families much longer
- *Children.* Took their status from their father in Roman marriages. Took status from mother in extralegal marriages. Were expected to submit to their parents and honor them by caring for them in their old age. Sons set up their own households when they got married, but they were still under the legal authority of their paterfamilias until they died
- Families were small (typically no more than two or three children)

- Women
  - Were free to take part in the public life of the cities of the Empire during NT times
  - Ideal wife: Does not cheat on her spouse, but puts up with his affairs. Does not reject his friends. Does not leave behind his gods for foreign religions. Does not make a public

spectacle of herself. Manages her husband's household
- If a wife became a Christian, it could lead to serious problems
- Women in non-legal marriages could get away with a lot more because they weren't monitored by the state

- Divorce
  - Simple procedure: send one's spouse a letter of intent to divorce
  - Reasons: Failure to have children (assumed to be the woman's fault), political reasons, continued adultery, desire to initiate and start a new marriage
  - Roman divorce included separating a mother from her children because the children legally belonged to the father
- Food
  - Food was produced in the country and manufactured in the city
- Education
  - Facilities were typically very simple—a hut or shed in front of a house or separated from the public by a thin partition
  - The students began with wax tablets for writing and progressed to papyrus sheets or parchments of worthless manuscripts
  - Boys and girls were educated equally until around age fourteen, when the boys would prepare for a public career
  - Curriculum was based almost entirely on Greek and Latin literature
  - Rome offered no formal technical education.

Children of lower classes depended entirely upon learning the family trade
- Professions
    - "They gave the greatest honor to those wealthy persons whose income came from agriculture."[2]
    - Commercial fishing was a huge profession, but fishermen were not independent because of the high cost of tools/resources
    - Trading: "Roman aristocrats considered trade to be a dirty business in which no self-respecting member of the upper class would be involved."[3]
- Banking/Debt
    - Many deposited their money into temples, thinking the gods would protect it
    - Wealthy Roman families practiced money-lending, becoming their own private banks
    - Were permitted under Roman law to bind into permanent slavery for temporary debt bondage
    - Women were excluded from banking
- Manufacturing
    - For the most part left to small businesses and individuals (large manufacturing centers were rare)
    - Merchants were known by their occupations (much like today)
    - Included weaving, bakeries, pottery, engravers, fullers, fine dyes, tent making, tanning
- Religion
    - Rome was not successful at controlling religious

---

[2] Greco Roman World, 19.
[3] Greco Roman World, 22.

innovation. Christianity benefited greatly from this
- Rome didn't recognize the difference between Christianity and Judaism until AD 60s.

4. Are there any political/governmental differences between them and me?

How to find: Bible background book, commentary, encyclopedia, dictionary

Answer: (Original audience: Roman Empire)
- Army
  - Made up of men "whose character was essentially that of mercenaries, and whose term of continuous service varied in different divisions from 16-26 years."[4] Comprised of the Imperial Guard, The Legions. "Auxilia", Numeri (didn't develop until the second century AD), and the Fleet—highest officials in the equestrian class
- Roman Empire
  - Octavian (Augustus) was the founder of the Roman Empire which formally began on January 16, 27 BC—signalized by the bestowal of the title "Augustus." Augustus controlled legislation, administration and the armies
  - Pax Romana: "Roman Peace." First established when Augustus reigned and the temple of Janus was closed. The Romans conquered like barbarians and ruled their conquests like a humane statesman, forcing everyone into peace under their rule. All national barriers were

---
[4] http://bibleencyclopedia.com/roman.htm

removed. Famous cities like Alexandria, Rome, Antioch were meeting places of all races and languages.[5]
- The Roman Empire was a one-man show. Augustus Caesar or nothing!

5. **Is there a difference of covenant between them and me? (If so, what theological truths are different/have changed since then?)**

   How to find: Use the information from Step One, asking what covenant the passage is under. If there's a difference, write about it

   Answer: There is no difference in covenant between the Philippians and us

6. **Are there any situational differences between them and me? (Economy, struggles, challenges, specific historical events)**

   How to find: Bible background books, commentaries, encyclopedias, dictionaries, study Bibles, etc.

   Answer: We covered this in the first question. But if something sticks out that wasn't included in the aforementioned answers, write it here.

REFLECT

My goodness, we're learning a bunch! I should say so! After all that, we deserve a break, but not for long! But before we do, can you see

---

[5] http://bibleencyclopedia.com/roman.htm

how vast are the differences in nationality, language, culture, politics, and government between the original audience of Philippians and us? And they're more similar to us than most cultures from biblical times.

Understanding these differences impacts the way you and I read and interpret Philippians and our passage within it. After going through Steps One and Two, it's impossible to read this passage the same again. The monotone transforms to magnificence as our minds wrap around what it was like to be the Philippian church, instructed by the apostle Paul himself.

Steps One and Two allow us to make a connection with the Philippian believers. Think about it. When you meet someone who strikes you as pleasant, you begin spending time with him in order to develop a relationship. Somewhere in the beginning of this process, you make a connection that creates a bond between the two of you. That connection is crucial to the development of any relationship because if you're not on the same page with him, your relationship probably won't develop much further.

That's why Steps One and Two are vital to the development and understanding of our passage—or any other passage in Scripture, for that matter. Learning the context and understanding the differences between the original audience and ourselves enables us to establish a connection or bond with them. We're on their same wavelength now! We're clued into what they experienced—how it was for them, living in a radical time in God's plan of redemption for the world!

When we place ourselves in their shoes, we bond with them. This bond keeps our perspective on par with God's. The more we connect with the original audience (getting into their mindsets and situations) the more objective we become when we get to the interpretation phase of our hermeneutics process (which, by golly, is coming up rather soon)! Savor this time in your studies of and with the Word. Take delight in the wealth of knowledge you're accumulating. It has far greater benefits than you realize; this I promise you!

Step Three—Scripture in Light of Scripture

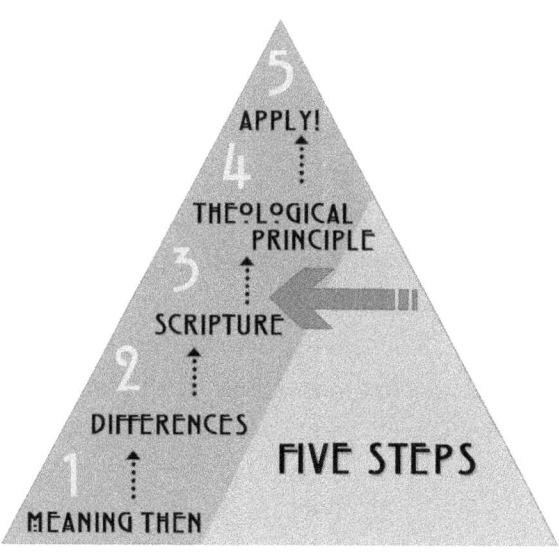

We now move from gathering information *about* the passage to *interpreting* the passage itself. The key word to this Step is *expand*. We first observe, then think, and now we expand upon what we have learned. We started with the passage, went beyond it to discover a host of information, and now we're returning our focus back to the passage, at least at first.

This Step asks two questions. First, "What are the main themes represented in the passage?" It's super-important to grasp the main themes of our passage because our next question is: "What other passages of Scripture teach, talk about, and/or address these themes?" With this question, we take the general themes, usually three to five in number, and find other passages of Scripture that reference them. Why? Because then we get a fuller, more vibrant understanding of the truths God reveals throughout the rest of His Word.

Remember, the first part of the goal of hermeneutics is to find the theological principle of the passage (Step Four) so we can be transformed by applying it to our lives (Step Five). Going from Step Two to Step Four without a bridge poses a daunting task! Enter: Step Three.

In Step Three we glean the main themes of the passage and then explore the rest of Scripture to see what else is said about those themes. It is actually a lot of fun because contexts of other chapters/books shed light on the themes represented in our passage. By exploring the rest of Scripture, we perceive a more complete picture of those particular themes. This prevents us from getting a narrow-minded view of the theme in our passage. Also, we get to see different characteristics and views of the themes, which makes His Truth that much more real in our lives and hearts. Let's dig in so you can see for yourself!

MAIN THEMES

What are the main themes in our Philippian passage? A mini-caveat here: there's no absolute right answer. Some of us will come up with one or two, others three or four. Verbiage and phrasing might be different because these are general themes, but you'll learn to spot them easily, especially after all the groundwork we've laid through Steps One and Two.

A couple of questions making theme hunting easier are: "What is the author trying to communicate with the audience?" and "Are there any key action words (verbs are often repeated) that show us what a theme would be?" When we read our Philippian passage for the umpteenth time, certain themes stand out, do they not?

Verses 1 and 2 touch upon a common theme in Scripture, especially the New Testament: unity. Notice Paul's repetitive instruction to be of the *same* mind, maintaining the *same* love, *united* in spirit, intent on *one* purpose. Sounds like unity to me. Unity definitely comprises a key theme in this passage.

Verse 3 introduces a theme that carries through the remainder of the passage. The key word here: humility (theme #2). Paul desperately wants the Philippian believers to be united, and the only way to do that is to be humble. Pride and unity are mutually exclusive. Paul addresses this and moves on to the third major theme of the passage: obedience. With Christ as the ultimate example of both unity and humility, Paul also uses Him to exemplify the theme of obedience.

Unity and humility before God and others is accomplished only when we live in obedience to Him—as Christ does. He doesn't display a small amount of obedience; rather, Christ remains obedient to the greatest extent—to the point of death. He holds nothing back, letting the Father accomplish His mission and purposes. This is the kind of obedience it takes to remain united and humble before both God and man.

What is the result of Christ's obedience (vs. 9-10)? He is exalted and lifted up (theme #4). This passage exalts Christ and lifts Him up as the ultimate example for us to follow. We've now articulated the four major themes in this passage: unity, humility, obedience, and Christ's exaltation. Quite an amazing collection of thematic goodness!

Exploring Our Themes in the Rest of Scripture

Now let's explore each theme in other passages in Scripture. We'll start with the first one: unity. We'll look for this word in the rest of Philippians, then in the New Testament, and then in the Old Testament. We'll practice this pattern with each theme—starting close to home and working outward (reverse funnel style). This way, we ensure our understanding of what our author was trying to communicate about each theme. Then we'll see what the other authors of his testament have to say about it, and then we'll get input from the authors of the other testament. (For future studies in other books, follow this same pattern: same book, same testament, other testament.)

Before we begin, let's walk through our method of accomplishing this. Get out those resources, friends! First we discover other passages that use the word describing our theme. If you remember from our word-study discussion, we look up the word in our concordances, either in print or online. So, for our humility theme, we look up the word humility, but also other words that correspond with that theme, such as humble, humbled, etc.

When looking for themes, we're not bound to one particular word. In fact, sometimes a story exemplifies the theme perfectly. Take the well-known story of Mary, the mother of Jesus. Think back to the story and look it up in Luke chapter one. The angel of the Lord appeared and told Mary she will give birth to the Messiah.

Say what? Perplexed, but once again confirmed by the angel, Mary responds, "Behold, the bondslave of the Lord; may it be done to me according to your word." Such a wonderful example of humility!

An angel appears to Mary, a teenageer about to be married, and says, "Hey, you're going to get pregnant (not by natural means, mind you), and the baby you deliver and will raise with your future husband, Joseph, is the Messiah of the universe. And oh, by the way, this means people will ridicule you and gossip about you because everyone is going to think you cheated on Joseph, or that you and Joseph weren't righteous enough to wait until you were married."

Obviously, that's mucho paraphrased, but you can imagine these things going through her mind. Her life was not her own anymore. Her plans, hopes, and dreams for her future were thrown off completely. Of course, God's plans always trump ours, and she realized this. With great humility, she said, "Let's do it!"

See how Mary sets an example of humility, yet the word humility is not in the story? This is perfectly acceptable (and actually totally awesome) to use for Step Three. Humility, like any other of our four themes, is not limited to words or obvious stories. If God brings to mind another story that displays humility, include it in your examples!

This brings us back to the process of Step Three. Start in Philippians. Find every mention of unity, humility, obedience, and exaltation of Christ. Then do the same for the rest of the New Testament and the Old Testament.

A rule of thumb is to find two or three examples for each one. (You can certainly give more if you like.) Find three examples of unity in Philippians, three in the New Testament, and three the Old Testament, then three examples of humility, and so on.

Is it clicking yet? I hope so. If not, it will when we put it into practice, so let's go! (FYI, two or three examples of every theme are written out for you; the others are included as references to show that there are lots more! You never have to settle on just three!)

STEP THREE: IN PHILIPPIANS

Humility

We may begin by looking up the words for "humility" and "humbled," which are used in our passage. This isn't necessary, but I find it helps sometimes. The word for "humility" in the original Greek is "tapeinophrosyne," which means, "a) having a humble opinion of one's self, b) a deep sense of one's (moral) littleness, c) modesty, humility, lowliness of mind."[1]

The word "humbled" is "tapeinoo," which means, "a) to make low, bring low, b) metaphor: to bring into a humble condition, reduce to meaner circumstances, c) to lower, depress—of one's soul; to bring down one's pride, to have a modest opinion of one's self, to behave in an unassuming manner, devoid of all haughtiness."[2]

Now that we grasp the words, let's see where else the words and theme of humility are represented throughout the rest of Philippians.

- Philippians 2:17—"But even if I am poured out like a drink offering on the sacrifice and service of your faith, I am glad and rejoice together with all of you."
  - Paul was being "poured out like a drink offering." (Lots of humility there!) for the Philippian believers
- Philippians 4:11-12—"I am not saying this because I am in need, for I have learned to be content in any circumstance. I have experienced times of need and times of abundance. In any and every circumstance I have learned the secret of contentment, whether I go satisfied or hungry, have plenty or nothing."
  - Pride is incompatible with contentment. But humility goes hand in hand with it

Unity

- Philippians 1:4-5—"I always pray with joy in my every prayer for all of you because of your participation in the gospel from the first day until now."

---

[1] http://www.blueletterbible.org/lang/lexicon/lexicon.cfm?Strong s=G5012&t=NASB
[2] http://www.blueletterbible.org/lang/lexicon/lexicon.cfm? Strongs=G5013&t=NASB

- Philippians 1:27—"Only conduct yourselves in a manner worthy of the gospel of Christ so that—whether I come to see you or whether I remain absent—I should hear that you are standing firm in one spirit, with one mind, by contending side by side for the faith of the gospel."

- Philippians 1:29-30—"For it has been granted to you not only to believe in Christ but also to suffer for Him, since you are encountering the same conflict that you saw me face and now hear that I am facing."

- Philippians 3:10-11; 4:14

Obedience

"Obedient" in 2:8—"hypekoos" means "giving ear, obedient."[3]

- Philippians 1:27—"Only conduct yourselves in a manner worthy of the gospel of Christ. . . ."

- Philippians 3:17—"Be imitators of me, brothers and sisters, and watch carefully those who are living this way, just as you have us as an example."

- Philippians 4:8-9—"Finally, brothers and sisters, whatever is true, whatever is worthy of respect, whatever is just, whatever is pure, whatever is lovely, whatever is commendable, if something is excellent or praiseworthy, think about these things. And what you have learned and received and heard and saw in me, do these things. And the God of peace will be with you."

---

[3] http://www.blueletterbible.org/lang/lexicon/lexicon.cfm? Strongs=G5255&t=NASB

Christ Lifted Up

"Christ" is used thirty-five times in Philippians, which is proportionally more than any other of Paul's writings. Romans uses it sixty-six times with sixteen chapters, 1 Corinthians: fifty-four times with sixteen chapters, 2 Corinthians: forty-four times with thirteen chapters, Ephesians: forty-three times with six chapters.

"Jesus" is referred to twenty-one times in Philippians, proportionally more than any other of Paul's writings. Romans comes closest with thirty-seven uses within sixteen chapters.

- Philippians 1:12-13—"Now I want you to know, brethren, that my circumstances have turned out for the greater progress of the gospel, so that my imprisonment in the cause of Christ has become well known throughout the whole praetorian guard and to everyone else."

- Philippians 1:18—"What then? Only that in every way, whether in pretense or in truth, Christ is proclaimed; and in this I rejoice."

- Philippians 1:20—"According to my earnest expectation and hope, that I will not be put to shame in anything, but that with all boldness, Christ will even now, as always, be exalted in my body, whether by life or by death."

- Philippians 3:7-8; Philippians 3:14; 3:20

THEMES IN THE SAME TESTAMENT

Humility

Another option we have with themes is to break them up. First we study what Jesus said about humility and how He demonstrated humility. Second, we study other examples and teachings in the rest of the New Testament. This is just an option, but a good one!

Jesus' examples:
- Matthew 20:26-28—"It is not this way among you, but whoever wishes to become great among you shall be your servant and whoever wishes to be first among you shall be your slave; just as the Son of Man did not come to be served, but to serve, and to give His life a ransom for many."

- Luke 22:27—"For who is greater, the one who reclines at the table or the one who serves? Is it not the one who reclines at the table? But I am among you as the one who serves."

- John 13:3, 13-15—"Jesus, knowing that the Father had given all things into His hands, and that He had come forth from God and was going back to God, got up from supper, and laid aside His garments, and taking a towel, He girded Himself . . . and began to wash the disciples feet. . . . 'You call Me Teacher and Lord; and you are right, for so I am. If I then, the Lord and Teacher washed your feet, you also ought to wash each other's feet. For I have given you an example that you also should do as I did to you.'"

- Ephesians 5:1-2

Other Examples/Teachings

- Romans 12:1—"Therefore I urge you, brethren, by the mercies of God, to present your bodies a living and holy sacrifice, acceptable to God, which is your spiritual service of worship. And do not be conformed to this world, but be transformed by the renewing of your mind, so that you may prove what the will of God is, that which is good and acceptable and perfect."

- James 4:6,10—"But He gives a greater grace. Therefore, it says, 'God is opposed to the proud, but gives grace to the humble.' . . . "humble yourselves in the presence of the Lord, and He will exalt you."

- 1 Peter 5:5-6—"In the same way, you who are younger, be subject to the elders. And all of you, clothe yourselves with humility toward one another, because God opposes the proud but gives grace to the humble. And God will exalt you in due time, if you humble yourselves under His mighty hand."

- Luke 1: 38; 18:14; John 12:3; Ephesians 5:21

Unity

- 1 Peter 4:8-10—"Above all, keep fervent in your love for one another, because love covers a multitude of sins. Be hospitable to one another without complaint. As each one has received a special gift, employ it in serving one another as good stewards of the manifold grace of God."

- Acts 1:14—"These all with one mind were continually devoting themselves to prayer, along with the women, and Mary the mother of Jesus, and with His disciples."

- John 17:11—"I am no longer in the world; and yet they themselves are in the world, and I come to You. Holy father, keep them in Your name, the name which You have given Me, that they may be one even as We are."

- Romans 12:16; 1 Corinthians 1:10; 12:11; 2 Corinthians 4:13; Ephesians 4:1-6

Obedience

Jesus

- Matthew 26:39—"Going a little farther, He threw Himself down with His face to the ground and prayed, 'My Father, if possible, let this cup pass from Me! Yet not what I will, but what you will.'"

- John 15:10—"'If you obey My commandments, you will remain in My love, just as I have obeyed My Father's commandments and remain in His love.'"

- Hebrews 5:8—"Although He was a son, He learned obedience through the things He suffered. And by being perfected in this way, He became the source of eternal salvation to all who obey Him."

- John 4:34

Other Examples/Teachings

- Luke 11:28—"But He replied, 'Blessed rather are those who hear the Word of God and obey it!'"

- John 14:15—"'If you love Me, you will obey My commandments.'"

- 1 John 5:2—"By this we know that we love the children of God: whenever we love God and obey His commandments."

- Hebrews 5:9; Revelation 1:3; Acts 9:10-22; 1 Timothy 6:11-14; John 9:6-7; Matthew 28:18-20

Christ Lifted Up

- John 13:31-32—"'Now the Son of Man is glorified, and God is glorified in Him. If God is glorified in Him, God will also glorify Him in Himself, and He will glorify Him right away.'"

- Acts 2:32-33—"This Jesus God raised up, and we are all witnesses of it. So then, exalted to the right hand of God, and having received the promise of the Holy Spirit from the Father, He has poured out what you both see and hear."

- Romans 14:9,11—"For this reason Christ died and returned to life, so that He may be the Lord of both the dead and the living . . . for it is written, 'As I live, says the Lord, every knee will bow to me, and every tongue will give praise to God.'"

- Acts 5:31; 1 Corinthians 15:23-25; Hebrews 2:9-11; 3:1-3; 7:22; 8:1,6; 12:2; 2 Peter 1:17; Revelation 1:5; 3:21; 5:13

THEMES IN THE OTHER TESTAMENT

Humility

- Genesis 50:19-21—"But Joseph said to them, 'Do not be afraid, for am I in God's place? As for you, you meant evil against me, but God meant it for good in order to bring about this present result, to preserve many people alive. So therefore, do not be afraid: I will provide for you and your little ones.' So he comforted them and spoke kindly to them."

- Ruth 1:16-18 — "But Ruth said, 'Do not urge me to leave you or turn back from following you, for where you go, I will go, and where you lodge, I will lodge. Your people shall be my people, and your God, my God. Where you die, I will die, and there I will be buried. Thus may the Lord do to me, and worse, if anything but death parts you and me.'"

- Esther 4:13-17 — "Then Mordecai told them to reply to Esther, 'Do not imagine that you in the king's palace can escape any more than all the Jews. For if you remain silent at this time, relief and deliverance will arise for the Jews from another place and you and your father's house will perish. And who knows whether you have not attained royalty for such a time as this?'"

- Job 1:20-22

Unity

- Exodus 19:8 — "All the people answered together and said, 'All that the Lord has spoken we will do!' And Moses brought back the words of the people to the Lord."

- Feasts and Celebrations

- The people of Israel gathered together and did things as a community. They stuck together more than before because they were proud of their heritage as God's chosen people. Numbers 1:18, Judges 20:11

- 1 Samuel 18:1 — "When David had finished talking with Saul, Jonathan and David became bound together in close friendship. Jonathan loved David as much as he did his own life."

- Nehemiah 1:4-6 — "When I heard these things I sat down abruptly, crying and mourning for several days. I continued fasting and praying before the God of heaven. Then I said, 'Please, O Lord God of heaven, great and awesome God, who keeps his loving covenant with those who love him and obey his commandments, may your ear be attentive and your eyes be open to hear the prayer of your servant that I am praying to you today throughout both day and night on behalf of your servant the Israelites.'"

Obedience

- Genesis 6:22 — "And Noah did all that God commanded him — he did indeed."

- Genesis 12:1-4 ". . . So Abram left, just as the Lord had told him to do, and Lot went with him."

- Sacrificing Isaac — Genesis 22:1-19

- 1-3 — "Some time after these things God tested Abraham. He said to him, 'Abraham!' 'Here I am!' Abraham replied. God said, 'Take your son — your only son, whom you love, Isaac — and go to the land of Moria! Offer him up there as a burnt offering on one of the mountains which I will indicate to you.' Early in the morning Abraham got up and saddled his donkey. He took two of his young servants with him, along with his son, Isaac. When he had cut the wood for the burnt offering, he started out for the place God had spoken to him about."

- Exodus 15:26 — "He said, 'If you will diligently obey the Lord your God, and do what is right in His sight, and pay attention to His commandments and keep His statutes, then all the diseases that I brought on the Egyptians I will not bring on you, for I, the Lord, am your healer.'"

- Joshua 4:24; Hosea 1:2-3; Ezekiel 4; Isaiah 1:18-20

Christ Lifted Up

- Psalm 2:6-8—"'I Myself have installed My King on Zion, My holy hill.' The King says, 'I will announce the Lord's decree. He said to Me: 'You are My Son! This very day I have become Your Father! Ask Me, and I will give you the nations as your inheritance, the ends of the earth as your personal property.'"

- Psalm 72:17—"May His fame endure! May His dynasty last as long as the sun remains in the sky! May they use His name when they formulate their blessings!"

- Isaiah 9:1-7—"For a child will be born to us . . . and the government will rest on His shoulders; and His name will be called Wonderful Counselor, Mighty God, Eternal Father, Prince of Peace. There will be no end to the increase of His government or of peace, on the throne of David and over His kingdom, to establish and to uphold it with justice and righteousness from then on and forevermore."

- Micah 5:2-5; Isaiah 49:7-8; 53:12; Daniel 7:14

Do you see how bold these themes become when we expand our vision beyond our current passage and view them in light of all Scripture? Themes boasts many facets. It's like looking into our diamond (we like this example) from a million different angles and learning something about it from each of them!

We've said this once or twice before, but God is not bland, boring, or monotone! He doesn't give us just one truth or example of a theme; He gives us lots so we gain a fuller picture. In our fallen nature, our feeble minds remain unable to grasp any theme in its entirety, but practicing Step Three with different passages will certainly be a brain-booster!

We must read Scripture in light of itself. Only when we have the whole Word in the back of our minds can we arrive at a greater depth of understanding of a particular verse. Remember, many human authors penned Scripture, but only one Divine Author inspired them to write His holy Word. This Word stands united, which is why His themes and truths are found everywhere in various forms and fashions!

Scripture is the inerrant, infallible, inspired, and living Word of God, given to us to glean from and pore over so we may know, love, and be transformed by Him—and tell others about it! What a gift! We must be responsible stewards of this gift, not reading whatever we want into a passage, but rather discovering the truth already present. This is the theological principle of the passage, which is our next Step!

Step Four—Determining the Theological Principle

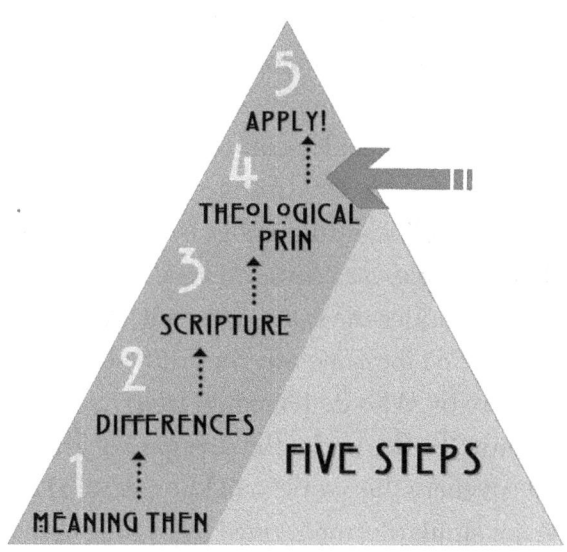

Now we're getting into it, folks! First, we *observed* by discovering lots of background information to give our passage context and by dissecting the passage itself. Then we used our brains to *think* by connecting with the original audience through noting all kinds of differences between them and us. Next, we *explored* the major themes in our passage by comparing them with other representations throughout the rest of Scripture.

What an accomplished bunch we are! Now we're ready to *focus* on those themes directly in our passage and comprise our theological principle!

SIMILARITIES

One mini-step I recommend at this point is to return to Step Two: Differences Between Then and Now. This time, instead of focusing on the differences, we focus on the similarities between the original audience and ourselves. This won't require a ton of work because much of the work rests in our answers from Step Two, but this mini-step is important because the theological principle applies to both the original audience and us. Finding the similarities bridges the gap and allows us to discover what God is communicating *through* them *to* us.

The main similarities we look for are general, not necessarily nit-picking cultural and political differences like the ones we fleshed out in Step Two. For example, a major similarity between the Philippians and us is that we are under the same covenant. Why is this important? Because we relate to God the same way they did—we trust in Jesus Christ as our Lord and Savior, Who delivered us from our sins and sealed us with His Holy Spirit. We live under the covenant of grace established by Christ—the last covenant this world will know until He returns.

Another major similarity, mentioned in passing above, is that of the Holy Spirit. Scripture reveals the Spirit has been active in this world since the beginning. However, His role came to fruition at Pentecost after Christ accomplished His redemptive work on Earth. We, like the Philippian believers, are sealed, led, and being sanctified by the Holy Spirit through His Word.

These two main similarities suffice for our mini-step of Step

Four. Again, we just want to grasp general similarities so we're better prepared for the task at hand—determining the theological principle.

THE THEOLOGICAL PRINCIPLE

The theological principle(s) of a passage answers the question, "What's the point?" What is the broad, general principle God communicates with us through the passage? Answer these questions, and you've got your theological principle!

Let's go over a couple of tips before articulating our principle for the Philippian passage:

- The theological principle(s) should be no more than one or two sentences

- There can be more than one principle, but usually no more than three

- The theological principle(s) usually corresponds with your major themes from Step Three (hint, hint!)

- Write the theological principle(s) in present tense, not past.[1] (Remember, you can apply this principle directly to your life now; it's not limited to the Philippian believers!)

Ask the following questions to help you determine the principle:[2]

- "Does the author state a principle?"

    If he does, then you've got it! Ephesians 6:1 exemplifies this when Paul said, "Children, obey your parents in the Lord." Pretty self-explanatory! It's a general, timeless principle

---
[1] Duvall and Hays, *Grasping God's Word*, 24.
[2] The first three points are referenced from Duvall and Hays, *Grasping God's Word*, 237.

that applied not only to the Philippian church, but also to the church today.

- "Does the broader context reveal the theological principle?"

The passage you're reading may involve an aspect or a specific part of a principle the author is trying to convey. Sometimes backing up and reading the context around it reveals a principle in blazing glory! Can't go wrong with context, friends!

- If you have a particular command or instruction, ask why it was given.

For example, in Galatians 5:2, Paul told the Galatian church, "If you receive circumcision, Christ will be of no benefit to you." If you come across a tricky verse like this, ask yourself why Paul said it. Look at the context. Just four verses later Paul explained himself by saying, "For in Christ Jesus neither circumcision nor uncircumcision means anything, but faith working through love." Always look at the context of a verse and passage! It will never let you down, and often the theological principle is right there waiting for you to discover!

- Reference your themes

You've discovered the themes of the passage from Step Three, so now it's time to glean the individual principle(s) from them. If a major theme is humility, you can bet that the theological principle will include it! Write your principle(s) with the themes in mind. Let them pave the way.

So what's the theological principle(s) in our passage? Read the passage again, look over Steps One through Three, and do it! Write out a sentence or two that explains the point. You got it!

After you've spent a few minutes writing one out, check it against/with these criteria:[3]

- The theological principle should represent what is being said in the text.

- The principle should be timeless and should not be tied to a specific historical situation. For example, when Paul told Euodia and Syntyche to live in harmony with each other in the Lord in Philippians 4, he's talking about these two women. If by some random, freaky chance there are two ladies with these names in your church, Scripture is not talking directly about them!

- The principle should not be culturally bound (applicable only to the culture/time period in which it was written).

- The principle should be relevant to both the biblical audience and modern-day audience.

- The principle should fit well within the surrounding context (of the chapter and the book).

- The principle should be true. It should be consistent with what the rest of Scripture speaks on the subject.

- The principle should be straightforward, not strained. If you derive a principle that seems complicated, messy, long-winded, or "not quite there," keep trying!

- The principle should reflect and remain consistent with the major themes of the passage.

Does your theological principle pass the test? I'm sure it does!

---

[3] The first five of these criteria are paraphrased from the points found in Duvall and Hays, *Grasping God's Word*, 24.

To help you make sure you're on the right path, here are a couple of good options for a theological principle for the Philippians 2:1-10 passage.

> **Option One:** Genuine unity with each other and with God cannot occur unless we make a deliberate and purposeful decision to act as Christ did—humbling ourselves before God and becoming obedient to Him and His Son, who is above and beyond all else in the world.
>
> **Option Two:** Pure humility cannot fully be realized apart from obedience to the Father. Humility, obedience, and/or Christ glorified must be practiced in order to experience genuine unity with Christ and/or within His church.

As with themes, there's no absolute, correct, and proper verbiage to theological principles. You can word them any way you want, as long as they reflect the major themes we talked about in Step Three. The theological principle stands as the crux of the entire hermeneutic process, because it's the nugget of truth we apply directly to our lives. Again, your theological principle and mine will vary in word choice and grammatical structure. You may even find a different theme emphasized than I do, depending on where the Spirit is leading us both at any given moment.

The point isn't to have the same word-for-word theological principle everyone else finds in their studies. How boring would that be? Uber-boring! We are each different—each coming from a myriad of experiences, talents, backgrounds, skills, gifts, and abilities. God created us uniquely, and our relationships with Him are expressed just as uniquely.

Just as parents enjoy the different character traits of their children, our Father enjoys and relates to us differently, yet with the same truth in love. It's no surprise then that He communicates with us differently!

His Spirit may emphasize the humility portion of the passage to one person, while to another, unity is key.

Emphases also vary quite a bit as you enter different phases in life. The reason God may emphasize humility over unity to Carla is because she struggles with pride at this junction in her life. The Word acts like a mirror that reveals both our strengths and weaknesses, and the Spirit is a Master at pointing out areas we need to work on! If He's been convicting you about being more united with your family, friends, and brothers and sisters in Christ, the theme of unity will probably stick out most to you in this passage.

That's the beauty of Scripture and the Spirit. God speaks to us individually, but He speaks the same truth to everyone. The truth never changes, but how it is received varies slightly among its recipients! Notice we said it varies *slightly*. Again, the Spirit does not reveal new truth or revelation from person to person. Through His Word, He reveals to us the same truth he revealed to other believers for centuries past. Yet He giftwraps that truth beautifully distinctly for each of us.

God challenges us to embrace and express gratitude for our uniqueness. As the authors of Scripture wrote in different styles based on their backgrounds, experiences, and personalities, so the Spirit uses our unique makeup in helping us interpret His truth. Isn't that amazing?! The best part is that when we're in community, growing in His Word together, we discover the different emphases He's presenting to each of us. When we combine those perspectives, we get a fuller, more enticing picture of His truth.

While we can learn and grow on our own, it's even better when we do it together. When we apply God's principles of truth to our lives, the Spirit uses them to transform us into His image—the best part and the whole point of hermeneutics! Are you getting goose-bumps? I sure am! Now that we've articulated our principle, we get to see how we can apply it to our lives!

Step Five—Meaning for Today

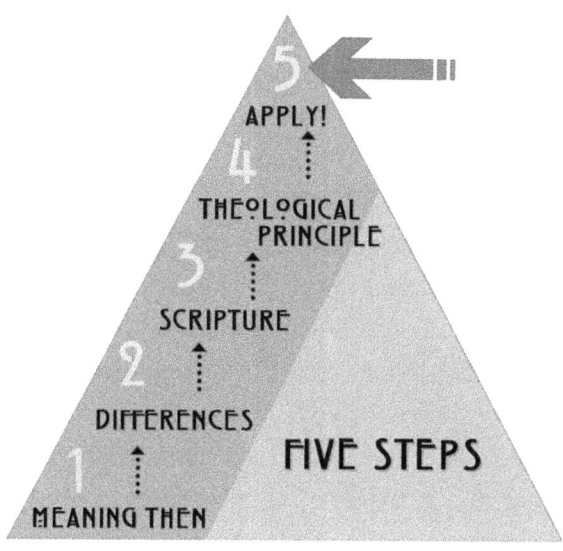

Oh boy, we're almost done! Hasn't time just flown by? At the beginning, when we started to learn about the infallibility and inspiration of Scripture, most of us were probably clueless about hermeneutics. Yet after learning about the Word (in addition to some fancy new vocabulary words), you are just about to cross the finish line of your first hermeneutical journey! And it couldn't be more exciting! (Actually, that's not true. It gets more exciting every time you go through it. Guaranteed!)

We finally arrive at Step Five: Meaning for Today. We've *observed, thought, expanded,* and *focused;* now we're going to *apply*! We've got the ammo, now we need to fire! Naturally, the question to ask in this Step is, "How should we apply the theological principle of this passage to our lives?"

Think back to our previous study about how to read and interpret Scripture (the eisegesis vs. exegesis discussion). We learned the distinction between the question, "What does the text mean to me?" and "What does this text mean? And how can I apply that to my life?" We understand now what a crucial difference that is. It's not our job to read anything into the text. It speaks quite well on its own!

As we near the finish line, that question returns in full force. We avoided reading anything into the text; in fact, we've taken every precaution against it! With the theological principle set, we're ready to embrace its personal application.

Before we go further, we must clarify a point. How many times have you been in a situation in which the world seemed to be in utter and total chaos? Nothing made sense, you had no idea which way was up or down, and couldn't for the life of you remember such simple things as where you put your keys. We've all had these moments.

Now think with me. In the midst of chaotic stress and confusion, are you thinking about theological principles to apply to your life? Do you go down a list of truths and see which one applies to the current situation? Maybe some of you do, and if so, kudos to you! But that's hardly a reality for most of us. This is why Step Five is critical. Applying a theological principle involves plugging it into a real-life situation. If we put a face with a name, then we are far more likely to remember and use it when a similar situation confronts us head-on in our lives.

Step Five involves just that—giving a face to the theological principle from Step Four. We put it to action by thinking of a situation it would apply to. Then, one day when we or a friend go through a similar situation, we trust the Holy Spirit to remind us of the truths we learned when we studied His Word. Rest assured that He certainly will!

So how do we go about giving the name a face? Think of a story, true or fictional, in which a character can and should apply the theological principle to her life. It can be one paragraph or ten, formal or informal. However, it should be modern-day. If you've tracked with us through this whole process, you've learned the original audience's context, saw how it differs from ours, gleaned the themes from it, and focused on the theological purpose statement from those themes. Now we bring it home!

The process begins when we remove ourselves from the equation because we weren't in the equation when the passage was written. But once we've discovered the truth or point of the passage, He wants us to apply it to our lives! We do this when we give the principle a modern-day context.

Another way to think of it is this: the biblical passage is how the truth was realized back in the day it was written. Now that we know that truth, how can it be realized today—in our present lives? Make sense? This is what application is all about. We apply the non-negotiable, always-right truth to our lives today. So let's put it to the test together.

Here again is our theological principle. For the sake of clarity, we'll use the first theological principle from our previous example.

> Genuine unity with each other and with God cannot occur unless we make a deliberate and purposeful decision to act as Christ did—humbling ourselves before God and

> becoming obedient to Him and His Son, Who is above and beyond all else in the world.

Awesome. Now, what's a modern-day story that's compatible with this truth? What story can you think of that demonstrates this principle in action—that we must follow Christ's example of humble obedience in order to be united with Him and each other? Think about it. Write it down.

Got one? Hope so! If not, read the example below for some inspiration, then try it for yourself.

> Lauren loves going on mission trips. She and her husband have travelled to several countries all over the world, serving Christ and caring for those in need. Even with two children, she seeks to remain faithful to the burden God placed on her heart for underprivileged families in third-world countries. Sending the kids to Grandma's, she and her husband, Tom, make a trip at least once a year.
>
> Two months before their trip this year, Tom lost his job. They'd invested a small amount financially already, but moving forward with the trip would strain their finances considerably since Lauren doesn't have an income. Lauren strongly believed they should pursue the trip and trust God to provide. Tom, on the other hand, felt very uneasy about making such an investment, especially in light of their depleting funds.
>
> Lauren wrestled with this predicament for days. She prayed fervently, begging God to change her husband's heart. Forfeiting this trip would mean waiting an entire extra year to go—a consequence she wasn't keen on enduring.
>
> Through her prayers and studies of Scripture, God spoke to her heart. He wanted her to use this opportunity to

honor her husband and submit to his desires, even if it cost her dearly. Though not thrilled at first, she slowly began surrendering to God's desires. She humbled herself to His will and obeyed Him, which resulted in greater unity with her husband and Christ's exaltation in her marriage.

As the saying goes, that's how it's done! It doesn't take much, and it can be as elaborate or simple as you want it to be. But the point is to put the theological principle in action by wrapping it in a modern-day context and one day (if not today), applying it to our lives.

Scripture is relevant today, friends. All we have to do is find the truth within its proper context so we can glean it from the passage and plant it in our lives. The Holy Spirit then works with us and the Word to grow and nurture His truth as we apply and live it out in our daily lives. How exciting!

Ah! We did it! We crossed the finish line of our very own hermeneutical study together, and I'm thrilled for you! Let's briefly recap everything we've learned, infusing it in your minds.

Let's Wrap it Up!

Our first lesson was dedicated to Scripture itself. Hermeneutics remains a mystery if we don't grasp what Scripture is. We asked the question, "What is the Bible?" and learned that it is the inerrant, infallible, inspired, and living Word of God. It's all or nothing when it comes to Scripture, and we're taking it all.

Next we discussed the canon—the actual composition of the Bible. We learned that its sixty-six books were widely accepted as God's Word until a couple hundred years after Christ. When doubts arose, the Councils of Hippo in AD 393 and Carthage in AD 397 solidified it (remember how we said we couldn't make up those names if we tried?).

Once we discovered how the canon was put together, we looked into the authors of Scripture—who they were and how the Holy Spirit directed them to write what they did. That discussion led to the authors' unique writing styles (shout-out for the literary style talk!) which confirmed yet again that Scripture is not mundane or boring! Literary styles directed us to languages, which segued nicely to the topic of translations. This provided a marvelous conclusion to our study of the Bible.

Next we dug into a hermeneutics study! We defined it, learned how and how not to conduct it, talked about the Holy Spirit's role with us in it, articulated its goal, then went through the four main rules of hermeneutics one by one: 1) The Literal, Grammatical, Historical Method, 2) Scripture is Our Ultimate Authority, 3) Context, Context, Context! and 4) Scripture Interprets Scripture.

Once we grasped the definitions, principles, and rules of hermeneutics, we explored the main genres in Scripture: historical narrative, the Law, wisdom literature, prophecy, the Gospels, parables, Acts, New Testament letters, and Revelation.

After laying that mighty solid foundation, we began exploring the process itself, with an example passage to work on too! Step One, of course, was to discover the passage's Meaning In Its Day by *observing* all we could about the passage, its surrounding context, and its book by answering a boatload of questions. Step Two came along to help us see the Differences Between Then and Now, which we accomplished by *thinking* through the many differences between the original audience and ourselves.

This transitioned nicely to Step Three, which enforces and supplements hermeneutic Rule #4—Scripture In Light of Scripture. We *expanded* on the main themes of the passage and researched them in the rest of the book, then the testament it's located in, then the other testament. Once marking these down, we hit the crux of our study with Step Four—*focusing* on the theological principle. Our main themes helped us narrow down the principle, and once we did, we moved on to our final Step, finding the Meaning for Today. In other words, we *applied* the principle we derived from the passage and put it into action with a modern-day story that exemplified it superbly!

Quite the little study we accomplished together, isn't it? And again, this is only the beginning of all the amazing adventures to come between you and God through His Word. You've heard the expression "ignorance is bliss," but I'm here to tell you once again that knowledge is the ultimate bliss when it's knowledge of His Word! The more you know, the more you crave! And it only gets better with time and commitment.

Here's your challenge after going through this beast of a process. One, take a deep breath and give yourself time to reflect on what you've just learned. Two, go through it again with another passage. Three, do it again with another passage. Four, do it a fourth time with yet another passage! Why? Because the more you do it, the more you'll learn, and the more He'll transform you into His image!

Don't neglect your personal devotional time with the Lord, and don't kill yourself thinking you have to do an in-depth hermeneutic study 24/7. That's a bit much. But don't shy away from it, either. Absorb it. Let His truth pour over you as you go deeper and mature in your understanding and in your relationship with Him and His Word. Get intimate with it. You will never regret it, and He'll never let you down. Thanks for taking this journey with me, friends! You now better understand Scripture as More Than Words: how to understand the ancient Book in a modern world!

We'll end with an encouragement and commission straight from His Word. Continue to "be diligent to present yourself approved to God as a workman who does not need to be ashamed, accurately handling the Word of Truth" (2 Timothy 2:15).

About the Author

Mindi Jo Furby grew up in the Superficial Capital of the World—Southern California. Image drives everything there, even some churches and faith.

The mirage looked great from a distance, but the closer she got the further she wanted to run.

And she did.

But God has this funny attribute called love; and only He can bring us back to a place we've never been!

God led her through a door (which ended up including a degree in Biblical Studies and a Masters in Religion) that re-introduced her to Scripture and a real life with Him. Now, she's thrilled to offer you the keys to that same door—no mirages, hypocrisy, or superficiality. Guaranteed.

Mindi Jo Furby makes her home in Savannah, GA, with her husband, ministry staff, friends, and little pup Tozer (yes, after A.W. Tozer). When she's not speaking, teaching, or writing, she finds herself most enjoying long chats, strong coffee, and relaxing walks downtown or on the beach.

To connect with Mindi Jo Furby, visit www.mindijofurby.com

BIBLIOGRAPHY

Alexander, Ralph. Abstract of "Hermeneutics of Old Testament Apocalyptic Literature," doctor's dissertation.

http://www.allgreatquotes.com/law_quotes.shtml.

Barker, Kenneth L., Donald W. Burdick, and Kenneth Boa. *Zondervan NASB study Bible*. Grand Rapids, Mich.: Zondervan Pub. House, 1999.

"Bible Encyclopedia: Philippians." Bible Encyclopedia Online. http://bibleencyclopedia.com/search--philippians.

"Bible Scripture - The Canon of the Old Testament." http://biblescripture.net/Canon.html.

"Blue Letter Bible - Home." Blue Letter Bible. www.blueletterbible.org.

Boa, Kenneth. "The Reliability of the Bible | Bible.org - Worlds Largest Bible Study Site." Free NET Bible and Thousands of Bible Studies | Bible.org - Worlds Largest Bible Study Site. http://bible.org/seriespage/reliability-bible.

Boa, Kenneth. "Interpreting the Bible | Bible.org - Worlds Largest Bible Study Site." Free NET Bible and Thousands of Bible Studies | Bible.org - Worlds Largest Bible Study Site. http://bible.org/seriespage/interpreting-bible.

Boa, Kenneth. "Uniqueness of the Bible | Bible.org - Worlds Largest Bible Study Site." Free NET Bible and Thousands of Bible Studies | Bible.org - Worlds Largest Bible Study Site. http://bible.org/seriespage/uniqueness-bible.

Boice, James Montgomery. *Does Inerrancy Matter?*, Oakland: International Council on Biblical Inerrancy, 1979, p. 13

Bromily, Geoffrey W. *International Standard Bible Encyclopedia*, Fully revised. ed. Grand Rapids, Michigan: Wm. B. Eerdmans, 1979. http://bibleencyclopedia.com/

Browning, Elizabeth. "How Do I Love Thee?" (Sonnet 43).

Carson, D.A.. *The Gospel According to John*. Grand Rapids: Wm.B. Eerdmans, 1990.

Christian Answers, "About the Bible." http://www.christiananswers.net/bible/about.html

Douglas, J. D., and Merrill C. Tenney. *Zondervan Bible Dictionary*. Grand Rapids, Mich: Zondervan, 2008.

Duvall, J. Scott, and J. Daniel Hays. *Grasping God's Word: A Hands-on Approach to Reading, Interpreting, and Applying the Bible*. Grand Rapids, Mich.: Zondervan, 2001.

Fee, Douglas and Gordon Stuart, *How to Read the Bible*. Grand Rapids, Mich: Zondervan, 2002.

Fee, Douglas and Gordon Stuart. *How to Read the Bible for All it's Worth*. Grand Rapids, Mich: Zondervan, 2003.

Gasque, Ward. "Bibles: Available, Accessible, Ignored." Christian Week, February 1, 2008, 22. http://www.christianweek.org/features.php?id=15

Geisler, Norman L, and William E. Nix. *A General Introduction to the Bible*. Chicago: Moody Press, 1968.

Got God Questions Ministries, "Textual Criticism – What Is It?" http://www.gotquestions.org/textual-criticism.html

Hansen, G. Walter. *The Letter to the Philippians*. Grand Rapids, Mich: William B. Eerdmans Pub. Co: 2009.

Hemingway, Ernest. *Death in the Afternoon*. New York, New York: Scribner, 1996. Via http://www.goodreads.com/quotes/ show/2955

Jeffers, James S. *The Greco-Roman World of the New Testament Era: Exploring the Background of Early Christianity*. Downers Grove, Ill: InterVarsity Press, 1999.

Keathley III, J. Hampton. "The Bible: The Holy Canon of Scripture | Bible. org - Worlds Largest Bible Study Site." Free NET Bible and Thousands of Bible Studies | Bible.org - Worlds Largest Bible Study Site. http://bible.org/seriespage/bible-holy-canon-scripture.

Litke, Sid. "Canonicity | Bible.org - Worlds Largest Bible Study Site." Free NET Bible and Thousands of Bible Studies | Bible.org - Worlds Largest Bible Study Site. http://bible.org/seriespage/canonicity.

Lockman Foundation. http://www.lockman.org/nasb/.

"NET Bible." Free NET Bible and Thousands of Bible Studies | Bible.org - Worlds Largest Bible Study Site. http://www.bible.org.

NIV Study Bible. Grand Rapids, MI: Zondervan, 2008.

Pfeiffer, Charles F. *Baker's Bible Atlas*. 2003 ed. Grand Rapids: Baker Book House, 2003.

Ryrie, Charles. *Today in the World*. MBI, December, 1989, p. 7.

Utley, Bob. "The Bible | Bible.org - Worlds Largest Bible Study Site." Free NET Bible and Thousands of Bible Studies | Bible.org - Worlds Largest Bible Study Site. http://bible.org/seriespage/bible.

White, Brian. "BuddhaNet" http://www.buddhanet.net/e-learning/5minbud.htm. 1993.

Young, Robert. *Young's Analytical Concordance to the Bible*. Peabody, MA: Hendrickson Pub, 1984.

Zukeran, Patrick. "Authority of the Bible | Bible.org - Worlds Largest Bible Study Site." Free NET Bible and Thousands of Bible Studies | Bible.org - Worlds Largest Bible Study Site. http://bible.org/article/authority-bible.

www.ingramcontent.com/pod-product-compliance
Lightning Source LLC
Chambersburg PA
CBHW071306110426
42743CB00042B/1194